*All the Best Rubbish*

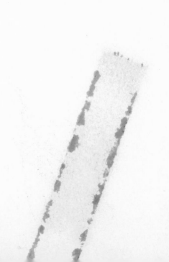

*Books by Ivor Noël Hume*

All the Best Rubbish

A Guide to Artifacts of Colonial America

Historical Archaeology

1775: Another Part of the Field

Here Lies Virginia

Great Moments in Archaeology

Treasure in the Thames

Archaeology in Britain

Men do mightily wrong
themselves: when they
refuse to be present in
all Ages: and Neglect
to see the Beauty of
all Kingdoms.
                —Thomas Traherne, c. 1637–1674

# All the Best Rubbish

## by Ivor Noël Hume

**HARPER & ROW, PUBLISHERS**

New York
Evanston
San Francisco
London

1817

*Frontispiece: From a late-seventeenth-century Italian book on antiquities. Translation of Latin—"Whatever is under the earth the present age brings to light."*

FIRST EDITION

*Designed by Sidney Feinberg*

8-74 BT 10⁶⁰

Library of Congress Cataloging in Publication Data

Noël Hume, Ivor.
    All the best rubbish.
    Bibliography:  p.
    1.  Collectors and collecting.  I.  Title.
AM231.N63      745.1      73–4093
ISBN  0–06–011997–7

*To my Father*
*for whom love and laughter*
*were the only treasures*

# Contents

# *Acknowledgments*

AN AUTHOR who chooses a subject as uncontroversial as the beauty of motherhood must still expect to be denounced by a few irate readers, but the archaeologist who dares to write in praise of collecting is asking for all sorts of trouble. No matter how clearly and vehemently he may condemn the looting of objects from the ground or of later parting them from their historical documentation, he can expect to be charged with promoting every crime from trespass to treason. If he should be so foolhardy as to suggest that rather than seeing objects only as things to measure, catalogue, and hoard away in museum storerooms, they can legitimately serve as catalysts for fact-borne flights of imagination, then he is liable to be thought as irrational as he is irresponsible. Consequently the brickbats are rightfully mine, and the many people who have provided the hard facts are wholly blameless for the manner in which I have used them.

I am indebted to many dealers in antiques and antiquities both in the United States and in Britain who, over the years, have been more than generous with their advice, and from whom I obtained many of the objects that made this book possible; but I am particularly grateful to Robert Allbrook, John May, Anthony Oliver, and Howard Phillips in London, and to Joan Morris of Stamford, Connecticut, and Ricks Wilson of Williamsburg, Virginia. I am equally in the debt of the museum curators and librarians who have helped me pursue the histories of the objects discussed or have provided me with illustrations. They are: Thomas N. Armstrong III, director of the Pennsylvania Academy of The Fine Arts; Barry A. Greenlaw, John D. Davis, and John C. Austin, curators in the department of collections, and Julia Davis, historian in the department of research, all of the Colonial Williamsburg Foundation; Donovan Dawe, principal keeper at the Corporation of London's Guildhall Library; James L. Howgego, keeper of prints and paintings, Guildhall Library; Ralph Merrifield, deputy keeper at London's Guildhall Museum, and Norman C. Cook, its retired keeper; Ian Lowe, curator of Western Art, Ashmolean Museum, Oxford; Mary Clapinson, assistant in the department of Western MSs., Bodleian Library, Oxford; Michael Moad, curator of the Eastgate House Museum, Rochester, Kent; G. A. Morris, librarian at the North Devon Athenaeum, Barnstaple; Joyce L. Sears, librarian at the Prince Consort's Library, Aldershot; Michael Webb of Greenborough House, Hartlip, who allowed me to explore and excavate on his Medway marshlands; and A. de Franciscis, superintendent of antiquities for the province of Naples and Caserta, Italy. I am also greatly obliged to William M. Jones and J. E. Hardy of Jacksonville, Florida, for the use of hitherto unpublished information, and to Helen Camp of Pemaquid, Maine, for similar courtesies. In Jamaica I owe much to the assistance of C. Bernard Lewis, director of the Institute of Jamaica at Kingston, and to Thomas A. L. Concannon, Ivor Cornman, and Ray Fremmer; and on the island of St. Eustatius to my good friend Robert Grodé, without whom the book would have no title. I am appreciative, too, of the help given me by Anne Able Smith at A. P. Watt & Son in London.

For the provision and use of photographs I wish to express my appreciation to the following institutions and individuals: to Burnley Corporation, Towneley Hall Art Gallery and Museum for Fig. 1; the *Western Morning News* (Plymouth, England) for Figs. 3 and 4; Eastgate House Museum, Rochester, for Fig. 11; The Society of Antiquaries of London for Fig. 12;

the Ashmolean Museum, Oxford, for Figs. 13 and 14; the University Museum, Oxford, for Fig. 16; the Victoria and Albert Museum, London, for Figs. 19 and 123; the Pennsylvania Academy of The Fine Arts for Fig. 20; the North Devon Athenaeum, Barnstaple, for Figs. 24 and 26; Parke-Bernet Galleries, New York, for Fig. 27; Florida State Division of Archives and History for Fig. 28; the Mariners' Museum at Newport News, Virginia, for Fig. 31; J. M. Harrison of Edinboro, Pennsylvania, for Fig. 44b; the British Museum for Figs. 49, 55, 64, and 108; the Institute of Jamaica for Figs. 50 and 51; the DeHardit Press, Gloucester, Virginia, for Fig. 54; the Colonial Williamsburg Foundation for Figs. 10, 67, 90, 94, 102, and 113; the United States National Park Service for Fig. 82c; Washington and Lee University, Lexington, Virginia, for Fig. 84; The Guildhall Library, London, for Figs. 45 and 99; Weidenfeld and Nicolson Ltd., for Fig. 104; Richard Green (Fine Paintings) Ltd., for Fig. 105; and Ivor Cornman of Stony Hill, Jamaica, for Fig. 116.

For permission to photograph objects in museums and private collections, I am obliged to the following: the Colonial Williamsburg Foundation for Figs. 8, 83, 85, 92, 94, 101-103, and 120; the Association for the Preservation of Virginia Antiquities for Fig. 18; the Guildhall Museum, London, for Figs. 5, 38, 40, 42, 77, 80, 109, and 119 (right); Mary Watkins of Wilmington, Delaware, for Fig. 53; the British Museum for Fig. 61; the Ashmolean Museum, Oxford, for Fig. 63; John V. N. Dunton of Louisbourg, Nova Scotia, for Fig. 76; Henekey's, Ltd., of London, for Fig. 79; Portsmouth City Museums in England for Fig. 96; and Charles T. Hotchkiss of Williamsburg, Virginia, for Fig. 118. I am grateful, too, to Hans E. Lorenz, whose printing has done much to make my photography seem better than it is.

For permission to quote from copyrighted sources I am obliged to Atheneum Publishers, Inc., for the extract from Maurice Rheims's *The Strange Life of Objects*, and to the Oxford University Press for the excerpt from Flora Thompson's *Lark Rise to Candleford*.

Finally, I want to express my lasting appreciation to Marilyn

Marlow, who believed in this project even when I faltered; to Jean Patton of Bloomington, Indiana, who introduced me to Flora Thompson and who provided the Traherne quotation, and to Audrey, my wife, who reviewed the manuscript and suggested that I rewrite the last chapter—which I did.

*January, 1973*                                                    I.N.H.

# ◆§ ONE

# "What's Past Is Prologue . . ."

JUST AS A PAINTING is viewed with greater respect if the
canvas bears the name of a distinguished artist, and as an oft-
voiced plan is suddenly adopted when heard from the mouth of
a costly consultant, so authors seek stature for their paltry
thoughts by quoting someone else. Not wishing to lose points so
early in the game I, too, propose to begin with a quotation. The
words are those of the respected French art expert and auc-
tioneer Maurice Rheims, who, in his book *The Strange Life of
Objects,* had this to say:

> An object's date is of prime importance to a collector with an
> obsession for the past. He values it for its associations, that it be-
> longed to and was handled by a man he can visualize as himself.
> The object bears witness: its possession is an introduction to history.
> One of a collector's most entrancing daydreams is the imaginary joy
> of uncovering the past in the guise of an archaeologist. In reality
> most finds are a few fragments of bone, two or three bronze rings,
> or at most a necklace of some precious material.[1] *

Mr. Rheims's reference to collectors with an *obsession* for the
past leaves little doubt that he holds small brief for such
people and their folksy approach to collecting. Nevertheless,
setting the offending word aside, I must own that he has succinctly described the satisfaction of one aspect of collecting,

* Notes to the chapters begin on p. 303.

one that I happen to find fascinating and which is to be the warp if not the weft of this book.

Collectable objects can indeed provide an introduction to history, and it follows that if they are to do so we must know to which period they belonged. It is equally true that the use of objects as signposts to the past inescapably carries the explorer into the realms of archaeology. After all, Webster's primary definition of the word is that archaeology involves "the scientific study of the material remains of past human life and activity."[2] Although rather a superficial definition, it does serve to support M. Rheims's contention, for to me collecting and archaeology are two tines of the same fork; they are a means of learning about the past. With that said, we part company. M. Rheims's vision of archaeology smacks too much of grave robbing and his disappointment at the poor quality of his imagined loot echoes the chagrin of the foiled treasure hunter. It is a venerable but outdated concept that lingers on among booksellers' cataloguers who lump "Art and Archaeology" together, and in auction houses that still mount sales devoted to "Antiquities and Works of Art." Archaeology had earned its place there as the means of acquiring works of art from out of the ground: marble statuary, bronzes, burial urns, gold and silver cups, and painted Grecian vases, all objects of sufficient artistic caliber to be admired, and bid for, alongside the works of medieval masters.

When we look, say, at John Zoffany's picture of London antiquaries swamped in a sea of classical statuary in Charles Towneley's library (Fig. 1) it is evident that the Age of Enlightenment had fostered an appreciation for beauty rather than a burning enthusiasm for studying the past through its material remains. It was an outlook that in 1803 prompted Lord Elgin to ship home two hundred crates of marbles from the Athenian Acropolis for display in his private museum in London, and which encouraged President Lincoln's consul to Cyprus, Luigi Palma di Cesnola, to bring back the vast collection of antiquities that in 1870 would become the pride of the new Metropolitan Museum of Art in New York. Nobody was much concerned with broken household pottery, ancient tools,

1. An antiquary, his dog, his friends, and one or two odds and ends. John Zoffany's 1782 painting of Charles Towneley in the library of his home in Park Street, Westminster. The clutter is artist's license; the objects had been brought together for the picture from various parts of the house.

cooking utensils, or other humble artifacts, which were shoveled back into the ground. It is an attitude that dies hard, particularly in those countries where ancient art objects of great size, beauty, and worth are still to be found. I was dramatically reminded of this in 1968 on a visit to the village of

Miseno on the Bay of Naples. There a farmer flattening a tiresome and unproductive hillock was in the process of destroying the cella of a subterranean shrine dating from the first century A.D. When I got there only its end wall was still more or less intact, temporarily reprieved because a magnificent pair of life-sized statues of the Emperor Vespasian and his son Titus stood in niches set into it, flanking the standing altar. These, I was assured, would be saved, for they were works of art, and valuable; as for the rest of the shrine, it was already rubble, and only the fragments of painted plaster still clinging to the remaining wall testified to the quality of what had been destroyed. Awed though I was by the splendor of the figures (Fig. 2), I found myself more interested in trying to make sense out of the piles of debris. It was evident then, as it has been for years, that as far as traditional antiquarianism was concerned, I was an unrepentant radical.

I hasten to add that this is not to be a book about archaeol-

2. Archaeology by bulldozer. The remains of a Roman shrine at Miseno, Italy, accidentally discovered while grading in 1968. The figures are those of the Emperor Vespasian (A.D. 69–79) and his son Titus. They were claimed by the state and are preserved at Baia.

ogy as such, though it will inevitably slip in now and again. It can hardly do otherwise, for this is to be a personal view of collecting, and I happen to have plied the trade of an archaeologist for most of my working life. If, however, we interpret archaeology in its loose, Websterian sense, using it to mean searching for, finding, and interpreting elderly objects, then indeed archaeology is the name of the game. While working on the manuscript, I have been asked repeatedly by friends and colleagues to describe it, and when I told them it was about collecting, they were prone to reply "Oh, no, not another one of those!" It was fair, if none too encouraging comment. Libraries and remainder bookstores are full of books on antiques by specialists for specialists, grab-bag A to Z compendia—the Complete Book of this, or the Concise Encyclopedia of that; and grand coffee-table volumes of greater size than substance. It will be evident from the present format that mine will do nothing for the nation's coffee tables (except, perhaps, for those having one leg shorter than the others). There are some other things that the book is not: its concept of collecting does not extend to botany, gemology, lepidopterology, mineralogy, philately, or to birds' eggs. Furthermore, I have no intention of trying to tell anyone all he needs to know about anything— even supposing I was able to do so. On the other hand, the book *is* about antiquities, bygones, memorabilia, books, manuscripts, a miscellany of antiques, and a dash of numismatics, which when all lumped together comprise what used to be known as *curiosities*. It is not a bad term at that; it identifies the objects as being out of the ordinary, exciting curiosity— and that is what collecting and the book are all about.

The objects in any collection generally reflect their owner's taste and interests, but in my case taste—by which I mean artistic appreciation—has little to do with it. I have collected not for aesthetic satisfaction but to bring together objects having something to say about themselves, about the people who made them, or about the times wherein they were used or enjoyed. This may sound a bit stuffy, even pompous, but I hope to be able to show that in reality there is tremendous fun and satisfaction to be derived both from finding and finding out, and that can be a far cry from collecting objects for what they may be worth or for the impression they may make on one's peers. I am as interested in the idea of collecting as I am in the objects themselves, and with luck this will emerge not only from the text but also through the illustrations. Many of the pots, bottles, and miscellaneous odds and ends are of no great artistic merit, but they are typical or evocative of their times, and that is what makes them worthy of one's attention.

It is questionable whether the collector is ever as interesting as the collection, but it cannot exist without him, and for this reason I cannot escape from these pages. Nevertheless, in an effort to present as fleeting a target as possible, I propose to dispose of a few essential autobiographical confessions at once in the hope that I can be kept firmly in my place thereafter.

I was raised as an only child in England in a family whose memories of the way things used to be served as a bulwark against the cold wind of present reality, and so from a very early age I was drawn toward a world of make-believe, to the theater, to history, to archaeology, and to a fierce but outdated patriotism. Tales of past British glory, of battles, heroes, kings, and castles, were more important to me than mathematics, football—or even cricket. I was dispatched to my first boarding school at the age of six, and thereafter my thrice yearly return home for the vacation months was met with minimal rejoicing. Under the eye of a succession of housekeepers, I was deterred from making unsuitable friends by being denied the opportunity, and was encouraged to make my own amusements—quietly. Consequently I learned to find pleasure in solitude.

Early in 1942 we moved to the prewar yachting haven at Salcombe in south Devonshire, where the wild, spray-swept headlands and deserted coves well suited my developing temperament. Local legends told of hidden treasure, of lantern-waving wreckers who had lured eighteenth-century merchantmen onto the rocks, and of smugglers' caves and of tunnels cut through the cliffs from the beach to a distant village church. Intoxicated by these stories, I spent months searching but found only one tunnel, and that turned out to be well known. Nevertheless, the tales of wrecks and wreckers were often true;

there were documentary records to prove it, but more convincing to a treasure-hunting boy was the sight of the occasional Spanish silver coins found in the sand after a winter's gale. There were cannon, too, salvaged years ago from the 90-gun man-of-war H.M.S. *Ramillies* that went down near Bolt Head in 1760. Beaten to pieces on the granite rocks, little of the great ship remained to be salvaged, but another four-masted sailing ship, the *Herzogin Cecilie*, which went aground close by on the Hamstone Rock, was pulled off and towed to a sheltered bay—where she sank (Fig. 3). On a still day, at slack tide, and with the sun at the right angle, her hull and barnacle-covered spars were visible resting on the bottom, and by the hour I would hang over the side of my dinghy, peering down into the water and seeing in her all the romance of Britain's maritime past. It was not, as it happened, a very remote past; the *Herzogin Cecilie* was one of the last of the great clipper ships; built at Bremerhaven in 1902, she had been lost in 1936 homeward bound with a cargo of Australian grain. But that made no difference; to me she was the *Golden Hind*, the *Marie Celeste*, the *Flying Dutchman*, anything I wanted her to be.

Five miles east along the cliffs and clinging to a ledge no more than six or eight feet above normal high water stood the deserted remains of the fishing community of Hallsands (Fig. 4). The roofless and crumbling walls of a handful of cottages were all that was left of a village whose life had abruptly ended on a January night in 1917. A storm of unprecedented ferocity had hurled waves and shingle against the cliffs high over the houses, stripping the roofs and felling the chimneys, pouring thousands of gallons of water into the rooms until doors and windows burst out, and finally carrying more than half the buildings away in the undertow. When the seas subsided only one house remained habitable, and it continued to be lived in by a stubborn survivor until her death in 1964. The old lady's stories of life at Hallsands in the years before the storm (her father had been landlord of the London Inn) and her memories of the storm itself were as fascinating to me as the legendary seaman's tales that inspired the youthful Walter Ralegh.

3. The grain ship *Herzogin Cecilie* after hitting the Hamstone Rock on the South Devon coast in 1936. She subsequently broke her back and sank in Starehole Bay.

It was these ruins, the wreck of the *Herzogin Cecilie*, and a house that I will come to later, which were to be the principal influences directing my future—but not just yet. Realizing that my peculiar antiquarian and unfashionably jingoistic interests best fitted me for a life of dilettantish ease (and knowing that dilettantism and impecuniosity made impossible bedfellows), I

4. The ruins of Hallsands, a Devonshire village washed away in the great storm of 1917. The sea and the gulls make the only sounds still heard there.

took the only remotely appropriate course and volunteered to accept a commission in the Indian Army. Invalided back into the real world in 1945, a series of accidents of no relevance enabled me to escape into the never-never land of the museum profession. In 1949 I joined the staff of London's Guildhall Museum to assist the curator in the recovery of antiquities revealed during the rebuilding of the bombed city which was then beginning. A week later the curator came down with pneumonia and never returned, and his deputy quit, leaving me to do battle alone against the bulldozers and mechanical grabs for possession of the remains of two thousand years of London's history. Six years of hard-fought but generally losing battles ensued before I surrendered and accepted an invitation to move to Virginia and take over Colonial Williamsburg's department of archaeology. Ever since I have remained deep in the eighteenth century—with occasional forays deeper into the seventeenth century and forward into the nineteenth century.

Since I entered the museum world through the back door, it is, perhaps, no surprise that I am more at home in the storerooms and laboratories than in the ordered sterility of the galleries. I find potsherds as stimulating as intact objects, and the commonplace of yesterday more evocative than its treasures. As a collector I take the same view, being happier searching the dusty shelves of junk shops than being guided by obsequious assistants through the salons of expensive dealers. I find it infinitely more exciting to hunt the unrecognized and the unidentified through the antiquarian thicket than to have my prey handed to me all patched, polished, and packaged, with nothing left to do but pay. I must confess that the pursuit of a bargain has often been as much a necessity as a pleasure, for my desire to acquire has frequently been bludgeoned into whimpering quiescence by the need to remain solvent. Like most people, I dream of being free of such restraints, but as this is unlikely to occur, I argue that fiscal responsibility injects a useful hazard into the game and makes winning that much more delectable.

Limited not only by price but also by space, most of my collecting has been directed toward relatively small objects, most recently to ceramics in use in British and American homes from the sixteenth century onward. Always my interests have developed in step with my professional career, moving ever later as my "need to know" draws closer to our own era. When my digging days were devoted primarily to Roman London, I was enraptured by the sophistication of classical artifacts and could see no merit in anything surviving from the squalid, medieval world.

Later, however, I would be moved to see this supposed squalor as a captivating simplicity to which the florid vulgarity of the subsequent British renaissance was no better than whorehouse haberdashery. So it went, step by step through the seventeenth and eighteenth centuries, each alleged lowering of my standards punctuated by anguished cries of "Thus far and no farther!" I almost choked on the Industrial Revolution and swallowed it only by looking beyond its belching chimneys and its grimy terraced dwellings to the clean air of the countryside and the rural craftsmen who continued to do their own thing through most of the nineteenth century. For years I looked with disdain on the development of transfer printing on earthenwares and condemned it as the death knell of the creative potter's art. Today, the need to understand and evaluate these wares in their own contexts has taught me to see beyond the mechanical multiplication to the source of the engravings, to the hand that held the burin, and to the girl who applied the tissue-papered print to the vessel and whose efforts to conceal the joins revealed that there was still room for human frailty. I confess, nonetheless, that I have yet to coax my Vicar-of-Brayism past the mid-nineteenth century, and even if I should survive for another thirty years, I doubt whether I can expect to discover aesthetic pleasures in a plastic cup. But while I may balk, others will not; as the supplies of collectable antiques dwindle and as new generations of collectors grow up, so our yesterdays become their ancient history and our rubbish a legacy from another age.

My choice of pottery as the principal thrust of my collecting stems in part, as I have said, from the ease with which it can be housed, but more from the fact that pottery making is one of

5. Press molding, an early ceramic technique, seen here in the making of a Samian ware bowl attributed to the potter Comitialis of Rheinzabern in about A.D. 160–170. Diameter 9½ inches.

man's oldest artistic achievements; it survives from cultures that bloomed almost at the dawn of history, and through its stylistic and technological evolution one is able to trace the rise and decline of civilizations. Through ceramics we can watch the development of a nation's taste and, as often as not, the influence of foreigners upon it. I venture to suggest that we can read the character of an era in a single piece of pottery. A mold-decorated Gaulish Samian ware bowl of the second century A.D. (Fig. 5) epitomizes to me the brash, mass-produced provincial Roman culture, the glory of the gods glowing still, but

6. A London delftware dish, decorated in blue, green, orange, and yellow in a design of some antiquity. About 1640. Diameter 14 inches.

the sharpness of the Augustan Age weakened by repetition, the edges smeared, and the image not as clear as once it was.

We can see the England of the first Stuarts in a tin-glazed dish decorated with Adam and Eve in the garden, all in bright yellow, orange, blue, and green; the whole naïve, God-fearing, and not too far removed from the Catholicism of its Italian maiolica predecessors (Fig. 6). The maturity and elegance of mid-eighteenth-century Britain abides in a redware coffee pot adorned in relief with Chinese figures and rococo foliate scrolls, together embodying the lightness and purity of line, the taste for chinoiserie, and the slightly frightening confidence that was England at the end of the Seven Years' War (Fig. 7).

7. Sprig molding was an ancient technique, but it is seen here in its elegant eighteenth-century form, decorating an English redware coffee pot of about 1760. Height 7¼ inches.

8. An American tortoiseshell-glazed cuspidor, mold-decorated with stars and stripes. Perhaps made in Baltimore in about 1870. Diameter 10½ inches.

Such a piece is a far cry from the hideous, transfer-printed effusions of leaves and flowers garlanding a molded Gothic pitcher that is my ceramic portrait of Victorian Britain a century later, or the brown-glazed cuspidor which I see as the embodiment of the United States in the same period (Fig. 8). Such fanciful thinking will doubtless be condemned as thoroughly unprofessional, yet the collector who thinks along similar lines can find comfort in the realization that he can do so only after first acquiring a better than passing knowledge of the histories and ceramics of the periods thus portrayed.

With rare exceptions, hand-thrown ceramic objects, no matter how mundane, display a fluidity and unity of form that plastic clay simply cannot avoid. So, too, does glass in the hands of a craftsman, though it lends itself to being assembled from a miscellany of disparate parts (bowls, stems, knops, cushions, feet, handles, spouts, and bits of fiddlededee) and thus too often falls victim to its creator's bad judgment (Fig. 9). At its best, the splendor of glass lies in its simplicity, in its transparency, its reflective quality, its cold winter sparkle, and its strength in the guise of fragility. For me, however, glass remains aloof, evoking more respect than affection, and perhaps for this reason my interest in it has largely been directed toward wine bottles whose dark and often opaque colors pay no more than lip service to the material's potential. Indeed, I have never collected bottles as glass, but simply as bottles. Like household crockery, they evolved with the passing years, and to the collector seeking an entrée to the past, or to the archaeologist attempting to determine where he is in time as he digs into the ground, bottles are signposts most clearly marked (Fig. 10).

When I first became interested in bottles in the early 1950s, they were not widely collected. In England the few people who were collecting them were predominantly men in the wine trade, and in America they were sought by collectors with a fairly scholarly enthusiasm for relics of the early American glass industry. Today, bottle collecting has become one of the United States's most popular hobbies, and an early Coca-Cola is as prized as a sealed Piermont Water of the mid-eighteenth century is in Britain. A Dr. Davenport's Snake Root or a Bulmer's Bitters of the 1870s can aspire to the ultimate compliment of being copied for the benefit of connoisseurs unable to secure an original. The British have yet to come as far, and most collectors confine themselves to wine bottles; but as supplies shrink and prices escalate, it may not be too long before venerable milk bottles will be offered in the sale catalogues of Sotheby's and Christie's! If that prospect seems to tax credulity, it is worth noting that in the United States there already is a National Milk Bottle Collectors' Club colloquially

9. Ancient glassblowers were given to excesses. A green glass vase or unguentarium; probably from Syria, third to fourth century A.D. Height 7½ inches.

10. English wine bottles being excavated from a tavern site in Williamsburg, Virginia. The bottles were buried in about 1745–50.

known among its members as MOO—Milkbottles Only Organization! Given the smallest encouragement, a sense of competition, and a club to belong to, people will collect just about anything.

## ✂ TWO

# To Have and to Hold

WHY DO YOU COLLECT?" I asked the large lady in the small red dress at an Antiques Forum cocktail party.

"Have a sausage," she replied. "Oriental Lowestoft. We collect Oriental Lowestoft. My husband just loves porcelain. We collect it all the time."

"Why?" I persisted.

"Why what?"

"Why do you collect porcelain?"

"Why does anybody collect anything?"

"Ah," I replied, chewing on my sausage.

I realize that this was not one of the world's more profound conversations, but it was typical of the responses I have elicited to the apparently simple question, Why collect? It is generally received first with jaw-sagging surprise and then, when no neat answer leaps trippingly on the tongue, with a kind of dismayed and defensive belligerence. Why is this idiot asking such a question? In fact, of course, there are many possible answers, the simplest being that collecting is a fundamental human instinct, and everybody knows that instincts are there—they need no explaining. By adopting that stance we can conveniently avoid the glum truth that just as many instincts are singularly unattractive, so the urge to collect is not one of our better traits. If it is any consolation, it is not ours alone; we share it with magpies, crows (indeed with all the *Corvidae*), with squirrels, pack rats, dogs, and even with an archaeologically oriented groundhog of my acquaintance. Though we all like shiny things, the human animal does not confine his evaluation of an object's desirability to the quality of its reflective surface. We have the advantage over the aluminum-foil collecting crow in that, for us, paper money shines as brightly as silver or gold.

There can be no denying that value has much to do with the collecting instinct, for once two people want the same object it acquires a commercial price. Here it is that we differ from our animal cousins; they have no means of obtaining their neighbors' treasures short of theft or mayhem. We first try trading. Competition is a basic element of the collector's makeup, and the competitive spirit, as everyone knows, is thoroughly praiseworthy and should be fostered in every contributing member of society from Cub Scouts and baton-twirling moppets to football-playing assassins. In the world of collecting, this healthy philosophy is often tastefully interpreted as "screwing the dealer." It is, fortunately, a sufficiently reciprocal pursuit as to retain the essential element of sportsmanship.

Sport and sportsmanship, like collecting, are words capable of diverse interpretation. Smiting a diminutive white ball and riding after it in a small vehicle to see where it went (golf is such good exercise) is sport of a sort; so is sitting in a stick hut on a marsh making oral sexual advances to passing ducks. The sporting spirit of the collector is equally free and quite as bizarre. It is stimulated by greed, by love, by patriotism, by loneliness, even by madness—though the madness comes later as the collection takes command of the collector. I am not thinking of the little madnesses we display in hoarding pieces of string, collecting hotel match folders, or bringing home junk from trips to the beach. I am referring to the lunacy that will allow a collector to starve rather than sell his treasures, or to live in utter squalor so as to be able to buy things of beauty. It is the same mania that makes the collector so fearful for the safety of his possessions that he will lock them, and himself, away behind high walls and shuttered windows, eschewing almost all contact with the thieving and avaricious world outside. Through inanimate objects he finds the stimulation that the normal intercourse of life fails to provide; in short, either deliberately or through disuse, he loses touch with reality. Taken to its ultimate power, collectomania can transform one into Napoleon, Noah, or Queen Victoria.

It is easy enough to dismiss such observations as the product of an overindulgence in the rich fare of Dickens, Henry James, or Sheridan Le Fanu. Nevertheless, the gnomes of irrationality are locked within each of us, and it is fun, even a relief, to sometimes let them out—providing we can get them in again. There is nothing particularly odd, for example, about collecting furniture, or so my great-grandmother thought when the first wagons rolled up to the door. But when they kept coming, and coming, and coming, she realized that great-grandpapa had a problem. Finally, in a house stuffed with furniture, he shot himself. As a rule, however, nobody sees anything very peculiar about a collector of American eighteenth-century furniture. On the contrary, it is a pursuit that is looked upon as a sign of class in an allegedly classless society. Because it is virtually impossible to collect any category of antique without having at least some interest in the period to which it belonged, it is reasonable to assume that now and again our American furniture collector sits on his William Savery chair and imagines himself in colonial Philadelphia, which, if he happens to live in New York, is thoroughly sensible thinking. We might, however, be more quizzical if we knew that he habitually rushes home from the office and changes into a Ben Franklin suit; yet we would be flattered and amused to be invited to his Washington's Birthday colonial costume party. It is all a question of degree. How far dare we let our innate Walter Mittyism go before we draw the attention of neighbors, employers, or the police?

I once knew an elderly lady dealer in Egyptian antiquities; she was fat, dowdy, and not terribly clean, yet her stark white bedroom was furnished with superb reproductions of the bed, chairs, and tables from Tutankhamen's tomb. The floor was strewn with tiger-skin rugs, as was the magnificent bed whose frame was fashioned in the shape of a pair of golden cows, representing the goddess Hathor, each head supporting a gilded sun-disc between its horns. I would have wagered an asp to an obelisk that no sooner was that old lady alone than she would exchange her drab clothes for a lapis lazuli necklace and, lying back on the bed, be transformed into the Temptress of the Nile. And why not? There could have been little joy in spending her days amid flaking mummy cases and corroding bronzes, trying to sell ushabtis and canopic jars to a world that had shed its last bout of Egyptomania before the Second World War.

Escapism and nostalgia lie at the very roots of collecting, and the tree grows best in periods of national uncertainty, when the "good old days" seem safer and more desirable than either the present or the future. Those of us whose flights of fancy have difficulty getting off the ground look back no farther than our own youth; hence the recent enthusiasm for Mickey Mouse watches, old Sears catalogues, and ancient movie magazines. Psychiatrists consider this sort of thing unhealthy and intimate that it can turn us into a generation of emotional cripples. Perhaps; though such gentle aberrations seem infinitely preferable to those that promote the collecting of Nazi insignia, animal traps, and whips of the world.

It is true that people collect some very weird things, but as a rule such collections are but the tip of the iceberg; much greater depths of oddity lie beneath the surface of the collector himself. I became aware of this early in my career on a visit to the museum at Rochester in England. The town is best known as the setting for numerous episodes in the writings of Charles Dickens, and its museum is appropriately housed in one of the low-ceilinged and labyrinthine buildings which Dickens described so well. It is a typical county museum, rich in old farm tools, costumes, leather fire buckets, memorabilia, Dickensiana, and an extremely fine collection of Roman pottery. Many of the pots are large, immaculately preserved, and possessing a beauty of form and decoration that is quite breathtaking. Among them, in an unlit case, just inside a low doorway where few people stopped to notice it, had stood a small pitcher

11. A burglar's loot. This lead-glazed pitcher from Roman Gaul was stolen from the Rochester Museum in England more than twenty years ago and has not been seen since. Excavated at Bapchild, Kent, the jug dates from the first century A.D. Height 5⅞ inches.

coated with a dirty yellowish-green glaze, dating from the first century A.D., and made in France at what is now the small town of St. Rémy-en-Rollat (Fig. 11). By comparison with many other pots in the collection, it was a singularly unattractive little pitcher, but in terms of Roman ceramic history it was both rare and important, more so than any other vessel in the collection. The curator showed me where it had stood on the shelf, the place marked by a small circle in the dust. The case had been pried open and the jug stolen. Nothing else had been touched, though there must have been a dozen other small pieces to gladden the heart of any thief looking for a "starter" collection of Roman pottery.

As far as I can recall, the St. Rémy jug bore no label proclaiming its rarity, though it had been mentioned and occasionally illustrated in scholarly journals. There could be little doubt, therefore, that the thief knew precisely what he was taking and that he would never be able to dispose of it.

The museum subsequently published a photograph of the missing pitcher in journals read by museum curators, dealers, and auctioneers but, although the theft occurred some twenty years ago, the jug has not been seen from that day to this. One wonders what pleasure anyone could derive from possessing an object he could never show to his friends, never sell, never even talk about. What will happen when he dies? Will some respected antiquarian be revealed as a common thief—he surely must think about that—or will the jug be thrown away by relatives or executors who know nothing of its importance? He must think about that too, for if he risked his reputation to steal the pitcher because of its rarity, it is unlikely that he would be willing for it to be robbed of its significance at his death.

Equally hard to understand are collectors who will pay professionals to steal paintings and other well-known works of art, for in doing so they not only become prisoners of their own collections, they also lay themselves open to blackmail. Diamonds can be recut, silver melted down, and relatively common antiques sold to unsuspecting dealers. But what do you do with a hundred delftware plates from a famous collection, all photographed and ready to appear in a book soon to be in the hands of every dealer and collector? Thieves who knew the answer raided a London apartment, equipped with boxes and Styrofoam packing, cleaned out all the pieces of importance, and disappeared without trace—save for a few shreds of their packing material left behind on the floor. Police, dealers, and customs officers on both sides of the Atlantic have waited in vain for the loot to reappear, and presumably they will continue to do so until the statutes of limitation on the sale of stolen goods run out.

Sidestepping the lepidopterists whose delight it is to poison and impale, and the amateur botanists who have ruined many a rare book by staining its pages with the life juices of crushed flowers, it is a fair generalization to say that the history of English and American collecting stems both from a curiosity about distant places, people, and things and from the pursuit of beauty. In the eighteenth century the division between the two was often drawn along class lines; the scholars on one side and the possessors on the other, men of wonder and men of taste, the antiquaries and the dilettanti.

The Society of Antiquaries of London (which included Benjamin Franklin among its eighteenth-century fellows) was founded in 1707 and held its early meetings at taverns in Fleet Street and the Strand. The Dilettanti Society was born some years later, in 1732, and in spite of grandiose plans to build itself premises designed as an exact copy of a classical temple, it, too, settled for a tavern—the Star and Garter in Pall Mall. The Dilettanti were principally interested in works of art, preferably foreign works of art. Thus, in 1751, they sent two members to Greece to compile an account of the antiquities of Athens, a project whose publication in 1762 had a dramatic influence on English and American artistic and architectural taste in the latter part of the eighteenth century. Although the Dilettanti Society was ready enough to sponsor antiquarian travels to Greece and Asia Minor, it showed little interest in the Roman and later antiquities of its own country.

In this the Society can be compared to modern American state art museums which vie with each other to acquire costly French Impressionists, Tibetan scrolls, or Fabergé Easter eggs, while ignoring the material remains of their own nation's past. Thus the Dilettanti looked down on the Antiquaries (though a few were members of both societies), many of them subscribing to the view of one contemporary lexicographer who defined an antiquary as "a curious critick in old coins, stones, and inscriptions, in worm-eaten records and antient manuscripts; also one that affects and blindly doats on relicks, ruins, old customs, phrases, and fashions."[1] Nevertheless, the Society of Antiquaries went on to receive a Royal Charter in 1751, and to a permanent and handsome home in Burlington House, Piccadilly, which it has occupied for almost a century. It remains, as it has for more than two hundred years, Europe's most prestigious antiquarian society and, now as in the past, it counts a number of Americans among its fellows (Fig. 12).

In the eighteenth century, most antiquaries were collectors, in part for the pleasure of owning things that interested them,

12.   The president of the Society of Antiquarians receiving a new member. A watercolor cartoon by Thomas Rowlandson in the collection of the Society of Antiquaries of London. 1782.

but more because there were then few public museums wherein the relics of the past could be preserved and made available for scholarly study. The British Museum did not open its doors until 1759, and then only by appointment. Previously, anyone describing a visit to "The Museum" was likely to have been referring to the Ashmolean Museum which had been established at Oxford in 1679, through the efforts of Elias Ashmole—in whom resided all the demons of the manic collector.

The nucleus of the Ashmolean Museum's treasures, though donated by Ashmole as his, was actually the fruits of another man's labors, or, to be more exact, two other men's: the Johns Tradescant, father and son. Together they had been the parents of scholarly collecting and the museum in England and are deserving of vastly more recognition than posterity and Elias Ashmole have allowed them. The Tradescants lived in south Lambeth at Caron House, which had been acquired by John the Elder in 1626 and which would later earn renown as "Tradescant's Ark" wherein were housed all the wonders of the earth that diligence and friendly sea captains could secure. Both father and son were gardeners to kings, John the Elder also enjoying the patronage of Charles the First's favorite, George Villiers, Duke of Buckingham, and it was he who sponsored the Tradescants' assembling of a collection of exotic botanical and animal rarities.

The word went out to British captains trading around the world that they should try to obtain all manner of unusual, large, or otherwise interesting "Beasts & fowells and Birdes Alyve or If not Withe Heads Horns Beaks Clawes skins fethers" as well as "seeds Plants trees or shrubs" from Guinea, Benin, Senegal, and Turkey. In a postscript Tradescant was more specific, asking that the merchants of the Guinea Company should bring back an "Ellophants head with the teethe In," or a "River horsses head of the Bigest that can be Gotten." He also asked for the heads of "Seacowes" and "seabulles . . . with hornes," as well as any "strange sorts of fowells & Birds Skines and Beakes Leggs & phetheres that be Rare or not knowne to us," along with "All sorts of shining stones . . . of Any strang shapes"; in short "Any thing that is strang."[2]

The elder Tradescant died in 1638, shortly after being appointed keeper of the botanical garden at Oxford, and in his will he left most of his estate to his son, adding "That if hee shall desire to pte with or sell my Cabinett that hee shall first offer ye same to ye Prince."[3] But John the Younger (Fig. 13) had no intention of selling the "Cabinett"; on the contrary he intended to keep on enlarging it, and when the civil war broke out between King and Parliament in 1642, he was in Virginia doing just that. It was his second trip; he had been there when his father died, he would go again in 1654, and all the time the collection would continue to grow. John had taken as his second wife a girl with the improbable name of Hester Pooks, who fortunately shared his enthusiasm for exotic plants and all things weird and wonderful. So, too, did the public, and even during the sober years between the kings, Tradescant's Ark

*J. John Tradescant Jun.
in his Garden.*

13. John Tradescant, Jr., in his garden at Lambeth. A contemporary painting by Emanuel de Critz in the Ashmolean Museum at Oxford.

received a constant stream of visitors: dignitaries, men of science and curiosity, old men with tales to tell, youngsters with wide eyes and awe in their silence, travelers and seamen bearing packages and plants, all of them pilgrims.

By 1650 John and Hester were growing concerned about the future of the collection. What would become of it after they were gone? It was a question and a fear that have haunted every aging collector, and the Tradescants discussed it with their friend Elias Ashmole. He was a kindred spirit, a student of astronomy, natural philosophy, alchemy, and heraldry; he was also a bibliophile and a modest collector of coins, medals, and antiquities but, more importantly, he was an enthusiastic admirer of the Ark and everything in it. It was Ashmole's opinion that the Tradescant Collection should be preserved for the nation, and John and Hester agreed wholeheartedly. But first, Ashmole told them, a catalogue should be published, and he would underwrite the cost of it.

The catalogue took six years to produce, not because of its vast size or the depth of its research, but because, then as now, there was many a slip 'twixt pen and printer. There was John's absence in 1654 on his last trip to Virginia, then more delay caused by the tardiness of the celebrated engraver Wenceslaus Hollar, who had undertaken to provide portraits of the two Johns as the catalogue's only illustrations. At last, in 1656, the *Musaeum Tradescantianum* was published, and although it was not destined to become everybody's pocket companion, it did what it set out to do. It preserved for all time a record not only of the stuffed birds, animal heads, minerals, antiquities, and miscellaneous marvels, but also of the trees, shrubs, and plants that the Tradescants had introduced into their unique Lambeth garden. The garden was destined to disappear along with the house in 1881, and in 1894 the Ashmolean Museum dispersed the Ashmole–Tradescant Collection in a way that caused much of it to lose its identity. Consequently, most of the content of Tradescant's Ark is known to us only as a listing in the catalogue—a sobering thought for any modern collector who keeps his catalogue in his head.

By sophisticated, twentieth-century museum standards Tradescant's Ark was a mess, something akin to Noah's at the end of the Flood, disorganized, naïve in concept, and piloted more by love than scholarship. Yet, surely, it was a magic craft wherein seventeenth-century Englishmen could truly blow their minds; and if anyone thinks it would have no popular appeal today, he has only to recall the patient lines that waited at the Smithsonian to see a drab, gray rock from the moon!

There was nothing drab about Tradescant's treasures. Who could fail to thrill at the sight of his first "Dragon's egge," at "Two feathers of the Phoenix tayle," or at "The claw of the bird Rock; who, as Authors report, is able to trusse an Elephant"? There was a dodo from Mauritius, "a natural dragon, above two inches long," a "wilde Catt" from Virginia, birds' nests from China, a circumcision knife of stone, and "A Brazen-ball to warme the Nunnes hands." If these failed to excite, there was a trunnion from Sir Francis Drake's globe-girdling *Golden Hind,* a couple of Roman urns, and some "Blood that rained in the Isle of Wight, attested to by Sir Jo: Oglander." Other wonders ran a mind-boggling gamut from a "lacrymaticall Urne for Teares, of glasse" and "Nunnes penitentiall Girdles of Haire," to women's breeches from Abyssinia and "A Bracelet made of thighes of Indian flyes." There were turtles and tortoises, teeth from a sea horse, a sea wolf, and the *"unicornu marinum,"* the closest the Tradescants could get to the true unicorn. Though failure to find it was one of their greater disappointments, other marvels did much to soften the blow. It was not everyone who could claim ownership of "A copper Letter-case an inch long . . . with a Letter in it, which was swallowed by a Woman, and found." They owned porcelain from China decorated in purple and green, and thirty sorts of tobacco pipes from Brazil, Virginia, China, India, and Amazonia, as well as "Shooes to walk in Snow without sinking," and "Pohatan, King of *Virginia's* habit all embroidered with shells, or Roanoke." Luckily, this most evocative of all American Indian treasures still survives in the modern Ashmolean Museum (Fig. 14).

Upon publication of the catalogue and the even greater interest in the Ark that it aroused, the future of the collection was again under discussion, and Elias Ashmole once more expressed his deep concern for its ultimate safety. He mentioned in passing that if he could enlarge his own modest collection to comparable proportions he planned to build a museum for it. John and Hester were suitably impressed, and in 1659, under circumstances that remain unclear, they signed a

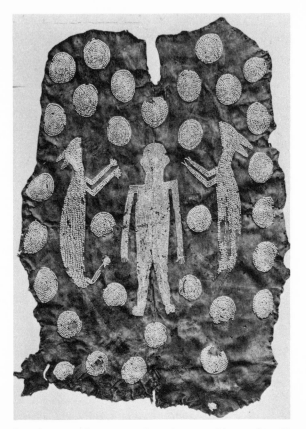

14.   The deerskin mantle presented to Captain Christopher Newport by
the Virginia Indian chief Powhatan in 1608. The cloak is decorated with
shell beadwork in designs comparable to others found on Virginia Indian
tobacco pipes in the seventeenth century. The garment was subsequently
part of the Tradescant Collection and is now in the Ashmolean Museum.

deed of gift assigning the contents of the Ark to Ashmole upon
their deaths. Hester, however, was suspicious of the document
and asked Ashmole to allow her to show it to lawyer friends,
and he made the mistake of letting her have it. On reading the
fine print, John Tradescant decided that he had been duped; he
cut his signature and the seals from the vellum, and when, in
1661, he made his will, he made no reference to any previous
disposition of the collection. Instead, he left everything to his
wife and asked that on her death the contents of the Ark
should be given either to Oxford or Cambridge University.

John died in 1662 and shortly afterward Ashmole visited his widow and demanded delivery of the deed. Hester told him that it had been destroyed, but Ashmole took her to court and had the agreement re-established. Nevertheless, Hester still had the collection, the house, and the garden—and Ashmole waited. In April, 1669, he bought the house next door and moved in beside her, presumably so that he could keep a proprietary eye on his inheritance. Before the year was out he had used an alleged robbery attempt as an excuse to prevail upon Hester to let him take the cream of the rarities into his protective custody. On November 26 she agreed, and a week later the move began.

The wrangle over the Tradescants' Cabinett of Rarities is a classic example of the power of inanimate objects to dominate the lives of otherwise sane, relatively educated, and respectable people, turning them into monsters and harridans ready to destroy each other's characters and reputations in order to gain possession of an assemblage of stuffed heads, rocks, oddities, and vegetables. It was a tale infinitely more bizarre than Henry James's classic novel *The Spoils of Poynton.*

Hester Tradescant continued to live in the depleted Ark, tending the garden and receiving old friends whom she regaled with stories of her neighbor's villainies. In 1676 Ashmole, an enthusiastic litigant, took her to court to force a retraction of some of Hester's more colorful accusations, and again he won. Less than two years later, on April 4, 1678, Ashmole was able to breathe a sign of relief and satisfaction, noting in his diary: "My wife told me, Mrs Tradescant was found drowned in her pond. She was drowned the day before about noon, as appeared by some circumstances."[4] It is hard to imagine that this could have been Ashmole's only epitaph to the last of the Tradescants, once such close friends without whom there would be no collection for him to enjoy. Eleven months later Ashmole purchased the Tradescant house and thus secured the last of the spoils, the contents of the garden. In her book *The Tradescants, Their Plants, Gardens and Museum, 1570–1662,* Mea Allen has noted the final irony. At the back of John Tradescant's own copy of herbalist John Parkinson's *Paradisus Terrestris* (1629), Ashmole wrote a list of "Trees found in Mrs. Tredescants Ground when it came into my possession."[5] He could not even spell her name.

The widow Tradescant did not live to see the foundations of the Ashmolean Museum laid at Oxford, and perhaps it was better that she was spared Elias's triumph; on the other hand, she was denied the satisfaction of knowing that an important part of his collection would never be seen. Ashmole's apartments in the Middle Temple were destroyed by fire on January 26, 1679/80, and in them his collections of antiquities and "curiosities of nature." His library and the rest of his collection was housed at Lambeth and thus escaped, and it was there that diarist John Evelyn went in July, 1678. He found Ashmole "not learned, but very industrious. . . . He showed me a toad included in amber," Evelyn wrote. "The famous John Tradescant bequeathed his Repository to this gentleman, who has given them to the University of Oxford."[6]

Ashmole died in 1692 and was buried in Lambeth parish church, the place at the east end of the south aisle marked by a substantial slab of blue marble. Outside, in the churchyard, in a tomb destined to be ravaged by centuries of London weather, lay the Tradescants: John the Elder; Jane, his wife; John the Younger; his son, and Hester, at whose direction the tomb was built (Fig. 15). Rebuilt in 1853, the sides are decorated in bas-relief with representations of Egyptian and Grecian ruins, shells, trees, and animals, and on the top are carved the names of its occupants, along with the following lines:

> Know stranger, ere thou pass, beneath
>     this stone
> Lye John Tradescant, grandsire, father,
>     son:
> The last dy'd in his spring: the other two
> Lived till they had travell'd Art and
>     Nature through,
> As by their choice collections may appear:
> Of what is rare, in land, in sea, in air:
> Whilst they (as Homer's Iliad in a nut)
> A world of wonders in one closet shut:

These famous Antiquarians that had been
Both Gardiners to the Rose and Lily
      Queen
Transplanted now themselves, sleep here:
      And when
Angels shall with their trumpets waken
      men,
And fire shall purge the world, these
      hence shall rise
And change this Garden for a Paradise.

The bones of the Tradescants still lie in Lambeth churchyard waiting for the last trump; meanwhile the world has
buried them deep beneath the memory of Elias Ashmole,
whose name and fame will endure at least as long as there is an
Oxford University and an Ashmolean Museum. The injustice to

15. The tomb monument to the Tradescants in the churchyard of St.
Mary's, Lambeth. The original was designed by John Tradescant, Jr.'s
widow, was restored in 1773, and entirely reconstructed in 1853 with a
heavier emphasis on Egyptian antiquities. The pylon to the right of the
relief is absent from drawings of the first tomb and probably was then
unrecognized as being typical of surviving ancient Egyptian architecture.

the shades of the Tradescants might have been more tolerable had the respect in which Ashmole was held been enough to insure the permanent safety of the collection. But it was not.

In 1738, Ephraim Chambers's *Cyclopaedia* described "The Museum at Oxford, called the Ashmolean Museum" as "a noble pile erected at the expense of the university, for the promoting and carrying on several parts of curious and useful learning." Completed in 1683, the museum housed "a valuable collection of curiosities . . . presented to the university by Elias Ashmole Esq; and the same day there deposited, and afterwards digested and put in a just order by Dr. Plot." Already the Tradescant name had disappeared, and the reference to curator Plot's digestion indicates that the collection had been shorn of much of its order before it reached the museum. This is hardly surprising, for having been hauled from Lambeth to Oxford in twelve large carts it is easy to conceive of ample opportunity for damage and curatorial chaos. The encyclopedia went on to say that "Divers considerable accessions have been since made to the museum; as of hieroglyphics, and other Egyptian antiquities, by Dr. Huntingdon; and of an entire mummy by Mr. Goodyear; of a cabinet of natural rarities by Dr. Lister; also of divers Roman antiquities, altars, medals, lamps, &c."

Thus, over the years, the original Ashmole–Tradescant Collection became no more than the grain of sand around which a pearl was to grow. As travel and expanding knowledge broadened men's minds, much that had been rare, shining, and strange in the seventeenth century had become commonplace, dull, and even an embarrassment a hundred years later. Few educated men still believed in dragons or unicorns, or in the "tayle" feathers of the phoenix, nor did they believe in the Great Roc and its ability to truss an elephant. Nevertheless, in 1845, the anonymous author of *Old England: A Pictorial Museum,* in writing about the Ashmolean Museum recalled the Tradescants, saying: "They believed in griffins; and rocs that can truss elephants; and why not? Did not the historian Sindbad see the birds? And yet, while we smile at these credulities, we forget how often they are in truth no credulities at all, but the mere readiness of the believer to own that there may be more mysteries in heaven and earth than are dreamt of in men's philosophy. The men of science of the present day," the Victorian author went on, "who would have rejected with scorn the Tradescants' relics of the griffin and the roc,—would, no doubt, have done the same with the marvellous relic of the dodo. . . . We own we would like to inquire at the museum what has become of the griffin and the roc—or their representative fragments."[7] In 1971 I made my own pilgrimage to Oxford to ask that very question, but I could find no one in the museum who knew the answer.

If, in some Oxford attic, Tradescant's "claw of the bird Rock" still survives, it will probably turn out to be no more than a stem from the raphia palm whose fronds were brought back from Madagascar as examples of the bird's feathers, and which may also have been the source of the "feathers of the Phoenix tayle." But do we really want to be sure? In a world that can still amaze us with a coelacanth or a walking catfish, and which once was home to the *Brontosaurus excelsus* and the flying Pterodactyl, surely there is room for a giant bird that fed elephants to its young? And what of the Tradescants' "Dodar, from the Island of Mauritius" that was so churlishly christened *Didus ineptus*, it being "not able to flie being so big"? This is believed to have been the bird that was exhibited alive in London in about 1638, but it is presumed to have been dead before it entered the Ark. Nevertheless, the catalogue listed it under "Whole BIRDS," and it remained so until 1755 when, by decree of the university's vice-chancellor and the museum's trustees it was ordered to be removed and destroyed. It was in fact burned, though someone with a conscience salvaged the head and one foot, and those still survive in the University Museum (Fig. 16).

For those of us who think of giving our collections to museums, the sad tale of the dodo serves as a reminder that the judgment of trustees is not always to be trusted. When the order was given to destroy the Tradescants' dodo, the species

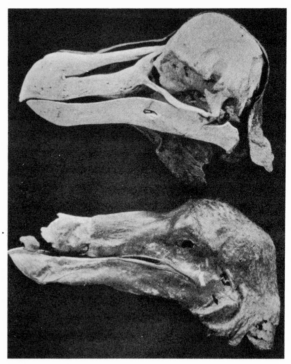

16. The skinned head of the Tradescants' dodo. The bird had been exhibited alive in London in about 1638 before entering the Ark—presumably feet first. In poor condition in 1755, the unique specimen was ordered to be destroyed and all but the head and one foot was burned. These melancholy remains survive in the University Museum at Oxford.

had been extinct for more than seventy years, and a century would pass before another intact skeleton would be found to enable ornithologists to reconstruct a model of the bird. As for the feathers, the world can only take the word of those lay bird watchers who saw the dodo on Mauritius or who visited the Ark and reported that the plumage was ash-colored, the breast and tail white, and the wings a whitish yellow.

# THREE

# Cabinets, Closets, and Dubitable Curiosities

THE VAST MAJORITY of the people who went to Lambeth to see the Tradescant Collection did so to be amazed rather than to learn; but before we condemn the seventeenth-century public for any shallowness of purpose, it does not hurt to remind ourselves that the world's largest stuffed elephant is still the centerpiece of the Smithsonian Institution's natural history museum in Washington, and that visitors remember it long after they have forgotten the okapi or the speckled snail. It is still true, too, that our capacity for amazement is enhanced by a modicum of bibulosity; consequently it need come as no surprise that in the eighteenth century some of the most celebrated collections of curiosities were housed in taverns and coffee houses.

One of the best remembered coffee-house collections was owned by a certain Don Saltero who, in 1717, was in business in Chelsea at No. 18, Cheyne Walk. He had previously earned a small niche in literary history through being satirized by Richard Steele in *The Tatler*. The catalogue of the Saltero collection smacked of the *Musaeum Tradescantianum* (which apparently was no accident) and included such wonders as "A Piece of Queen Catherine's skin . . . A painted ribbon from

Jerusalem with which our Saviour was tied to the pillar when scourged . . . Instruments for scratching Chinese ladies' backs . . . A pair of nun's stockings . . . A starved cat found between the walls of Westminster Abbey when repairing," and "Queen Elizabeth's chambermaid's hat." Commented Steele: "He shows you a straw hat, which I know to be made by Madge Peskad, within three miles of Bedford; and tells you 'It is Pontius Pilot's Wife's chambermaid's sister's hat!!'" Steele added that the Don was not descended, as he claimed, from John Tradescant, "but from that memorable companion of the Knight of Mancha."[1]

None of the eighteenth century's tavern collections survives, though many "olde inns" around the British Isles possess collections of horse brasses, man-traps, post horns, copper flagons, blunderbusses, and the like. As a rule, these displays' only relationship to their predecessors lies in the short measure of truth contained in the landlords' claims for them. Such rarities as are to be seen (with the possible exception of Dirty Dick's in London) have usually been installed by brewery interior decorators.

Besides the collections displayed in eighteenth-century taverns, there were others in now unidentifiable London apartments where, for a small fee, one could enjoy two or three rooms' worth of amazement. The German bibliophile Zacharius Conrad von Uffenback visited one of them in 1710 and found that it offered, among other things, a considerable collection of coins, some old musical instruments, a large Indian crab, a life-size wax figure of Cleopatra clasping her asp, and what passed for the head of Oliver Cromwell. The museum's owner told his visitor that he could get sixty guineas for the head, but Von Uffenbach later noted in his diary that there were many Cromwell heads to be found in England. "With this head of Cromwell there was also the head of a mummy," he added, "which I should infinitely have preferred."[2]

Britain's first truly national collection was acquired in the mid-eighteenth century and installed in the elegant Montagu House in London's Bloomsbury. It comprised three great collections: Sir John Cotton's library of books and manuscripts which he had given to the nation in 1700; Sir Robert Harley's manuscripts; and Sir Hans Sloane's much more varied collection of manuscripts, antiquities, coins, prints, precious stones, and natural history specimens. The Harley and Sloane collections were not gifts; they were acquired by means of a national lottery authorized by Act of Parliament in 1753. The money was also to be used to "provide one General Repository for the better Reception and more convenient Use of the said Collections, and of the Cottonian Library and the additions thereto." Thus did the British Museum come into being. Although designated as the home of national treasures and launched with money obtained from the populace, the museum was at first by no means as public as it is today. Up until 1820 it was open but three days a week, and then only to those who had made application in advance, admission being limited to five groups of fifteen people per day. When the young American Benjamin Silliman visited the museum in 1805, he noted in his journal: "The museum is now shut for two months."[3]

Silliman would later be described as the most prominent and influential scientific man in America during the first half of the nineteenth century. For fifty-two years he was Yale University's professor of chemistry and natural history, and as such one might expect him to have had little time for the wonderment and romanticism so characteristic of naturalists and antiquarians of the preceding centuries; but not a bit of it! Describing the British Museum's classical collection, Silliman wrote: "The Roman vases were extremely beautiful; modern arts have produced nothing superior in workmanship. I must not omit to mention," he went on, "that I saw the Roman Eagle which was carried aloft in their battles. All these things serve to carry one back to the Roman ages, to identify the past with the present, and to produce a very pleasing impression when you reflect that a Roman hand once held the article which is now in yours."[4]

Nowadays the average visitor to the "B.M." does not get to grip the goodies, and, ironically, those museum officials and scholars who do will generally go to considerable lengths to assure questioners that they derive no emotional satisfaction from it. Objects are not to be thought of in such childishly evocative terms; they are the remains of material culture, not memorials to the lives of individuals, but computer fodder to be reconstituted into cultural patterns. Similarly, many a modern archaeologist will go out of his way to convince us that in his digging he is not trying to prove anything but only to collect data which should not be interpreted until it, too, has been computer analyzed. Meanwhile, the public (whose taxes pay the scholars' salaries and whose children get the most out of museums) retains a stubborn and disconcerting interest in people, and displays such an ignorance and paucity of taste as to respond more readily to sensations than to statistics. Consequently, most small museums in Britain still get more mileage from their scold's bridle, whipping post, ducking stool, highwayman's boots, fossil footprints, and old fire engines than from their cabinets of coins and their type series of Acheulian, flint hand axes and Mousterian choppers. Although a faded slave poster may substitute for the whipping post, or a Civil War saddle for the highwayman's boot, the curators of America's lesser museums must cater to the same public. We are still ready and willing to be astounded by the largest this or the smallest that, still suckers for what, in the eighteenth century was called a *raree-show*—providing it is served to us in a contemporary and dramatic fashion.

Display techniques have never been as important as they are today; the medium, as Marshall McLuhan has pointed out, being as commanding as the message. But an eye-catching setting has always been appreciated, as we learn from Benjamin Silliman when he visited the Leverian Museum in London in 1805. He was much taken with the museum's ornithological display, calling it "a grand collection of birds in fine preservation, and beautifully, although not scientifically, arranged, in a Rotunda, with an interior gallery. In this," Silliman added, "the cases are placed, and the whole is illuminated by a fine sky light"[5] (Fig. 17).

The Leverian Museum was the late eighteenth century's version of the Tradescants' Ark. Assembled by Sir Ashton Lever of Alkerington Hall, near Manchester, it was first dis-

17.  The rotunda of the Leverian Museum, once considered the most remarkable "cabinet of curiosities" in Europe. After being won in a two-guinea lottery, the collection ended its life in Southwark where this engraving was drawn in about 1805.

played in London at Leicester House in what is now Leicester Square. Lever is reputed to have lavished more than £50,000 on the collection (a tremendous sum for that date), making it the most distinguished "cabinet of curiosities" in all Europe, none being "more rare, more curious, or more instructive." One visitor was so impressed that he sat down and composed lengthy verses in praise of it. Written in 1778 and later published in the *Gentleman's Magazine,* they began as follows:

> If I had Virgil's judgment, Homer's fire,
> And could with equal rapture strike the lyre,
> Could drink as large of the muse's spring,
> Then would I of Sir Ashton's merits sing . . .
> Here stands a tiger, mighty in his strength,
> There crocodiles extend their scaly length:
> Subtile, voracious to devour their food,
> Savage they look, and seem to pant for blood.
> Here shells and fish, and dolphins seen,
> Display their various colours blue and green.
> View there an urn which Roman ashes bore,
> And habits once that foreign nations wore. . . .[6]

And so on through diamonds, monsters, river horses, and the inevitable elephant. The verses, too, aspired to a place in the collection, being the work of a tiresomely precocious boy of ten.

According to Silliman, Sir Ashton Lever's collecting zeal brought him to a state of extreme pecuniary embarrassment. In 1790, Thomas Pennant, in his book *London,* wrote of the Leverian Museum that "To the disgrace of our kingdom, after the first burst of wonder was over, it became neglected." In 1785, however, when Lever decided to dispose of the collection by lottery, he firmly contended, "The very large sum expended in making [the collection], is the cause of its being thus disposed of, and not from the deficiency of the daily receipts (as is generally imagined) which have annually increased." He offered 36,000 tickets at a guinea apiece, but sold only 8,000, leaving himself with the 28,000 still in hand, and a more than sporting chance of retaining the collection—and the 8,000 guineas. But he was out of luck. The winning ticket belonged to a Mr. Parkinson (he bought only two) who transferred the museum to a new home across the river in Southwark, a move which apparently gave it another lease on life. It was there that Silliman saw the collection and admired the rotunda; but a year after his visit the doors closed for the last time, and everything in the building was auctioned and dispersed.

Although exhibitions of waxworks, sculptures, and miscellaneous marvels came and went in nineteenth-century London, the Leverian Museum was the last of the all-encompassing, private collections to be permanently exhibited on a pay-at-the-door basis. Once the British Museum opened its gates to a wider and less discerning public, no other cabinet of curiosities could compete with it. Although the British Museum's tremendous portico was not finished until 1847, the building had been constantly expanding, and by the 1830s it had become "The Museum," just as the Ashmolean had been at the end of the seventeenth century. Nevertheless, the grandeur of the B.M. did nothing to discourage the nineteenth-century's private collectors who were to be encountered at every turn, pursuing butterflies, desecrating burial mounds, chipping rocks in the Hebrides, and buying up classical and Egyptian antiquities as fast as they could be found or manufactured. In the seventeenth century the word *cabinett* had meant "the most retired place in the finest apartment of a building; set apart for writing, studying, or preserving any thing very precious."[7] The 1749 edition of Nathanial Bailey's *English Dictionary* was scarcely less grand in its interpretation: "a Closet in a Palace, or Nobleman's House; a Chest of Drawers or Casket to put Things of Value in." By the nineteenth century, however, the word *cabinet* meant pretty much what it does today, and every educated man aspired to some kind of cupboard or glass-topped case in which he exhibited the tangible evidence of his travels and erudition. He hung his hat on the horns of an antelope, kept his umbrella in the brassbound foot of an elephant, and scared the life out of the between-maid with a glass-eyed tiger's head mounted on the wall of the second-floor landing. There were mini-Tradescants all over England, but with the decline of the benefits of clergy and the dissolution of the gentry, their coins have been sold, their hippo heads given to the Women's Institute jumble sale, and a myriad mite-eaten butterflies have been consigned to the incinerator. The Harry

Lauder walking sticks, and the cavalry sabers, assegais, and Zulu shields that were once the pride of stiff-collared and mustachioed Victorian patriarchs are now the property of limp-wristed and droopy-whiskered dealers in the Portobello Road, hoping to catch the eye of a visiting American "Scotchman" or a Soul Brother in search of a heritage.

The connoisseurship that was so much a part of the Victorian English gentleman's life-style was not widely paralleled in America. The old, colonial plantation aristocracy had fallen on hard times, and, with a few notable exceptions, the new, landed and monied men were too busy making it and developing it to spare time for butterflies or Roman coins. Relatively few American men traveled in Europe or the Near East simply for the pleasure of it, and they had no empire to patronize.[8] Furthermore, American army officers were more at home on the prairie than with the polka and expected to end their days at a log fort at Laramie rather than in a bath chair at Leamington Spa. Britain's outposts of empire were imagined with a romantic yearning by those who stayed at home; the enemy was a noble adversary, medieval in his armored gallantry, his face fierce but fine as engraved in the *Illustrated London News*. Consequently, his helmet, plated gauntlets, jeweled daggers, and brass trays were welcome in English homes. White Americans, on the other hand, looked upon their Indians as child-murdering savages whose war bonnets, beads, pots, and scalps would not be appreciated in polite Eastern homes. Nevertheless, just as there had been kings and princes in Europe to assemble great private art collections, so in the late nineteenth century there were potentates of industry to do the same in America. At their forefront stood John Pierpont Morgan (1837–1913) who would become president of the Metropolitan Museum of Art in 1905 and whose generosity, along with that of his son, did much to improve the buildings and enhance the collections of Hartford's Wadsworth Atheneum— which opened its doors in 1844 and can thus claim to be the nation's oldest surviving art museum. It is not, however, the Morgans, Carnegies, Rockefellers, Hearsts, Du Ponts, or Mellons, and their ability to buy masterpieces as other less fortunate men relish the acquisition of an arrowhead or a mustache cup, who truly represent American collectors.

The rise of patriotic interest after the 1876 centennial celebrations saw the creation of numerous historical and preservationist societies to which gravitated all sorts of local curiosities. Lacking professional curators or proper display facilities, the gifts were often stored away in boxes and drawers where they languished until they fell apart or were thrown out. Now and then in the course of house cleaning, a long-neglected treasure would be found amid the trash, and with luck somebody would be around to tell one from the other. Thus, for example, the turning out of an old desk drawer by a newly appointed director of the Association for the Preservation of Virginia Antiquities led to the discovery of a mutilated bronze figure and a faded label stating that it had been found on an Indian site in the 1930s. Although, when the figure was first shown to me, I did not recognize it for what it proved to be, I was certain of its importance and incorrectly deduced that it was Spanish and dated from the late fifteenth century (Fig. 18). On a subsequent trip to England I found a close parallel in the Ashmolean Museum and another in the Victoria and Albert Museum and learned that the figure was part of a German-made candelabrum dating from the first half of the sixteenth century (Fig. 19). It can lay claim to being one of the earliest, if not *the* earliest, European art object yet found in the eastern United States, and it is certainly the oldest surviving colonial lighting appliance. One shudders to think what might have become of it, had the desk cleaning at the A.P.V.A. headquarters been in the hands of a clerk rather than a professional with museum training.

In addition to the major American historical societies with their sometimes opulently clublike quarters in big cities, there are many small societies and local branches of larger organizations that maintain museums of their own. Rarely have they inherited collections of importance; instead they have become useful repositories for memorabilia. Throughout the nineteenth century, the family was America's most valuable possession, and kinship the greatest honor. Consequently, these local mu-

18. Part of the standing figure supporting a German bronze candelabrum dating from the first half of the sixteenth century. Found on an Indian site in King William County, Virginia, it is believed to be the oldest example of European art metalwork yet found in America. Height 4½ inches.

seums became artifactual mausoleums for the satisfaction of the donors, with exhibits having no need to appeal to a public much broader than was to be found in the neighboring counties. Now, of course, even the smallest American museum can expect to receive tourists from every state in the Union, and if they happen to own Jefferson's gimlet, Jim Bowie's knife, or General Grant's whisky flask, they can still get by. But if all they have to offer is Mrs. Satterfield T. Wrightgard's glove "worn by her when she danced with President Buchanan at the Athenia Hotel on the occasion of his visit in 1858, and presented by her daughter Miss Amelia B. Loveless of Barren Hill, Fauquier County," then the curators are faced with a yawning communications gap.

It would be grossly misleading if I were to imply that

19. A German bronze candelabrum in the Victoria and Albert Museum, London, closely paralleling the Virginia fragment, 1500–1550. Height 9¼ inches.

eighteenth- and nineteenth-century America was without educated men for whom collecting was part of that education. On the contrary, there were colonial collectors of natural curiosities as early as the second half of the seventeenth century, and the archaeological discovery of ancient Indian pottery and implements on colonial home sites of the 1640s suggests a degree of interest in aboriginal artifacts. Thomas Jefferson's excavation of an Indian burial mound in Virginia in the 1760s attests to the "curiosity" of the colonial gentleman and reminds us also that Jefferson is acknowledged as having been one of the world's pioneers in the field of scientific archaeology. The Charleston Library Society had been founded in 1743, its members voting to add a museum in 1773; the American Philosophical Society was also created in 1743, and expressed interest in just about everything grown, born, or manufactured. In 1774 the Philadelphia-based society ordered its collections to be brought together to be housed in a "Cabinet" instead of being scattered through the homes of its members, and in 1789, with the building of Philosophical Hall, its treasures found a safe haven. But the catalogue of those treasures still smacked of Tradescantiana; thus, for example, a list of acquisitions received in 1797 included a lump of petrified buffalo dung, a stuffed swan's foot, and a pair of Indian garters. Other curiosities included a chair once sat in by Benjamin Franklin, a chip off Plymouth Rock, and a cannonball reputedly fired at Mary Queen of Scots.

When the American Philosophical Society opened its new building it had no professional curator and so a mutually convenient arrangement was made with the artist and naturalist Charles Willson Peale, who agreed to rent part of the hall to house his own natural history museum and to serve as caretaker for the Society's collection. In 1802, however, Peale moved next door, to Independence Hall, where he installed his museum on the second floor and ran it as a commercial enterprise (Fig. 20). In spite of a somewhat indigestible juxtaposition of stuffed birds and painted patriots, Peale's museum was long considered the best in the country—though supercilious European visitors claimed to find little to choose between the best and the worst. British author Frederick Marryat on a tour of the United States in 1837 observed that the nation's museum collections were of the caliber "as would be made by schoolboys" rather than by men of science. "Side by side with the most interesting and valuable specimens, such as the fossil mammoth [in the Peale Museum], etc.," Marryat told his hosts, "you have the greatest puerilities and absurdities in the world. . . . Then you invariably have a large collection of daubs, called portraits of eminent personages, one-half of whom a stranger never heard of."[9] A later British traveler was even less charitable. "A 'museum' in the American sense of the word," he declared, "means a place of amusement, wherein there shall be a theatre, some wax figures, a giant and a dwarf or two, a jumble of pictures, and a few live snakes. In order that there may be some excuse for the use of the word, there is in most instances a collection of stuffed birds, a few preserved animals, and a stock of oddly assorted and very dubitable curiosities."[10] It was a description that could well have applied, for example, to the once distinguished Western Museum of Cincinnati, which had begun life in 1820 as a genuinely scholarly institution but which, by the time it expired in 1867,

20. "The Artist in His Museum." Charles Willson Peale's self-portrait standing in his gallery at Independence Hall, Philadelphia, in 1822. Behind and to his right can be seen part of the mammoth skeleton which Peale himself had excavated.

had slipped to exhibiting a pig with eight feet and two tails, the pickled head of a local murderer, and a waxwork chamber of horrors.

No such charges of cheap sensationalism have ever been laid at the door of America's version of the British Museum. From the outset, and throughout its long life, the collections and staff of the Smithsonian Institution in Washington have played key roles in many of the most significant ethnological, anthropological, geological, and astronomical studies of the nineteenth and twentieth centuries. Somewhat ironically, the funds to establish it were provided by an Englishman, James Smithson, a chemist and mineralogist, who died in 1829 leaving a sizable estate to a nephew with the stipulation that should he die without issue, the legacy would pass to the United States. It was there to be used "to found in Washington, under the name of the Smithsonian Institution, an establishment for the increase and diffusion of knowledge among men." The nephew did so die, and the rest is history—which needs no repeating, other than to note that the Institution was formally created in 1846 with the first meeting of its regents.

The Smithsonian differed from the British Museum not only in its commitment to research but in its inaccessibility. The B.M. was in the heart of London, and London was the road and rail hub of England, and in relatively easy reach of any Briton with a pound and a potsherd in his pocket. Conversely, however, all roads did not lead to Washington, and few nineteenth-century Americans had the time, the money, or a driving desire to go there. Those who did would have found the Smithsonian's collections weak in popular appeal and less extensive than might be expected of a national museum—due in some measure to a major fire in 1865. Though well able to open the visitors' eyes to the natural and aboriginal wonders of his own continent, the collections did little to encourage the kinds of eclectic collectors who abounded in the Old World—which was probably just as well.

Today the shoe is on the other foot; the Englishman has sold his rarities, and it is the American who collects everything in sight. This is, of course, a sweeping generalization; legions of Americans collect nothing more esoteric than trading stamps, while in England one can find connoisseurs of anything from constables' truncheons to manhole covers and lavatory pulls. Nevertheless, the fact remains that collecting calls for stability, leisure, money, mobility, and education (not necessarily in that order), and while the average American did not enjoy these advantages during the pioneer generations, he has them now to a greater extent than ever before. Speaking of the "average" present-day American is to risk another charge of irresponsible generalizing. It is, however, far less dangerous than referring to the "average" Englishman of the nineteenth century, for the cultural and social differences 'twixt top and bottom in the United States today bears no resemblance to the gulf that divided them in Georgian and Victorian England. In the heyday of British collecting, it was essentially the hobby of the gentry, the upper middle class, the clergy, and scholars of various stripes who might or might not stem from one or another of these groups, but who, in any case, through their scholarship aspired to social acceptability.

The United States is probably as close to being an open, classless society as is possible (or desirable) in an aging nation, and it is curious, therefore, that so much of American collecting is entwined with status. This was brought home to me in the early 1960s when one of the lectures scheduled for delivery at the prestigious Williamsburg Antiques Forum was to be devoted to what was described as "Pedigreed English Pottery." Assuming that the speaker would have something useful to say about pieces made by identified potters for recorded customers at known dates, I urged my archaeological colleagues to attend. To my dismay, and their amusement, the lecture was concerned not with makers and original owners but with the collectors through whose hands the pottery had passed and the prices it had commanded along the way. I have since learned that, regardless of its artistic or historical importance, the value of an object can be dramatically enhanced by its having lingered long enough in a well-known collection to be so labeled. Frequently, of course, the famed figure was insufficiently orderly in his collecting to aspire to a printed label, and so one's knowledge of his ownership comes from a sale catalogue or a dealer's whisper. Then, alas, the only way that the new owner can get any mileage out of this information is to pass it on orally, converting his treasure into that most devastating of antisocial weapons, the "conversation piece."

There probably are as many definitions of what is meant by

a *serious* collector as there are people who collect. I am well aware that some of the most single-minded and unsmiling are those who see each acquisition as an investment, but to me the serious collector is one who *learns* from whatever it is he collects,* and that applies as well to the collector of barbed wire as to the connoisseur of Battersea enamels. Make no mistake; there is tremendous snobbishness among both collectors and those who serve them, not only as to the quality of our specimens, but also as to what we collect. The operative word here, of course, is money. The Bond Street art dealer specializing in Italian old masters would not be caught dead holding the door for a little old lady who loves Landseer's dogs—unless Sir Edwin should enjoy a sudden, profitable renaissance. Similarly, the collector of fine Philadelphia furniture will not feel comfortable seated on the knotty pine brand of Americana, any more than the numismatist specializing in Spanish gold pieces from the Lima mint will be at ease in the company of a man whose collection of American pennies is ingeniously mounted to form a life-size portrait of Abraham Lincoln. Collectors of fine arts can just tolerate superior numismatists, armor specialists, and collectors of classical antiquities, but they warm not at all to folk art or to bygones. And so it goes—in more ways than one.

Wars, natural attrition, the proliferation of transatlantic collectors with money in their pockets, and the expanding interests of well-endowed foreign museums have taken a tremendous toll of Britain's collectable objects. Although, quantitatively, the museums take little of the loot, what they do buy is generally the best, and in doing so they remove the pieces from the market indefinitely. The result of all this has been a steady increase in prices as demand exceeds supply. Record salesroom bids make headlines in London and New York, causing those who own remotely comparable objects considerable satisfaction. The effect on the "have-not-who-wish-they-hads" is distinctly less stimulating, deterring them from risking the humili-

---

* I can but hope that liberated ladies will forgive my persistent use of the masculine gender. To give both equal emphasis would not speed the movement, it would only slow the book.

ation of doing more than breathing on the windows of quality antique shops.

In an effort to beguile the nervous small collector, British dealers are at pains to point out that while the pound has dwindled to a quarter of its value in the past thirty years, rising salaries have taken up the slack. Thus, an object that sold for £50 immediately before the Second World War can now command £200 without having increased either in price or value. Such consoling generalizations, however, do not take into consideration the all-important fact that popularity fluctuates and that some objects that were highly desirable in 1939 are not as sought after today, and therefore their prices have not marched as closely in step with inflation as have those of items whose popular appeal came later. Thus, for example, the still soaring enthusiasm for bottle collecting has had an amazing effect on the market. A bottle for which I paid less than $4 in 1952 was paralleled by another sold at Sotheby's in 1968 for twenty-six times that figure, while in 1972 a slightly later example was offered to me at a figure close to $300. Yet another bottle, this one of no great importance, was bought in London for less than $10 but increased its price twelve times by simply crossing the Atlantic. In spite of dealers' assurances to the contrary, it is prices such as these that are sidelining the less wealthy collector or thrusting him into new and as yet unexplored or exploited fields. Consequently, our interpretation of the collectors' vocabulary (antique, early, desirable, important, significant, rare) is forever being modified downward, a descent reflected by the decision of the United States Treasury to change its customs definition of an antique from an item made before 1830 to one that is a mere hundred years old. Nowadays, such things as Victorian and later patent medicine bottles, which a few years ago were thrown out with the junk, are considered "collectors' items," and the connoisseurs of American glass insulators are as enthusiastic hunters as those who once pursued French paperweights.

Changing interests are fostered, too, by lack of space. Homes are smaller than they used to be, particularly for urban people, and many a would-be furniture buff can be deterred as effectively by square footage problems as by an ailing bank balance. Small furniture, like oak joint stools (such cute side tables), has climbed in price much faster than larger pieces of comparable date and better quality. How many of us know just where to put an eighteen-foot Elizabethan refectory table? Spatial limitations may also have something to do with a growing interest in such small "collectables" as pot lids, card cases, mustache cups, infants' mugs, buttons, tobacco tokens, and scores of other odds and ends which until a few years ago were studiously ignored.

These small objects are not only easy to house but have the advantage of being relatively easy to find. As every novice collector knows, the one thing he cannot abide is being unable to find whatever it is he is after. Thus, at the outset at least, age and rarity are less important than availability. Alas, this is another factor leading to the drying of the wells—and to the burgeoning manufacture of reproductions, fakes, and unabashedly modern and totally worthless objects designed specifically for the "collector market."

Here and there, unaffected by fashion or the desire to compete, there still lurk a few descendants of the Tradescants, eccentrically collecting into their arks whatever pleases them, excites their curiosity, provokes their wonder, stirs their memory, or titillates their imagination. Though lacking relics of the Great Roc, the griffin, dodo, and unicorn, and bereft of an Abyssinian lady's breeches, their cabinets might yet arouse the avarice of a latter-day Ashmole. One wonders, for example, how he would respond to the following:

A vase of glass to hold a Roman's tears.
An ancient urn containing cremated human bones, and a red dish
    to cover it withall.
Three human hands from Egyptian mummies most marvelously
    preserved, and in a leather box contained.
Part of a fossilized worm.
A baby's leather shoe from the time of the Virgin Queen.
A likeness of King Charles the Second of blessed memory, done in
    oils in his lifetime.
A wine bottle made for Ralph Wormeley, Gent, of Jamestown in
    Virginia, before 1652.

Another of about 1660 of remarkable small size, made for WH at
the sign of the Rose, and found in Mrs. Ansty-Perks's garden
at Breaston, Derbyshire.
A bottle filled with beer, found in the sea off Sandwich, and believed lost aboard a vessel wrecked in the Great Storm of 1703.
Three pewter coins minted in the reign of King James the Second
for use in the American plantations, but found in the River
Thames at Billingsgate.
The notebook of a pornographic poet dated 1718, hidden behind a
mantel in a house in Smith Street, Westminster—and found.

Listed out of context, these objects appear to be less a collection than the contents of an idiot's mind. The truth, however, is
that they are indeed part of a collection. I have described them
in the language of the *Musaeum Tradescantianum* to make a
point, namely that rarities and oddities still hold the power to
intrigue—regardless of more than three centuries of education
and enlightenment. Furthermore, the objects listed do have
something in common; they reflect the changing interests,
adventures, and maturing of a single collector. They are, of
course, my own.

## ＄ FOUR

# In Search of Bald Sextons

Fʀᴏᴍ ᴛʜᴇ ᴠᴇʀʏ ꜰɪʀꜱᴛ ᴛɪᴍᴇ that I held an ancient artifact in my hand (it was an Athenian coin given to me by an
old Greek lady whose long-dead husband, so she claimed, returned to visit her on wet days), I have remained angrily frus-
trated by my inability to know what an object has known or
to see what it has seen. It was a frustration that took on a new
importance on my first day as the Corporation of London's
only archaeologist, and my first encounter with someone who
had known the answers to the questions I was asking (Fig.
21). It was a cold, wet Sunday in December, 1949; the prom-
ised volunteer helpers had failed to show up, and I was alone
in the midst of a vast construction site, working in drizzling
rain to uncover the bones of a Londoner who had died in the
sacking of the city during the Boudiccan Rebellion of A.D. 61.

Although I had been given the awesome responsibility of
salvaging two thousand years of London history before it was
swept away in the postwar rebuilding, I was the greenest
archaeologist who ever held a trowel. I did not know enough to
tell whether I was looking at the skeleton of a man or a woman,
and I do not recall whether I ever found out; but I shall always
remember peering into that rain-soaked face and silently asking, Who were you? What were the last sights you saw and the
last sounds you heard? What might we have had in common?

The City of London was virtually uninhabited at weekends, and on that miserable day there was hardly a sound to be heard, save for the occasional mournful hooting of tugs on the river and the steady patter of rain in the puddles. All around me the scorched red clay of the burned Roman town was being eroded by the rain, reddening the water as it ran down into the gravel below, and reminding me of the thousands of Londoners slaughtered in what had been one of history's most violent acts of retribution. The bones of this victim (if that was what they were) lay as I might have found them two years after burial; the succeeding years had changed nothing—except for the invisible carbon 14 and fluorine content of the bones. I was intrigued by the thought that for the person whose mind had inhabited that skull, time had ended in A.D. 61, but for me it would not begin until 1927, and so for the two of us the intervening 1,866 years did not exist. Perhaps by means of controllable retrocognition man will eventually find a way of bridging time, but until he does, conscious imagination remains our only vehicle, a time machine powered by the images and artifacts that the past has left in its wake.

Who has eaten at this table or sat on that chair? What kind of man was he who blew this bottle or who decorated that dish? What was he thinking about as he worked: his God, his children, his neighbor's wife? Here is a wine glass, a thing of fragile, colorless beauty, yet strong enough to have survived the centuries. How? Where? What role did it play—making weak men brave, strong men weak, happy men sad, or sad men merry? We can only guess; but in doing so the glass ceases to be a mere artifact, instead it becomes a fragment of life.

Fascinated as I am by the elusiveness of time, it is only natural that I should find clocks intriguing. No collector's home should be without at least one antique clock, preferably made in or before the period that most interests him—always supposing, of course, that he is not a collector of classical antiquities. There is something tremendously satisfying, almost hypnotic, about the sound of a ticking clock stoically commenting on the passage of one's own life just as it has through the lifetimes of its previous owners. The tall-cased grandfather varieties of the

late seventeenth century usually have a small window in the door through which we can watch their enameled pendulums swinging back and forth—an even more mesmerizing experience. Although my own tall case clock has such a pendulum, the case was not made until the 1740s and so lacks the window, and therefore I am denied the pleasure of peering into grandpa's navel. It is, however, the tick that entrances, representing as it does one of the few sounds that can claim to have survived unchanged through the centuries. Today, of course, the preservation of sound poses no problem; we transfer it to discs or to tapes, and can expect our voices to be heard a thousand years hence—providing there is someone left to listen.

It is true that many musical instruments have survived from earlier centuries, but with the exception of such mechanical devices as musical boxes and barrel organs they do not play themselves and therefore their sounds are controlled in large measure by the musicians; furthermore, the instruments have usually been restrung, reskinned, or rereeded. An argumentative reader may contend that natural sounds have remained the same—dogs still bark as they did, birds still sing, crickets chirp, and wind still whistles. But to the true historical audiophile (there must be such people somewhere) these are all modern copies. Clocks, on the other hand, tick and chime just as they did when first made. I submit, therefore, that there can be few more satisfying mental exercises than sitting beside the light and warmth of a log fire on a winter's night (preferably with port in hand) simply listening to the voice of a clock and trying to imagine the part it may have played in the great moments of history.

Figure 22 shows a clock far less elegant than the long-case

21. The first of London's bombed sites to be developed after the Second World War. To the right can be seen the church of St. Stephen's, Walbrook, which survived the German blitz. Below, the bending figure facing the dirt bank is trying to salvage painted wall plaster from the buried remains of a second-century Roman building. The human skeleton mentioned in the text had been found where the cement dispenser is standing.

patriarchs of the eighteenth century, yet with its bell, chain, and weight defiantly exposed, it has appreciably more character. Equipped with but one hand, as were most lantern clocks made before the 1670s, its dial reminds us that it was the work of "Edward Norris at ye [Crossed Keys] in Bethlehem." The keys are pictorially rendered, not spelled out, and refer to the sign by which Norris's shop was identified. Clearly it was located in the vicinity of London's Bethlehem Hospital for the Insane (better known as Bedlam), but the use of the crossed-keys symbol is less readily explained. Norris was not the only London clockmaker to use it, for there is another rather similar lantern clock in the Science Museum inscribed "Thomas Kniston at the Cross Keyes at Lothbury." As Saint Peter and his crossed keys were adopted as the patron and symbol of London's locksmiths, it is possible that early clockmakers also made locks, or vice versa. Although this is typical of the kind of puzzle that keeps a collector on his toes, my point is that this relatively simple and unsophisticated clock has survived in working order for three hundred years. It has outlived kings and emperors; it has seen the morning glory and the evening twilight of the British Empire; it ticked on unmoved while its

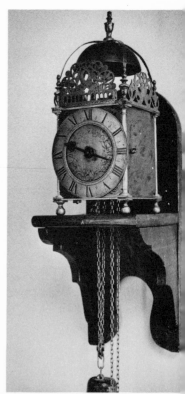

22. A brass lantern clock made by Edward Norris of London who became a freeman of the Clockmakers' Company in 1658 and its Master in 1686. Height 15 inches.

English owners feared lest their homes would be invaded by the Dutch, the Spaniards, the French, and the Germans, and now as an immigrant to Virginia its measured voice competes with the strident heralds of disaster heard each day on American radio and television. It is housed within sight of historic Jamestown Island, and within musket's sound of Green Spring battlefield (where, in 1781, Britain won her last small victory before the final humiliation at Yorktown), and I often wonder whose hands wound the clock through the years of the American Revolution—and where the winder's sympathies lay.

The Norris clock's bell was cracked when I bought it, and there is no knowing to what degree the tone has been altered in the repairing of it. Nevertheless, suspended openly above the movement, the old bell chimes out the hours with bold disregard for whatever embarrassing voice change it may have suffered. You will appreciate, no doubt, that one does not have to be a horologist (and probably cannot be) to appreciate a clock in this way. Indeed, it is a safe bet that such people would be horrified at the idea of thinking of a clock as a dream machine rather than as an ingenious assemblage of escapements, cogs, wheels, and whatnots. They probably would be equally scornful of Shakespeare's description of time as "the clock-setter, that bald sexton."[1]

Clock bells are by no means the only available source of antique tintinnabulation, and bells, as such, have a pleasurable and practical place in any antique collector's home. Those of us who have had the depressing experience of visiting houses with electric chiming doorbells must know that there has to be a more dignified method of enabling us to announce our arrival. A knocker, be it of iron or brass, has the dignity, but one has to be sure that the door and the house can take it. A return to the jangling, wired spring-bells of the eighteenth and nineteenth centuries can be an amusing alternative, but if the wires are to be hidden (as they were intended to be), it is an idea best left until major repairs are afoot or a new house is on the drawing board. I should add, too, that hanging such a spring-bell in the vicinity of the front door may be convenient and cute, but it is short on authenticity. Although resembling the bells used over shop doors, the domestic variety was not intended to be heard by the visitor; it was housed deep in the bowels of the building in earshot only of the servants.

Spring-bells attached to wire pulls were commonly used in uncommon English homes by the second quarter of the eighteenth century, and at least one rigger of such bells was plying his trade in Philadelphia as early as 1756. Nevertheless, not all fashionable American residences aspired to such campanological devices, and in 1800 Mrs. John Adams complained that in the executive mansion (not yet dubbed the White House) "Bells are wholly wanting, not one single one hung through the whole house."[2] By the second quarter of the nineteenth century, however, wired bells were common in town houses of quite modest proportions, the tones differing to let the servants know in which room the knob or cord was being pulled. Similar bells were hung on the outsides of houses in the deep South, usually on the wall closest to the kitchen or the quarters for domestic slaves. Much bigger bells, mounted in miniature belfries, were often employed to advise the field hands of meal breaks and the day's end. Not many people have a use for such large bells today; but for anyone with a sizable garden some kind of bell is a much more attractive means of summoning the family than standing at the door and yelling "Chow up!" or "Henry, it's for you!" Old wooden-handled school bells are ideal for this purpose, and although most of those to be found in antique shops are none too ancient, they have changed so little over the years that accurate dating is almost impossible. The principal clues are to be found inside the barrel (the bell-shaped part); a cast rather than a wrought-iron clapper is a bad sign, and so is a machine-made wire shaft. On the other hand, considerable wear at any point where the clapper can be made to touch the inside of the barrel is evidence of much, if not long usage.

For the would-be bell fancier who lacks a garden but has a maid, there are small silver or plated hand bells that tinkled imperiously from countless Victorian drawing rooms. To my coarse ear, however, they sound prissily pretentious. Bells of similar shape and materials were often hung in frames above the withers of wagon horses or attached to the yokes of eighteenth- and nineteenth-century oxen. Commonly called latten bells because most of them were of plated brass, these framed or boxed bells were both decorative and functional, serving to warn oncoming traffic of their approach along narrow, winding lanes.

One of the problems of collecting anything is that practically every class of object has its own vocabulary, or, to be more precise, collectors, historians, and dealers have *their* vocabularies—sometimes using terms that are misleading if not downright incorrect. Chinese export porcelain is called Oriental Lowestoft, cream-colored earthenware is collectively called Leeds, and Rhenish stoneware is often described as "tigerware" regardless of the fact that it is leopard spotted rather than tiger striped. Similarly, in the wonderful world of bells some writers (and there are not many) who discuss animal bells refer to the so-called latten type used on horse and ox harness as *crotals,* although the *Oxford English Dictionary* interprets the word as being of Irish origin meaning "a small globular or pear-shaped bell or rattle, the nature and use of which are obscure." This, however, is a description of a *rumbler* bell, a type often hung around the necks of pack horses or attached to sleigh harness. Then there were the bells worn by sheep, known as *cups, cannisters,* and *cluckets* (Fig. 23). Cups were generally of bell metal and looked as their name suggests, being cup-shaped but with their handles on the bottom. Cannister was an equally descriptive term, the bells being shaped like old-fashioned tobacco cans, cut out of sheet iron, and with two iron loops for suspension. Cluckets were made in the same way save that the barrel was wider at the top than at the mouth. All three varieties were occasionally made of brass, and sometimes those of iron were dipped in copper as a crude form of plating.

In discussing bells at such length I am not suggesting that they belong at the forefront of collectable curiosities; I mention them as a demonstration of the fact that even the most mundane objects have a lot to teach us, have their coterie of aficionados, and a terminology to confuse and intimidate the novice. I realize all too well that the reader who never saw a

23. Bells of types in use in colonial Virginia. At *left,* a copper-coated iron "cannister" normally used as a cow bell; in the *center,* brass "rumbler" bells of different sizes and used on everything from horse harness to bird scarers; and *right,* a bell-metal house or shop bell 3½ inches in height.

bell he liked will already have become bored stiff by all this campanological detail—and there is a lesson in that too. The more varied the things we collect, the better chance we have of avoiding becoming tiresome about them. The secret hoarders mentioned earlier are comparatively rare birds; most collectors want their treasures to be admired, to turn their friends on, not off. To that end, therefore, there is much to be said for collecting objects that are decorative or functional assets to the home. Small, obscure, unattractive, or now-useless things do not readily become the focus of attention, and so direct a ploy as asking "Who wants to see my collection of urethral syringes?" is considered unsportsmanlike conduct.

Antique furniture and works of art are the most obvious household assets, and they are the backbone of most dealers' business. From the point of view of the modest collector, however, space limitations necessitate that his furniture be used. Consequently, chairs too fragile to sit on or tables too valuable for glasses to be stood on serve only to promote heart failure in their owners whenever approached by a tired guest with drink in hand. Anyone wishing to become acutely aware of how heavily, untidily, and destructively male guests are prone to sit has only to buy a fragile antique chair. Concern for the safety of one's chairs, however, is not a new emotional hang-up. In 1806, Yale's Benjamin Silliman found himself being chided for leaning back in his chair "so as to make it stand upon the two hinder feet only." His British host had traveled in America and considered this practice to be peculiar to New Englanders. Silliman was unconvinced that this was so but noted in his journal that he was sure he would "never forget again that a chair ought to stand on four legs instead of two."[3]

Using antiques as furnishings, even if one has no interest in the objects as history, is perfectly legitimate if they are aesthetically pleasing or do a job that needs to be done. But it is rather sad when they are bought simply to have a few "nice pieces" dotted about to give the place class. Ironically, they tend to have the reverse effect, spotlighting their owners' lack of it—like admitting to being so uncertain of one's own good taste as to allow one's home furnishings to be chosen by an interior decorator. Taste is not something that can be pinned to a dissecting board or be analyzed in a test tube; it is measured on the yardstick of fashion, or by the opinions of a few accepted trend setters. In Europe until the Second World War the arbiters of taste were the wealthy upper classes obsequiously prompted by designers. Now, with the aristocracy either gone or reduced to impotent penury, it is the designers and manufacturers who openly tell us what we should enjoy, regardless of who we are or what we really like. Thus the glossy magazines, in cahoots with paint, fabric, and bathroom salesmen, will tell us that puce is the color for this year or that things Mexican are today's fashionable accent.

Taste in antique collecting is equally fickle and manipulable. Until a few years ago just about everything Victorian was considered the very nadir of tacky taste; now it is back in favor, and things which even the Victorians thought cheap and nasty are today hailed as nice—and expensive. Nevertheless, there still remain plenty of opportunities for the collector to show his individuality. If he is a speculator, he can expect to turn a respectable profit by concentrating on an area that is currently out of fashion or, better still, one hitherto unexplored. By assembling the "classic" collection and writing about it he becomes the acknowledged authority; then, while his book and his name are still in the minds of his readers, he sends the collection to auction where the pieces fetch more than they are intrinsically worth by virtue of their newly acquired pedigree.

"Yes, madam, there is a tiny age crack, but you see it's a documentary piece from the Adam Thoroughgood Collection. I expect you saw it illustrated in his article in the *Antique Connoisseur.*" The fact that the object is not so much age-cracked as held together with fish glue is instantly overlooked, swamped by the magic of the Thoroughgood name.

Personally I have never been interested in paying inflated prices for other collectors' castoffs. For me the fun lies in breaking new ground, in discovering unrecorded specimens and tracking down their histories. If you know that someone else has already been through the same exercise, the sense of adventure and of accomplishment are drastically diminished— which is why I remain a disciple of the Tradescants. The specialist collector is concerned with learning more and more about less and less, developing a tunnel vision that prevents him from looking anywhere but at the objects of his affection. He is concerned with their date of manufacture, and to a degree with their purpose, but primarily he is interested in assembling all possible sizes, variations, and styles of whatever it is. When, at last, the myopic collector of Welsh loving spoons sits grimly down to write his definitive article, "The Lure of the Love Spoon," the odds are that it will be all spoon and very little love, all whittling and no wedding. With the spoons illustrated a dozen at a time, the reader loses sight of the fact that each was once a prelude to courtship representing an emotional bridge between two young people, masculine desire in the carver being turned to maidenly delight in the recipient. Instead, seen as a collection, the spoons lose their message and become mere specimens of Welsh folk art. The old adage that "all work and no play makes Jack a dull boy" remains equally true when he becomes an old collector; a stodgy diet of facts leaves him too corpulent to soar on flights of fancy, and the magic of the past slips away from him like a morning mist before the sunrise.

I am not suggesting that listening to clocks ticking or bells tinkling is alone stimulus enough to send us tripping into history. Imagination must be bolstered by knowledge, although, alas, the possession of it is liable to destroy our pleasure in other people's time machines. An otherwise superb television play set in the seventeenth century can have its carefully woven spell broken by the sight of nineteenth-century jars, bottles, and glasses. A generally well-researched movie of an eighteenth-century classic is torpedoed when the hero points a flintlock pistol with its frizzen open (and thus incapable of firing) and the villain still throws in the towel. Similarly, the novelist who allows his Elizabethan heroine to throw *up* the window and listen to the dawn chorus (Hark, hark, is't not a meadow lark?) does so unencumbered by the knowledge that throw-upable windows would not be introduced until a century later. But for the readers who do know, their literary magician is transformed into an inky-fingered charlatan.

As long as writers, artists, and film directors are to be our guides, naïveté remains one of the time traveler's greatest assets. It was a lesson that was graphically demonstrated to me at the age of eleven, though I was not to realize it until thirty years later.

In the summer of 1938 I was taken by childless neighbors on a camping trip into the Taw Valley of central Devonshire and to a minuscule hamlet named Eggesford. It was my first escape into the wilder English countryside, and the woods around our campsite were all I had dreamed they might be. Turned loose to explore them on my own, my imagination ran riot. I was in the New Forest hunting with King William when he got the arrow in his eye; I was in Sherwood Forest helping Robin Hood outwit the Sheriff of Nottingham, and I am sure that had I by then been exposed to *As You Like It* I would have seen myself in the Forest of Arden listening for the voices of approaching courtiers, lovers, shepherdesses, comic servants, transvestites, and assorted hey-noninoers. In spite of more wet days than I deserved, I roamed the woods untiringly, and there, amid the ferns, the lichens, the fallen trees, and the tinkling streams, I painted myself a medieval dream world that would have done justice to the Pre-Raphaelite Brotherhood. I was small, the trees were tall, and when the sun had the grace to peek through, it studded the dripping leaves with diamonds. But nothing my youthful imagination could conceive matched the revelation that awaited me one gray and misty morning as I emerged from the woods into a broad, green meadow.

Beyond a herd of grazing cows stood a vast ruined mansion more romantically, yet awesomely evocative than Mr. Rochester's Thornfield, Rebecca's Mandelay, and Miss Havisham's Satis House all rolled into one (Fig. 24). There were towers and battlements, tall mullioned windows, parts of stone and parts of brick, a medley of medieval manor and Jacobean grange. One wing lay in a mountain of rubble, and the walled courts and terraces were thick with weeds, but there was still glass in some windows of the central block, and the collapsing roof still kept part of the first floor dry. Nevertheless, ceilings had fallen, and breached and rotten floorboards offered precipitous access to black cellars below, and I ventured only into one room whose floor seemed relatively safe. I took it to be a kitchen, for on a wall beside the massive hearth hung a glass-fronted box filled with little numbered windows—part of the wired bell system.

At that age I knew nothing of architecture, but I had read *Ivanhoe* and *The Black Arrow,* and I was entranced. I could see that this was a house that had grown over the centuries, yet no part of it failed to fit my romantic image of the past, and it may have been here that I first became aware that the passage of time is itself intriguing. Today, when people tell me that they have torn down a nineteenth-century wing to restore an eighteenth-century house to its original appearance, I remember the impact that the apparent continuum of Eggesford House had on an eleven-year-old boy, and I wonder whether to applaud or condemn.

So great an impression did the house make on me that more than twenty-five years later I was able to describe it to my wife in what proved to be almost photographic detail. There had been beauty in the way that nature had embraced the ruins, yet at the same time they remained more than a little frightening. My imaginary Merry Men of the woods had been replaced by sepulchral shadows, and the solitary cawing of a crow from a mist-shrouded chimney top left no doubt that this was a place to be avoided once the sun went down. (Fig. 25). I have revisited it over the years whenever a nightmare needed a setting, and I have doodled its towers and crumbling stones in countless moments of boredom. It was inevitable, therefore, that one day I should return to Eggesford, and I did so in the late summer of 1966.

The ruins were still standing almost exactly as I had remembered them, though less lofty than they once had seemed. The lone medieval tower was there, divorced from the body of the house by the collapsed wing, and the central block, now empty-windowed but still crenelated and impressive, remained as evocative as ever—from a distance. But as soon as I approached it across the meadow I realized that I had been taken. The house had made me what it was itself, a product of the *Ivanhoe* syndrome. It was a creation of the nineteenth century's medieval revival, architecture designed to stir the imagination and rekindle the romantic fires of English chivalry. I was living proof that the architect had done his job well. My initial disappointment, and annoyance at having been duped, were soon tempered by a growing interest in the house for what it was, and I would later discover that I had shared my youthful enchantment with some famous figures of Victorian letters.

The mansion was built in 1830 by the Honorable Newton Wallop Fellowes, afterward the Fifth Earl of Portsmouth (Fig. 26). For thirty years he was master of the Eggesford Hunt, and during that time he built it into one of the most renowned in England, establishing a pack of hounds of such distinction that his dogs provided the foundation stock for some of the best packs still running. Today, in spite of the earl's long life, his wealth, and his position, few people (even in the village) remember the name of Newton Fellowes; yet, ironically, that

24.  The ruins of Eggesford House, once the Devonshire seat of the Fifth Earl of Portsmouth.

25.  Jacobean-style chimneys still provide nesting places for crows above the wreck of Eggesford House.

26. Eggesford House shortly after its completion in 1830. The artist has added an extra story, but otherwise the surviving remains, from their medieval-style towers to the mock Tudor front, bear witness to the authenticity of the rendering. Designed to evoke the spirit of romantic chivalry, the house in ruins still weaves its spell.

of a neighbor, less noble, but a close friend and frequent visitor, will survive the centuries. He was the Reverend John "Jack" Russell, a perpetual curate of the village of Swymbridge, a celebrated "sporting parson" who gave his name to a breed of terrier. Jack Russell not only shared the earl's love for hunting but also his wife's birthday, as did another of their sporting friends, Charles Kingsley, author of two of my childhood favorites, *Westward Ho!* and *Hereward the Wake.* Although Kingsley left his Dartmoor home at the age of nineteen, he is said to have returned whenever he could to share a triple birthday party at Eggesford House, reputedly an annual bash of mammoth proportions. I like to think that if, on the night of each June 12, the villagers will turn down their radios and television sets, they may yet hear the strains of a polka borne on the wind as ghostly dancers cavort in the ruined ballroom.

In his book *The Buildings of England,* Nikolaus Pevsner has described Eggesford House as an "eminently picturesque large ruin, standing against the sky, surrounded by the woods of the Taw valley like the best of follies,"[4] and as such it is hard to realize that its past glories are barely a century old. Kingsley died in 1875, Russell in 1883, and the Fifth Earl as recently as 1891, the same year as did another of his literary guests, James Russell Lowell, the American poet, essayist, and minister to Britain from 1880 to 1885. So hard have blown the winds of change, and so far have the wheels of progress traveled, that those tranquil and lordly days of England's summer already defy comprehension. Attempting to imagine what it must have been like to have been mistress of Eggesford House in the reign of Queen Victoria is as difficult as accurately envisaging the life-style of Bess of Hardwick or of Thomas Jefferson at Monticello. The very idea of a 3,000-acre estate, stabling for forty horses, a house with thirty bedrooms, and two full-time servants just to take care of the lamps is enough to boggle the imagination of a two-bedroom apartment dweller. It is equally difficult to reconstruct in contemporary human terms the relationship (or lack of it) that existed between his lordship and the assistant lamplighter. The earl is not totally lost, his biographical data is recorded, and his portrait probably survives, but what of the lamplighter? No one painted her portrait; her legacy may be nothing more than one of the lamps she trimmed and polished, a lamp now gracing the shelf of a New York antique dealer or lying buried in the ruins of Eggesford House.

What, one may ask, has all this got to do with collecting? First, it reminds us that the twilight of the past has a knack of creeping up on us, allowing the lengthening shadows of forgetfulness to obscure people and places that are little more than a long lifetime into history. Next, it provides an object lesson for those of us who tend to scorn Victorian antiques as being too new to be worthy of our attention, and third, it puts a new shine on the cliché that ignorance is bliss. The nostalgia-covered walls of Eggesford House were built to evoke in anyone whose knowledge of the past extended no deeper than the pages of the *Waverley* novels precisely the same images of romantic medievalism as they did in me. Thus, as I suggested at the outset, when it comes to purely cerebral excursions into the past, what we do not know need not bother us—providing we remain ignorant of our ignorance.

*✑✐* FIVE

# Something for Nothing

THE LURE of the treasure hunt is more than the mere desire for wealth without work. It was the motivating force that built the Spanish empire in America, that sent Sir Walter Ralegh in search of El Dorado, and in recent years has caused large sums of modern treasure to be expended on diving expeditions off the Florida coast and around the islands and cays of the Caribbean. Most of these enterprises end up investing much more than they retrieve, but now and again the results are spectacular, and eventually less hardy, armchair adventurers can enjoy the vicarious pleasure of possessing a genuine piece of sunken treasure by bidding for it in the comparative safety of the auction room.

The most spectacular haul to be sold in America in this century was the loot recovered from the Spanish fleet wrecked off the Florida shore near Cape Canaveral on July 31, 1715. When sold at the Parke-Bernet Galleries in New York in 1967, the treasure realized $227,450 and was described in the catalogue as "the richest haul of sunken treasure ever to appear at public auction." Carried away by the romance of it all, the usually reserved auction house preceded the sale with a public exhibition—complete with reconstructed captain's cabin, canned thunder and lightning, and a live macaw, presumably standing in for Long John Silver's parrot. The lots were pri-

marily specie divided into 240 units, ranging from single specimens to clusters of coins fused together and sold by weight;
but for those who preferred their bullion in lumps, buyers
could bid for ingots of gold and silver. For my part, I find
wealth in these forms about as exciting as fat-and-fortyish
barmaids, and having examined one poorly struck Spanish
coin, I consider I have seen enough. Fortunately for the
salvors, this Philistine's view was not shared by the bidders.

By far the most beautiful and, to my mind, desirable object
in the Parke-Bernet sale was a Chinese gold whistle fashioned
in the shape of an open-mouthed dragon, a thing of exquisite
delicacy attached to an equally delicate chain more than
eleven feet long and comprising 2,176 gold links (Fig. 27). The
whistle is claimed to have belonged to the commander of the
fleet, Captain-General Juan Estéban de Ubilla, whose ship was
one of those that foundered off the Florida shore. The sale
catalogue states that the object was recovered from the wreck
of the flagship, and one immediately has visions of the whistle
being scooped up from the seabed by a diver who rises to the
surface with the gold chain streaming out behind him like the

27. Found on the Florida shore near Cape Canaveral, this gold whistle
and chain is one of the most valuable baubles ever retrieved from an
American shipwreck. The remarkable object was made in the Orient for
the European market and is believed to have been the emblem of office
thrown overboard by Captain-General Juan Estéban de Ubilla as his
Spanish Plate Fleet foundered in the hurricane of July 31, 1715.

glittering tail of a submarine comet. He breaks the surface in an exuberance of white spray, holding aloft his trophy and eloquently crying "Eureka!" or more probably, "Hey, man, look what I got me!" But in fact that was not the way it happened. This $50,000 bauble was found on the beach.

Simply picking things up is undoubtedly the ideal method of discovering monetary treasure or assembling a collection of anything from seashells to old bottles. The trick is to know where to look—and to get there first. Seashells, of course, are found on the seashore, but relics of antiquarian interest generally are not—the Spaniard's whistle notwithstanding. Rivers, on the other hand, were recognized repositories for the detritus of history long before the word pollution found a place in the English language, indeed, before there *was* an English language. Ever since man emerged from his cave, he has settled either on high ground for self-preservation or on low ground by the riverside for self-propulsion, and for extracting food from the water while replacing it with garbage. Thus the world's rivers have become storehouses of the past's unwanted treasures. Because their wet silt preserved organic materials that would otherwise have quickly rotted away, rivers have provided antiquarians and collectors with unparalleled opportunities. Unfortunately, however, these are rapidly diminishing as the destruction of river foreshores is added to the price of progress.

Here in America, the rivers have as much to offer as do those of the Old World, although, like them, their most productive sites are no longer accessible to the casual collector, buried as they are beneath the waterfront buildings of great cities. Their relics are revealed, therefore, only when new construction calls for deeper digging below previous basements and into silt hitherto undisturbed. Then the remains of boats, barrels, wooden boxes, clothing, leather goods, and countless other artifacts of earlier times are smashed, scooped up in the jaws of mechanical excavators, and dumped where no one will ever find them. Wharfside dredging can have comparable results, as was dramatically demonstrated in the Delaware River in 1948. There, off Woodbury Creek below Philadelphia, a commercial dredger cut into the hull of a wooden merchant ship sunk in the 1770s, perhaps early in the Revolutionary War. As the dredge and the tides continued to pull at the damaged hull, numerous wine bottles and other artifacts were washed ashore. Many more were sucked into the pipe, carried two miles downstream, and spewed out onto a riverside marsh where local antiquaries waded about in a sea of mud salvaging an amazing collection of pins, nails, spikes, shoe buckles, brass buttons, scissors, pocket knives, table cutlery, locks and keys, latches, waffle irons, and tools of all sorts.

After it became known that the dredging had disturbed something of importance, a telephone-equipped government diver went down to examine the wreck and reported what he saw to the surface. He found, none too surprisingly, that the ship was filled and covered with mud. "From what I can see of it," he added, "it appears to be about two hundred feet long and made completely of wood. There are two-inch plank frame boards, supported with four-by-fours around the hull. From where I am now standing," he went on, "I can see into part of what must have been the ship's hold. In it there are what appears to be scores of kegs of nails. I am now gathering a number of grubbing hoes, and I'll bring them to the surface with me."[1] The diver apparently did just that, for some of the hoes were subsequently given to the Philadelphia Historical Society and to other local antiquarian groups.

The artifacts from the Delaware wreck were quickly dispersed among the finders, and as far as I can determine no careful study was ever made of either the vessel or its cargo. It is evident, nevertheless, that the dredging had brought about the destruction of a "treasure" whose historical value was far greater than that of the Spanish Plate Fleet's bullion. Monetarily, of course, the yield from the Florida wrecks was infinitely larger; gold and silver coins have an easily determinable worth; iron padlocks and brass buttons do not. But apart from a group of Chinese porcelain cups which provided direct evidence of Spanish trade with the Orient through Manila and the East Indies, the Florida treasure had little to tell us about eighteenth-century life or even anything very important about the ships whence it came. The vessels had been beaten to pieces on the offshore shoals, the cargo had been dispersed, and most of the wood and other organic materials had been eaten by the teredo worm, leaving only ballast stone, and iron fittings and cannon to rust and become cased in coral. The Delaware wreck, on the other hand, had settled into mud and remained more or less intact; the iron had not rusted, the brass still shone, and there was life in the leather. It was an unparalleled American time capsule which, had it been saved, would today provide Philadelphia with a historical attraction that might rival Stockholm's *Vasa*, the ship which sank on her maiden voyage in 1628 and which was raised in 1962 and successfully towed back to port.

Raising ships, or even mounting expeditions to recover their treasures, is a dream out of reach of the average collector. In spite of the availability and efficiency of modern metal-detecting devices, searching for treasure on the seabed is much like looking for the proverbial needle in a haystack, and once in a while even that is easier to find. In 1971, divers working off Marathon in Florida discovered a sealed wooden box weighing 410 pounds and elaborately marked with its owner's initials. The press quickly dubbed the box a "treasure chest" and concluded that it came from another Spanish fleet lost in a hurricane in 1733 (Fig. 28). The finders, the Doubloon Salvage Company, Inc., duly turned over the box to the Florida Department of State to be appraised and the product shared (as their contract demanded), and between the time of its discovery and the day it was to be officially opened speculation as to its contents ran a mouth-watering gamut. When that day came, two months later, an audience of divers, stockholders in the salvage company, historians, archaeologists, and state officials held its breath as laboratory technicians slowly revealed "the tips of what appeared to be comb teeth or needles."[2] They later turned out to be steel awls, and although they came in different types, awls was all the box contained. Needless to say, the Doubloon Salvage Company and its stockholders were none too pleased with their treasure.

The Marathon box had been found by a metal detector

28. Every diver dreams of finding a treasure chest. This one was recovered near Marathon, Florida, and is seen here being opened in the University of Florida's archaeological laboratory. Unfortunately its contents were not all that the finders had expected.

"some four to eight feet beneath the ocean floor" and was retrieved at considerable expense and no little effort. Now and then, however, as in the case of the Captain-General's whistle, "sunken" treasure can be delivered to us without setting so much as foot or snorkel in the water.

British beachcombers walking the Kentish shore near Sandwich following the great gale that swept across England in January, 1953, found broken and intact glass wine bottles of the early eighteenth century strewn along the high-water line (Fig. 29). Some of the bottles were still corked and full, and a few were opened and sampled by the finders; others were deliberately broken. A local antiquarian suggested that they had contained whiskey or brandy and came from a smuggler's hoard that had been uncovered and scattered by the storm-driven waves; but although later analysis proved the contents

29. Bottles of early eighteenth-century beer found on a beach near Sandwich, England, in 1953. They are believed to have passed the intervening years sealed in the hold of a ship sunk in the Great Storm of 1703.

to have been only beer, the explanation for the bottles' presence on the beach turned out to be distinctly less mundane.

On being invited to examine some of the specimens picked up by Major-General and Mrs. I. D. Erskine of Sandwich, I found that all were of the same squat type datable within the time bracket of 1700 to 1715, and highly desirable additions to any bottle collection. The stretch of beach on which they were found was about 150 yards long, and as both the intact and broken bottles were all found close to the high-tide mark and did not stretch out to the low-water line, it at first seemed unlikely that they had washed in from some submarine repository. Furthermore, the lack of abrasion on the sides of the whole bottles precluded their having bowled any great distance over the sandy seabed. Had the bottles contained dutiable liquor, the smuggler's cache theory would have been entirely reasonable. But they didn't, and it wasn't.

The town of Sandwich lies inland a distance of about a mile and a half behind a tonguelike spit, and it was on the sea side of that projection that the bottles were found (Fig. 30). Seven miles offshore lies the long and treacherous bar of the Goodwin Sands, while to the north the projecting hook of the Isle of

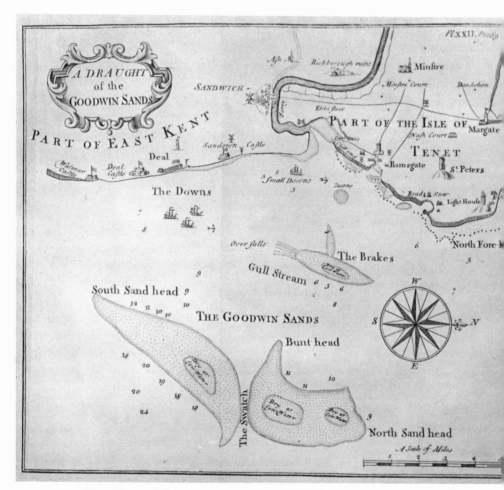

30. Chart of the Kentish coast and the Goodwin Sands in 1736. The bottled beer was found on the shore opposite the anchorage called the Small Downs.

Thanet protects the waters between sand and shore from the furies of the North Sea. This sheltered bay is still one of the world's most celebrated anchorages. It was there, in the Downs, that English convoys bound for America and the Orient assembled through the seventeenth, eighteenth, and early nineteenth centuries. But just as the Downs were known for their safety, the Goodwins, and their inshore cousin the Brakes, had a reputation as one of the most dangerous shoals known to mariners. Called the "shippe swalower" in the Middle Ages, and described by Shakespeare as "a very dangerous flat, and fatal, where the carcasses of many a tall ship lie buried,"[3] the Goodwin Sands continue to merit their ill repute, matched only by that of the banks off Cape Hatteras. The Goodwins differ, however, in that they are largely exposed at low tide and stretch in an ever-shifting strip up to five miles long, and ships driven onto them are gripped, dismasted by the surf, and finally buried in the sand. There they remain until wind and currents move the Goodwins in another direction, causing the carcasses to be disinterred. It seems possible, therefore, that in the 1953 storm, a long-buried hull had been breached and its cargo suddenly decanted. Reasonable though that explanation was, and even if the ship lay in the sands of the Brakes, the bottles would still have had to travel three miles across the seabed in a storm so wild that they would have been abraded all to pieces. Instead, the bottles all arrived together on a short stretch of shore, some in such mint condition that even the thin brass wire securing the corks remained undisturbed. There was an answer, however, and it had resided in a leather chest in a windowless room at the Manor of Cleeve Prior, near Evesham in Worcestershire, where it had been since 1713.

Exactly two hundred years later, the chest was found and its contents examined; they proved to be the papers of Captain Thomas Bowrey, a London adventurer in the East India trade in the late seventeenth and early eighteenth centuries, and a man who kept every last record of his business transactions. Among his papers are the accounts, invoices, inventories, letters, and journals relating to Bowrey's ship the *Rising Sun* and her voyage from Greenwich to India and back in 1703–1704. It was a journey that got off to a bad start, for on the night of November 27, 1703, while lying with the assembling fleet in the Downs, the ship faced what was to be one of the worst storms ever to rage across England. Dawn found the convoy scattered, wrecks littered the Goodwins, many large vessels had vanished without trace, and others, dismasted and helpless, were driven onto the Holland shore or were carried up the

North Sea to Scandinavia. The *Rising Sun* was luckier than most; she lost her masts but wound up at Texel with her hull so little damaged that after refitting she was able to continue and complete her voyage. The Bowrey Papers show, however, that had she foundered on the Goodwins, she would have gone down with no fewer than 2,500 bottles of beer in her holds. In all, the *Rising Sun* carried in excess of 5,000 glass bottles of beer and wine, all of it packed in wooden chests. So complete are the Bowrey Papers that they include invoices not only for the beer, the bottles, the corks, and the wire to hold them down, but also for the chest and the iron hinges and locks to secure them. The ship's inventories show that the chests were of two sizes, the larger holding up to 176 bottles, and the smaller around 116 bottles. Thus the ship's documents not only describe an occasion when ships carrying appropriate cargoes were wrecked on the Goodwins in the 1700–1715 period suggested by the salvaged bottles, they also show how such bottles could have traveled from wreck to shore and have arrived together and unbroken.

A chest better preserved than the rest could have been sucked out of the broken hull when the 1953 storm eroded the sand around it, have been carried across the Downs and cast onto the Kent shore where it burst, ejecting the bottles. That no sign of the chest was found is easily explained; beachcombers reported that the gale had left the shoreline littered with driftwood, and as no one was on the lookout for the remains of an eighteenth-century chest, it is unlikely that they would have seen any difference between its boards and the rest of the flotsam. Unfortunately it was some weeks before I was able to visit the site, and by then, tides and beachcombers had swept it clean. I did learn, however, that more bottles had been trawled up by fishermen in the area shown on the chart (Fig. 30) as the Small Downs, and I was able to acquire one of them from a Ramsgate antique dealer. Subsequent analysis revealed that this, too, contained beer. It seemed likely, therefore, that the bottles from the Small Downs came from another chest that broke open in deep water, and that hundreds more bottles like them were rolling about on the bottom of the bay. As far as

I have been able to determine, these salvaged bottles, probably no more than half a dozen in all, can claim to hold the oldest surviving specimens of bottled beer.

Although I shall have more to say about bottle collecting in a later chapter, it is worth noting that some of the best examples have come back to us after spending the intervening years under water. In America, the classic bottle haul was landed in 1934 when Virginia's Mariners' Museum and the United States National Park Service went prospecting in the York River for souvenirs from ships sunk at the Battle of Yorktown. Using both divers and a mechanical "clam-shell bucket," at least three vessels were found and explored, resulting in the recovery of many artifacts that included scores of glass wine bottles. The methods then employed would now be considered vandalism of the worst kind, but one has to remember that in 1934 the aqualung had not been invented and the discipline of historical archaeology was in its infancy. Nevertheless, one still blanches at the sight of a National Park Service photograph captioned "The clam-shell bucket comes up with an assortment of material from within a wreck."[4] Another equally graphic picture (Fig. 31) shows wine bottles being hauled aboard the salvage barge by means of a line looped around their necks like a necklace for a bibulous mermaid. So plentiful were the bottles that a later director of the Mariners' Museum decided to sell them off to collectors. Not knowing their worth, he

31. Bottles being hauled from the York River in Virginia during the search for the hulls of British ships sunk in 1781 at the Battle of Yorktown.

struck on the novel approach of doubling the price every time he sold one, commencing at two dollars and quitting when he could find no customer at two hundred. Today, of course, collectors would fall all over each other to secure a genuine Yorktown bottle at that price.

In the years that have passed since the Yorktown salvage project, many more eighteenth-century bottles have been recovered from the York River, most of them by fishermen dredging for oysters and clams. However, one of the best-preserved specimens was simply picked up by a local resident who, in 1970, found it sticking out of the mud farther upstream on the north bank. Be that as it may, the principal source of colonial and later bottles for the American collector has not been the York, but the mangrove swamps of the Florida Keys. Thrown overboard from passing ships, washed ashore from countless wrecks, or left behind by hunters and fishermen, the bottle relics of three centuries lay amid the roots awaiting the day when collectors would recognize their age and value. That recognition came about fifteen years ago, and since then the Keys have been picked over again and again by an ever-growing army of collectors and by entrepreneurs anxious to supply them. There may still be bottle treasures to be found there, but now the more enterprising seekers are moving farther afield, to the less well-trodden islands of the Caribbean and to South America.

Many late-seventeenth-century bottles have been brought up from submarine excavations on the site of the submerged Jamaican city of Port Royal, which sank in the great earthquake of 1692, but they were retrieved only with great difficulty and are in such poor condition that the effort was hardly worthwhile. Much better preserved, and lying in relatively clear water on the other side of Kingston harbor, were many later bottles discarded from the military post at Port Henderson, no small number of which have been rounded up by Sunday-afternoon scuba divers and shipped to America. That was before the Jamaican government very properly made it an offense to export its national antiquities; but unfortunately it is a law that is hard to enforce, and not long ago I saw four excellent mid-eighteenth-century bottles that had passed through the hands of a Charleston dealer after being smuggled off the island. The government of Guyana (previously British Guiana) has taken a similar step to protect its treasures—but not before literally hundreds of bottles and other artifacts were shipped out by a single team of prospectors.

It is thoroughly desirable that national governments should concern themselves with the protection and retention of their antiquities, for if they do not, no one else will. Furthermore, even if many of the relics are barely a century old, there is still no reason for letting foreigners carry them off—particularly if their motives are strictly mercenary. Any of us who tampers with the remains of the past has a moral responsibility to it, and that is in no way diminished by the claim that we are absconding with the loot in the name of historical research. Besides, the responsibility is not only moral, it is one of legality. Hardly a square inch of the earth exists that is not on record as being owned by someone, and therefore the removal of anything from it (or even setting foot on it) without permission can land us in trouble.

As an antiquary who resorts to archaeological excavation as a means of obtaining artifactual information, I am well aware that digging is inherently destructive. The earth should never be disturbed solely to obtain collectable objects no matter whether the collector is a curator in a great museum or a kid with a metal detector. It is the relationship between the artifacts and the layers of the soil in which they lie that reveals when and how they got there; deny us that information and the object has no more to say than if it had been bought from an antique dealer who declined to reveal where or from whom it was obtained. Unfortunately, the vast majority of the small and collectable items that have been found in the ground and now grace museum and private collections have been robbed of their pedigrees and can tell us no more of their history than is to be learned from their physical appearance. Not all "found" objects are imbued with heavy archaeological significance, however. The girl who picked up the wine bottle at low tide on the York River was not wresting her treasure from some immensely meaningful mud. There was no telling how the bottle came to be where it was; it could have been thrown from the shore, washed out of a refuse pit dug into a now eroded bank, or lost from a capsized boat.

What must rank as the easiest and, perhaps, the biggest bonanza for the something-for-nothing collector was discovered in London during the Second World War. The first to exploit it was the late Robin Green, who claimed that while serving as a member of the London Fire Brigade fighting a blaze in an incendiary-bombed warehouse, he fell overboard from a fireboat into the Thames, sank to the river bottom, and then rose to the surface with the bowl of an eighteenth-century tobacco pipe in his hand. This, so he said, led him to return to the river at low tide where he found the shore strewn with pipes, broken pottery, jewelry, coins, and a multitude of other artifacts of every age from Roman times to the twentieth century. In the years following his archaeological baptism by immersion, Green assembled a large collection of small antiquities from the Thames and eventually sold them to London's Guildhall Museum.

Robin Green was by no means the first collector to recognize that the Thames foreshore had much to offer, but he was the first to appreciate that comparatively recent and fragmentary objects were historically interesting. For more than a century before he came on the scene, the river had been supplying collectors (and eventually, museums) with some of the finest of Britain's ancient art objects. Perhaps the most famous of these antiquities are the magnificent Iron Age bronze shield found at Battersea and a horned helmet of the first century B.C., found near Waterloo Bridge. Many of the most spectacular discoveries were made in the second quarter of the nineteenth century by two indefatigable antiquaries, Thomas Layton and Charles Roach Smith, who not only patroled the shores themselves, but also paid watermen and laborers to bring them whatever they found.

Layton lived at Brentford and confined his river hunting largely to the stretch of it that flowed from Teddington down to Chelsea, while Roach Smith concentrated on the lower reaches that passed through the City of London. Though both were private collectors, their collections ended up in the public domain; Layton's was first given to the Brentford Museum and later to the London Museum, and, in 1856, Roach Smith's principal London discoveries were sold for the then princely sum of £2,000 to provide the British Museum with a nucleus for its Romano-British gallery. The kinds of objects that both men collected were generally self-evidently interesting and ancient: Bronze Age swords, bronze cauldrons, Neolithic urns, an Iron Age wooden tankard bound in bronze, a water clock, coins, and medieval weapons. They were not excited by broken seventeenth-century pottery and would have expressed no enthusiasm for Robin Green's clay pipe.

Although a tremendous number of archaeologically valuable objects have been recovered from the Thames all the way from Reading to Greenwich, many of the most significant have come from the vicinity of London Bridge. There have now been at least five bridges in that general location, beginning with a Roman bridge leading into Londinium, and ending with the present structure built in 1972. The latter replaced the 1832 bridge which was transplanted to Lake Havasu City, Arizona, to become what must surely rank as one of the world's more improbable collector's items.

The most dramatic relic retrieved during the building of the nineteenth-century London Bridge was a massive bronze head of the emperor Hadrian believed to have come from a statue that once stood in the city's forum. The majority of the treasures from the bridge site were not of such large size, however, and although some clearly found their way into the water by accident, most of them were thrown there deliberately, for luck—though that can hardly explain the presence there of a pair of elaborately decorated bronze forceps thought to have been used in the ritual of self-emasculation practiced by candidates for priesthood in the temple of Cybele, the Roman mother goddess.

The forceps were among Roach Smith's more remarkable discoveries, but they were no more remarkable than his astonishing collector's luck. Two examples will suffice. Among the relics he recovered from dredgers working on the bridge site was a headless, armless, and partly legless bronze figure of either Jupiter or Mercury. The gravel in which it was found was dumped into barges, carried upriver, and deposited along the banks at Hammersmith, Barnes, and Putney to build up the towpaths, and cottagers living nearby would sift through it in search of old coins which they later sold to London collectors. One such haul that happened to be offered to Roach Smith included a leg from his statue. From another of the bridge dredgers came a small bronze, fanlike object that neither Roach Smith nor his antiquarian friends could identify. Two years later, while watching further dredging in the same spot, he saw the bronze figure of a chickenlike bird lying amid the pebbles. It had lost its tail—which of course turned out to be the fan-shaped object and which, when reunited, turned the chicken into a peacock (Fig. 32).

Unfortunately I had but one opportunity to follow that closely in Roach Smith's footsteps. On a cold and rainy November day in 1952 I stood in the open hold of a dredger's barge, lying immediately below the 1832 bridge and over the site of the medieval London Bridge of nursery rhyme renown. As the river mud and gravel were dumped aboard, I had great hopes of being showered with treasures of every shape and age; but all I found was a single coin from the reign of the Roman emperor Vespasian (A.D. 69–79) and a small collection of Victorian pennies and halfpennies. It was not one of my better days, though I suppose that over the years I have enjoyed more than my share of good luck, coincidences, or whatever one cares to call being in the right place at the right time. In the summer of the same year, 1952, I found the base of a small delftware bowl lying face down in the mud at Queenhithe Dock. I use the word face advisedly for that was what was painted on the inside of the bowl, a smiling, mustachioed profile with so roguish an eye that it seemed to be shouting, "Hey, look at me!" In the twenty years that have passed since I found it, I have shown the fragment to most of the foremost specialists in English ceramics, but no one admits to having seen anything like it. The best they have been able to suggest is

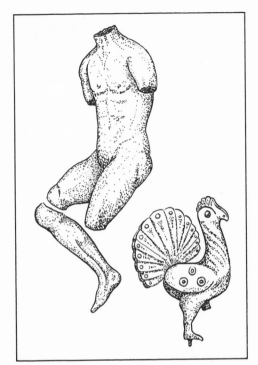

32. Roman figures of Jupiter and a peacock found in the 1820s during the building of London Bridge. The bird and its tail were found at the same spot, though two years apart, but the disarticulated leg was picked up ten miles upstream at Barnes, where the dredged gravel was dumped along the shore. Jupiter height 12⅛ inches, peacock 2¼ inches.

that the painting was the work of a bored delft decorator who was simply playing around, in which case it would almost certainly be one of a kind, a unique piece. But it isn't. In 1961, while excavating at Tutter's Neck plantation in Virginia, I found another identical base, and although in poor condition, the laughing eye and the twirling mustache leave no doubt that the American example is the work of the same painter (Fig. 33). So now there are two identical objects that no living collector or specialist has seen before, and I often wonder why fortune should have chosen me to find them both.

My own searches along the shores of the Thames extended over a period of eight years and provided some of the most stimulating and exciting hours of my life. I cannot deny that this was something-for-nothing treasure hunting in its simplest form, yet at the same time it was vastly instructive. The shores were strewn with artifacts of every period of London's history—just as Robin Green had said they were (Figs. 34–36). The trick was to avoid sinking into the mud and then to distin-

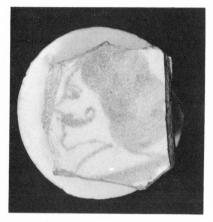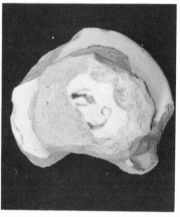

33. Base fragments from two delftware salts, both decorated on the interior with a caricature of a mustachioed gallant. That on the left was found in the Thames and that on the right at Tutter's Neck in Virginia. No other examples are known. About 1670. Base diameter 1¾ inches.

34. Mudlarking on the Thames foreshore at Dowgate below Southwark Bridge.

35. An unposed "still life" on the Thames foreshore near Southwark Bridge. Visible in the picture are numerous fragments of clay tobacco-pipe stems; at left center is a pipe bowl of about 1670 and above it another dating from the early eighteenth century. Below the latter is a Roman or medieval earthenware spindle whorl used in spinning wool. In the center is a seventeenth- or eighteenth-century iron buckle lying on the remains of an eighteenth-century shoe; to its upper right is the inverted base of an early-sixteenth-century Rhenish stoneware mug. The fish is modern.

guish between the historically interesting and the purely junky junk. On a single outing my discoveries ranged from a coin of the third-century Roman emperor Gallienus and a fifteenth-century leather shoe, to a German incendiary bomb and a portable bus stop, this last presumably thrown from nearby

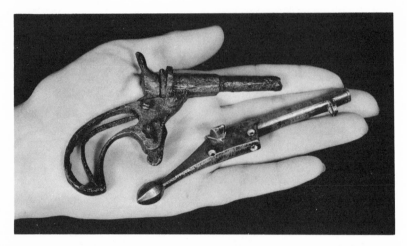

36. The trick is telling the best rubbish from the worst. Both these toy pistols were found on the Thames foreshore near Queenhithe Dock; the brass example dates from about 1600 and the iron one from around 1920.

Southwark Bridge by a disgruntled, would-be passenger whose bus failed to show up.

About fifty yards below Southwark Bridge a tributary named the Walbrook had once flowed into the Thames, and it was there that the Roman city wall had an opening to permit sea-going ships to enter and unload alongside the Walbrook's wharves; at least that has been the conclusion long favored by London historians. Although the Walbrook had been roofed over in medieval times, and when I knew it emerged into the Thames through an unromantic sewer pipe, it was there, at Dowgate, that many of the more interesting Roman objects were found, not the least of them being a Roman matron's bronze manicure set. From the same area came a miniature wine jar cast in lead and whose shape strongly suggests that it, too, may be of Roman date. This spot was also a good source of Roman coins, though most of them dated from the third and fourth centuries and were of poor quality and small size. Indeed, the smallest were barely five millimeters in diameter and took a good deal of finding!

Although, as I have noted, the Walbrook was vaulted over and squeezed into a conduit in the fifteenth century, its ancient bed has been revealed whenever buildings have been erected over it. Thus, for example, foundation digging in Queen Victoria Street in 1871 exposed the river's peatlike silt and in it what was reported to be a barge containing the calcined remains of a cargo of grain. Unfortunately, few details of this discovery have been preserved, and its age was either undetermined or unrecorded.

I first saw and smelled the rich, black silt of the Walbrook in 1949 when the eastern edge of its flood plain was exposed during the construction of the first city office building to be erected after the war. Roman houses had stood on piles driven into the silt, and many of the oak pilings survived in a perfect state of preservation, as did leather sandals, pieces of bronze and brass jewelry, iron tools, and a small, sparrowlike bird whose feathers had lasted for more than eighteen hundred years. In 1954, construction began on another office block that was to straddle the main channel of the Roman Walbrook, though it was not this that was to earn for Bucklersbury House its slightly cracked niche in the annals of British archaeology. That distinction stemmed from the finding of the remains of a Mithraic temple that had stood on the east bank of the river, a discovery that attracted tremendous popular attention and a cacophony of demands that it be preserved beneath the new building (Fig. 37). Instead, the remains were dug out with jackhammers, converted to a mountain of rubble, and later "reconstructed" as a kind of office workers' conversation piece in the forecourt of the new block. Promise of this archaeologically worthless compromise successfully muzzled the preservationists, and there were no public champions to call for time for the riverbed itself to be explored and its treasures salvaged—and treasures there were, in such quantities that in one afternoon's digging I retrieved enough Roman metal objects to fill two hundredweight coal sacks (Fig. 38). They included iron chains, hooks, chisels, lock parts, knives, hinges, goads, and vast quantities of nails from tacks to seven-inch spikes, as well as brass objects that ranged from brooches and pieces of decorative chain to needles, surgical tools, stili (for writing on wax-coated tablets), and coins, all of them from a section of

37. London's 1955 Nine Day Wonder, the temple of Mithras revealed beneath the basements of buildings destroyed in the blitz. The furor over whether or not the foundations of the Mithraeum should be preserved did much to generate popular interest in British archaeology. The temple, seen from beyond its apsidal west end, measured approximately 60 by 20 feet and was built in the mid-second century A.D.

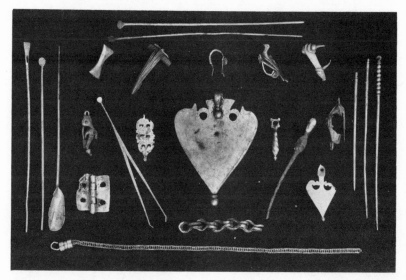

38. A few of the small brass and bronze items recovered from the bed of the Roman river Walbrook and now in the Museum of London. Among them are brooches, hairpins, a needle, spatula-ended "ear-picks," surgical or cosmetic tweezers, a small box hinge, chain for linking brooches, and two pendants probably from horse harness. The largest of the pendants is 3½ inches in length. All date from the first or second centuries A.D.

the Walbrook's east bank about twenty feet long by eight wide.

Stunning though the scope, quantity, and state of preservation exhibited by these treasures undoubtedly was, they were but the tip of the iceberg. Had it been possible to excavate properly and study the full length and breadth of the stream that flowed through this city block, there is every reason to believe that we would have learned much more about the life and evolution of Roman London than could have been obtained from the temple ruins even if they had been preserved in their original location. The delays already suffered by the builders because of the temple controversy had reduced both their enthusiasm for antiquities and their tolerance for archaeologists to an unprecedented low. Although, as representative for the City's museum, I was allowed on the site, I was unable to halt the contractors' work for even a matter of minutes. Only on those occasions when the building program took the crews away from ground yet to be dug out was I able to do any digging of my own, and then I could not extend beyond the lines established for the new foundations. The builders' point of view was understandable and their restrictions reasonable, even though it meant leaving behind countless marvelous Roman objects that lay half in and half out of the forbidden banks. Unfortunately the rules of the game were not understood or adhered to by private collectors who invaded the site after working hours and dug through the night by the aid of flashlights, burrowing into the banks in pursuit of artifacts so easily come by that it was like prying fruit from a cake. In the morning the once smoothly vertical sides of the foundation holes looked as though they had been attacked by armies of groundhogs. After two or three nights of this, and in spite of my protestations that the museum staff had no part in and did not condone the vandalism, we were barred from the site. Thenceforth, the builders went about their business, destroying the riverbed and its timber-revetted banks without so much as a photographic record being kept (Fig. 39). The silt was scooped out by mechanical draglines and dropped into waiting trucks, which, I was told, hauled it to barges on the Thames and which in turn carried it downriver to be dumped in the North Sea. There were to be no second chances like those Roach Smith had enjoyed a hundred years before. For two weeks the trucks rolled out through the gates, their backs piled high with the black silt and bristling with the splintered fragments of Roman oak piles.

Although professional archaeologists were denied any further opportunity to save the Walbrook's treasures, laborers employed on the site pocketed whatever they could pick up, and their take-home pay was considerably bolstered by the sale of coins and other small artifacts that they were able to sell as souvenirs in the neighborhood bars. The museum had long pursued a policy of paying workmen for salvaging artifacts, but it did so only with the prior concurrence of the landowners. It was not about to be party to the purchasing of stolen property. The artifacts from Bucklersbury House belonged to

39. The course of the river Walbrook as first exposed in 1955. Most of the objects shown in Figure 38 came from the area in the foreground behind the gasoline-driven winch where some of the Roman oak revetment piles can be seen protruding from the bank.

its owners, and they had a perfect right to dump them in the sea. Fortunately, however, two engineers working on the site gave what they picked up to the museum, while other finders and purchasers brought their goodies in for identification, and thus enabled an inventory to be made of what we knew to have been found. Much later, some items from one of the largest collections of privately excavated treasures from the site were presented to the City and received with florid expressions of gratitude by officials who had conveniently forgotten that the garnering of them had contributed to the loss of so much more.

Crying over missed opportunities has long been one of the most popular antiquarian pastimes, and in 1873, when another stretch of the Walbrook was exposed during the construction of the London National Safe Deposit Company's premises near the Mansion House, John E. Price, who was responsible for archaeological salvage work on the site, had this to say:

> There can be no question but that much has been overlooked, and that, had circumstances permitted, a more accurate investigation would have been of value and importance. . . . We institute researches abroad, sometimes on doubtful sites, and critically examine every shovelful of earth, often with no certain prospect of reward; but in a comparatively small space situate at home, and illustrative alike of the origin and progressive growth of this the chief city of the empire, sufficient interest has not been manifested to induce a properly organized investigation of any given site.[5]

It was a plea that would go unheard in London for more than seventy years and an accusation that would be voiced in almost precisely the same terms nearly a century later before the city council of Alexandria, Virginia, when the Smithsonian Institution was being urged to support archaeological salvage on urban renewal sites rather than sponsoring excavations abroad. The outcome was both predictable and depressing.

# SIX

# Billie and Charlie
# and Margaret North

IN HIS BOOK on Roman antiquities John Price complained that many objects offered to him as having been found on London construction sites had either been imported from abroad or were deliberate fakes. He was certainly not alone in making such charges, and because of these deceptions some of the most potentially significant European artifacts allegedly found in London and the Thames still have to be treated with caution if not downright disbelief. When he spoke of fakes, Price was almost certainly still smarting from the great "Billie and Charlie" caper of the 1850s, when two illiterates were apparently able to fool Britain's most respected antiquaries and to manufacture an amazing array of forgeries, many of which are still circulating today.

The story of Billie and Charlie began and ended in the London riverside slums that Charles Dickens and Henry Mayhew so graphically recorded for the discomfort of comfortable Victorians. Amid the warehouses, the alleyways, and the green fog that swirled up them from the river mud lived the fictional Fagins, Bill Sikeses, and Nancys—as well as the real-life William Smith and Charles Eaton. These two eked out a precarious existence as shore-rakers, a term used to describe those who earned a muddy living cleaning the foreshores for the owners of Thames-side warehouses, and at the same time salvaging bits of coal, copper, rope, nails, and anything else they could pick up or steal. They were also known as "mudlarks," a rather more romantic name since borrowed by collectors who, today, tread the same wet ground in search of the past.

The Victorian mudlarks were also aware that ancient curiosities were to be found along the shores, and, as I have noted, they sold them to gentleman collectors like Roach Smith, Charles Layton, John Price, and others who wrote nothing and therefore are not remembered. Among the more interesting and easily recognizable relics to be found in the vicinity of London Bridge were cast lead badges worn in the caps of medieval pilgrims as souvenirs of their pious travels: Saint Catherine's spiked wheel, the blessing of Saint Richard of Chichester, the heart of Saint Joseph of Arimathaea, the foot of Saint Victor of Marseilles, the mitered head of Saint Thomas à Becket of Canterbury, and a score of emblems from other less famous shrines at home and abroad (Fig. 40). Thus, in the fourteenth century, William Langland's *Vision of William Concerning Piers the Plowman* described a pilgrim who had traveled as far afield as Bethlehem and Babylon, the proof of which, he reminded doubters, "Ye may se by my signes that sitten on myn hatte."

Just how the signs that sat on the pilgrims' hats came to be in the river remains debatable, but the fact remains that they did, and when retrieved by the Victorian shore-rakers four centuries later, the badges probably did their finders more good than they had their original owners. Unfortunately, the collectors' demand far outstripped the supply, and the large specimens that fetched the best prices and were easiest to spot soon became few and far between. It was a sad state of affairs to which I can personally attest, for in all my years of hunting I found only three small and battered examples—two broken Beckets and an Our Lady of Boulogne. Yet, suddenly, in 1857, a saintly miracle was visited upon the antiquarians of London; excavations for the new docks at Shadwell began to yield

40.  Pewter badges like these from the Thames were worn by medieval pilgrims as souvenirs of the shrines they had visited. *Top left:* The foot of Saint Victor of Marseilles; *center:* the heart of Saint Joseph; *right:* the blessing of Saint Richard of Chichester; *below left:* the wheel of Saint Catherine; *right:* the shrine of Saint Thomas of Canterbury, its height 3½ inches. Fifteenth century.

leaden pilgrim relics, bigger, better, and more desirable than any found before. What made the discoveries all the more remarkable was the fact that the docks were being built well down river from the medieval city limits in an area that had previously yielded no relics of any period, and which had no known connection with the route of the pilgrims. The connection, as it eventually turned out, was not between Shadwell and the pious pedestrians but between the new dock and

Rosemary Lane, a street of tenements behind the Tower of London, wherein lived Messrs. Smith and Eaton. The two men were then employed as laborers digging out the dock, and it was they who were the first to "find" the Shadwell treasures. As word of the discoveries spread, collectors drove in hansom cabs to be shown the latest finds and to be assured by the seller that he "Just fished 'er aht not five minutes ago!" So remunerative did their charade become that Billie and Charlie soon delegated the "finding" to laborer friends who worked on a percentage basis, while they stayed at home in Rosemary Lane casting the products.

How two illiterate laborers got into the business of faking medieval antiquities will never be known, any more than we can ever hope to explain the astonishing gullibility of the antiquarian world. The forgers' first efforts were flat discs cast in two-piece molds, about three inches in diameter, and decorated with figures of saints (or perhaps kings) and surrounded by an indecipherable inscription and a date, usually a year between 1080 and about 1510 (Fig. 41). Not only did these objects bear some resemblance to genuine pilgrim badges, they also possessed an impressively ancient patina.

Before long, comparable but more elaborately molded leaden "antiquities" began to turn up on building sites elsewhere in London—reliquaries containing reclining figures of saints, intricately decorated mace heads, hollow-cast figures of Babylonian-style kings, and even an occasional dagger cast in brass, the hilt in the shape of a titillatingly naked goddess in bold relief (Fig. 42). All found a ready market and were carried off by delighted purchasers, eventually to be shown to hopefully jealous friends. Soon, however, the response "You mean, like mine?" became disturbingly commonplace, and in 1858, at a meeting of the British Archaeological Association, its president, Syer Cummings, announced that he considered these newfound treasures to be fakes. He went on to charge that many of them had been bought from a dealer who knew them to be spurious. Cummings's speech was reported in the *Athenaeum*, where it was read by an antique dealer named Eastwood who promptly sued the periodical for libel.

41. A typical "Billie and Charlie" medallion cast in lead and decorated on one side with a head that could belong to a saint or a late Roman emperor, and on the other with a pair of standing figures. Diameter 3 inches.

42. More fake antiquities attributed to Billie and Charlie. *Left,* a wise man or some such patriarchal figure; *center,* a barbarian; *right,* a shrine containing a recumbent figure. All three are of lead. *Below,* a brass dagger, its hilt in the shape of a female nude; length 9½ inches.

The action was brought before the Guildford assizes in August, 1858, and was attended by a crowd of the most respected and learned antiquaries—as well as a good many dealers who had a more than passing interest in the outcome. In his opening testimony, Eastwood declared himself to be an authority on medieval relics and said he was satisfied that the London discoveries were genuine. He added that more than a thousand had passed through his hands and that he had paid about £350 for them. William "Billie" Smith told the court that he had found, or acquired from fellow laborers, about two thousand relics and that he had sold them for £400. His partner, Charlie, did not testify; he had recently married, and the court was told that his wife would not let him attend.

It was beholden upon the plaintiff to prove the *Athenaeum* to be wrong, and to that end the dealer was able to marshal some of the biggest guns in London's antiquarian circle. Charles Roach Smith took the stand to testify that in his educated opinion the objects in question were "genuine relics of antiquity," adding that in spite of the wide range of dates embossed on them, he considered them all to have been made in the sixteenth century. Another leading antiquary supported him but thought the relics to be older. Inexplicably, the sample shown to the court was different from the rest of the Rosemary Lane products and the waters were muddied by the learned gentlemen's inability to identify it. The record shows that the best they could offer was that it was a "model of some ancient extinguisher." Before the trial could go any further and before any defense witnesses were called, the judge ruled that as the *Athenaeum* had merely reported Syer Cummings's remarks without editorial comment, there was no case to answer.

The court had failed to rule on the authenticity of the disputed objects, yet distinguished voices had been heard in favor of them, and none in opposition. Thus, the outcome was quite satisfactory enough to send Billie and Charlie back to work with new enthusiasm. Syer Cummings, on the other hand, was not ready to give up, and he and another Fellow of the Society of Antiquaries, Charles Reed, began to employ spies to watch Smith and Eaton, spies who reported that at no time did they see either man finding anything while raking the foreshore or digging on construction sites. This was what Cummings wanted to hear, but in retrospect it raises some unanswered questions. Why were Billie and Charlie back at their old menial and poorly rewarded labors when they had made the princely sum of £400 from previous sales and when business was never better? More important, why did nearly a year go by without Cummings being able to learn anything that connected the men to the forgeries? At the end of it, however, a laborer engaged in laying sewers in the City approached Reed with a collection of pottery and other artifacts which he claimed to have found. Among them were examples of "Billie and Charlie" medallions. When questioned, the laborer admitted that he had not dug them up but had obtained them directly from Smith and Eaton. Suitably bribed, he agreed to try to worm his way into the forgers' confidence and to gain admission to the factory. He did so, and when he left, some of the molds went with him. They were subsequently exhibited by Cummings at a meeting of the Society of Antiquaries— much, one supposes, to the chagrin of Roach Smith.

Although Cummings's evidence could not be denied, collectors were slow to admit that they had been duped, and the entrepreneurs of Rosemary Lane did not immediately go out of business. On the contrary, they seem to have continued at least until the death of Charlie in 1870. In the same year Syer Cummings took another swing at the old firm, exhibiting what he described as "a new type of forgery, made last September by William Monk, of the late notorious [partnership] of 'Billie and Charlie.'" Cummings's reference to Monk was no slip of the tongue, for in referring to Charlie, he observed that "bad as this fellow was, he was an honourable man in comparison with his co-partner, William Monk." The answer may be that Billie used an alias, or that Charlie later obtained a new partner. Either way it is a less troubling problem than the question of how two mudlarks could have acquired the technical skill to cast many of the highly intricate objects that are attributed to them, and how they could have known enough about medieval relics to design them—all without being able to read or write.

There remains the intriguing possibility that what we do *not* know about the Rosemary Lane gang may be more astonishing than what we do.

Today, most serious collectors of antiquities can recognize a "Billie and Charlie" at fifty paces, though many of the new breed of stall-holding, hole-in-the-wall dealers apparently do not (or hope that *we* do not), and Rosemary Lane products are still sold as "genuine relics of antiquity." Since, however, the United States Customs Service has decreed that any object needs only to be a century old to be classified as an antique, "Billies and Charlies" can at last claim a genuine measure of respectability. If corroboration be needed, I can relate that some months after the preceding sentence was drafted (and qualified by perhapses and possiblys), I found myself making cocktail-party small talk with a local Virginia realtor and an English antique dealer on a brief visit to Williamsburg. Both proved to be "Billie and Charlie" collectors, neither had met the other before, neither knew that I, too, shared their interest, and both expressed astonishment that anyone but he should take these Victorian oddities seriously. But they do, and nowadays the better and more complicated specimens command sufficiently respectable prices to be given lot room at Sotheby's or Christie's. The ultimate mark of acceptance, of course, is to be copied, or, as the antiquarian marketers would have it, to be reproduced. "Billie and Charlie" medallions enjoyed that distinction when, in 1963, a British magazine offered copies described as exact reproductions of those "the Crusaders used to wear," calling them an "up-to-the-minute fashion—and so versatile!"[1]

Rivers of deceit have always ebbed and flowed around the pillars of integrity, and while Billie and Charlie were going through the fiction of fishing relics out of the Thames, honest tradesmen were throwing other forgeries back into it. Forging the king's (or the queen's) coin was a relatively common means of improving one's lot in the eighteenth and nineteenth centuries, and consequently a great many spurious coins of every denomination were in circulation, most of them visually very convincing. It was only when dropped that they clunked.

When an honest man found himself stuck, it was his responsibility to take the coin out of circulation and to absorb the loss. It was also common sense, for passing dud coins was a serious offense. At least half of the high "value" coins that I found in the Thames were forgeries and must have been deliberately thrown away. Most of them came from the vicinity of Billingsgate fish market and included sixpences, shillings, and halfcrowns of George III, George IV, Victoria, and one half-crown of George V that dated as recently as 1924 (Fig. 43). The quality of their detail was uniformly excellent, occasioned in part by the need to fool the public and in part to protect the forger, for the crime of coining was classified as petty treason and until the nineteenth century the penalty was a most unpleasant death.

In 1794, diarist John Stedman noted that "Our civil laws are

43.  Forged British coins from the Thames. *Top* (from left to right): copper halfpenny of 1771 reading BRUTUS SEXTUS in the legend instead of GEORGIVS·III·REX; lead half-crown of George III, 1819; brass shilling of George III, 1819; *below,* gilt brass sovereign of George IV, 1822; lead half-crown of Victoria, 1891; and a lead half-crown of George V, 1924.

altered for the better of late. No malefactors to be crushed to death for want of pleading, and no more women to be burnt for coining as formerly, but to be hang'd to the gallows as men."[2] The law had actually been changed in 1789, one year after the last woman had been burned before the debtors' door of Newgate Prison. However, it was only treason to forge British coins, and it was not until 1797 that the law was amended to make it an offense to counterfeit foreign money. Consequently, there had long been a lucrative London export business in fake French louis d'or, German florins, Spanish dollars, Turkish sequins, and Indian pagodas. For the home market, and for the hawkers, market women, and hackney coach drivers who were the principal passers of dud coins, English low denominations changed hands most easily. Sometimes the nervous coiner tried to get over the treason hurdle by changing the name around the royal portrait so that he could claim that he was not copying English halfpennies. Two of the forgeries that I found on the Southwark shore of the Thames were dated 1771 and bore the name BRUTUS SEXTUS instead of the normal GEORGIVS·III·REX (Fig. 43). Such neat prevarications were rare, nevertheless, and the vast majority of counterfeit coins were straight copies of the current specie, made in the wrong metal if they were supposed to be of gold or silver, or thinner and lighter when they were of copper denominations. So widespread was this last practice that in the 1770s it was estimated that half the copper coins then in circulation were forgeries, and excavations on American colonial sites suggest that the same was true wherever British coinage was used.

Not all the leaden-sounding coins were forgeries, for in the reigns of Charles II, James II, and William and Mary, tin alloy farthings and halfpennies were issued by the royal mint in an effort to bring business to the depressed Cornish tin industry. Because the metal was soft the coins wore quickly, and because they were easily (though not very profitably) counterfeited, a copper plug was inserted in their centers. The plug was prone to drop out, and that problem coupled with the coins' soft surfaces ensured that few have survived in good condition. Examples ranging from fairly good to pretty miserable turned up on the Thames foreshore near Queenhithe Dock over an eighteen-month period in 1949 and 1950, never more than one at a time and always within an area of about two square yards. It took me a while to realize that there was any relationship between those isolated discoveries, but I eventually deduced that someone had lost a purse and that its contents were slowly working their way to the surface. Thereupon I armed myself with a shovel and sieve, and, to the politely unquestioning astonishment of lunchtime crowds peering down at me from Southwark Bridge, I proceeded to sieve the beach. But though I removed and screened the top nine inches of silt over the coin-bearing area, not one did I find. A week later, as the tide went down, there was another farthing glistening on the surface. In all, I found thirty-three coins in that two-yard area, ranging in date from 1677 to 1700; twenty-nine farthings, three halfpennies, and a silver sixpence.

The most recent of the coins in the Queenhithe group was a William III halfpenny whose patina indicated that it was made of tin, but no tin coinage was issued after April, 1694, and this was dated 1700. Thus baffled, I sent the coin to one of Britain's best-known dealers, explaining that I thought it to be of tin or pewter and asking for his opinion. Back came a prompt and courteous reply saying:

> I have looked at this coin very carefully and have shown it to my colleagues here and we all doubt whether it is in fact tin, as you suggest. It certainly does not look like tin and we have never seen a tin coin with this sort of surface.

The dealer went on to suggest that the halfpenny should be sent to the Ashmolean Museum for analysis so that we could be sure of its composition. I did so, and the answer was that "The coin is not a true pewter alloy which normally does not contain more than 4% copper, but is what we might call a high copper alloy of tin and lead."[3] The coin did in fact contain sixty parts of tin to twenty of lead and twenty of copper. Shortly after receiving this confirmation, I heard again from the dealer who had discussed the coin both with the author of the British Museum's catalogue of copper coins, and with the chief clerk of the Royal Mint. The latter had noted that the coin appeared to have been struck from dies of very good quality, and he recalled that during the reign of William III there were instances of official dies being smuggled out of the mint and sold by the engravers to professional counterfeiters. He suggested, therefore, that this apparently unique coin may have been the product of one such forger.

The coin is of obvious interest in its own right, but more pertinent is its reminder that collectors, curators, dealers, and antiquarians in general have a dangerous tendency to assume that if they have not previously seen an unusual object or if it is not to be found in published sources, it cannot exist. Thus, for example, the discovery of a fragment of German stoneware on an archaeological site in Virginia prompted such a response from a distinguished and immensely knowledgeable British collector. The sherd appeared to be dated 1632, but my collector friend would have none of it, contending that it was of much later style and that the date was really a blurred 1682. The point was of some importance, for not only was the date significant to the historical interpretation of the site, but it appeared also to be the earliest dated stoneware fragment yet discovered in an American excavation. Two months after the Virginia fragment was shown to me, a colleague came to my office with some potsherds he had picked up from the dirt heap of a roadside utility trench in Frankfurt, Germany. Among them was another small fragment decorated with a medallion cast from the same mold as the Virginia sherd, and with the date again appearing to be 1632 (Fig. 44a). Soon afterward I learned of a third, identical fragment that had been unearthed by United States National Park Service archaeologists digging at Jamestown. I took the two newly found fragments (and a photograph of the Jamestown sherd) to England and showed them to the expert, and still he insisted that they had to be blurred impressions of the date 1682.

"Why?" I asked.

"Because," he replied, "I have never, in a lifetime of collecting, seen this type of decoration dating as early as the 1630s."

A year later, and two weeks after I received word of my old

44a. Fragments from identical blue-decorated medallions from Rhenish stoneware jugs dated 1632; *left* from Virginia, *right* from Frankfurt, Germany. The pin measures 1 inch.

44b. A jug with comparable medallions, but dated 1634 and embellished both in cobalt blue and manganese purple. Height 11⅝ inches.

friend's death, I was sent a photograph of an intact jug recently bought in New England by an American collector. On its sides were three medallions identical to the Virginia and Frankfurt sherds, save for being cleanly and unequivocally dated 1634. The jug is decorated both with cobalt blue and manganese purple, the latter color previously thought to have been used no earlier than 1665 ( Fig. 44b).

Often, over the years, I have caught myself slipping into the trap of assuming that the last word has been said on a subject—particularly if the word happens to have been mine.

Someone asks, "Can this be a so-and-so?"

"No," I firmly reply.

"Why not?"

"Because I've never seen . . ." Then I remember the German jug and the Queenhithe halfpenny and quickly substitute a more open-minded response.

The dock at Queenhithe lies about sixty yards upriver from the spot where the coins were found. It is one of the oldest in London's history and one of the few still retaining something of its original shape, cutting back amid the waterfront warehouses as it did in the Middle Ages ( Fig. 45). Although the tide ebbs to leave the dock high, it is by no means dry; the floor is generally covered with a thick layer of slimy mud, too wet to walk on, and in places so deep and soft that one can sink to the knees in seconds—how far *above* the knees I never discovered. The only artifact that I ever discovered in the dock was an eighteenth-century leather shoe in whose toe was hidden a brass "coin" resembling a gold half-guinea of Queen Anne ( Fig. 46). It was a counter made in Nuremburg for the English market, and it said as much on the reverse: IOHANN-IACOB-DIETZ-REICH·COUNTERS, but in letters so small that it could well have passed for a half-guinea. Indeed, it probably did so, for why else would someone hide it in his shoe?

On the day that I was writing this part of the chapter I was visited by Mrs. Helen Camp, director of the archaeological excavations at Pemaquid in Maine, who brought with her an extremely corroded and, at first sight, unidentifiable coin. All

45. The Thames waterfront in 1749. Queenhithe Dock is to be seen to the left below the spires of St. Paul's Cathedral; the steps to the right are now close to the site of the modern Southwark Bridge. It was between these points that most of the postwar Thames mudlarks found their treasures.

46. This brass counter, resembling a Queen Anne half-guinea, had been hidden in the toe of a shoe lost into Queenhithe Dock. Diameter 1.9 centimeters.

that was visible on one side was the nape of a neck and the letters RE, and on the other, traces of four shields and the letters CO, half a B, and a D, but their spacing left little doubt that the inscription had originally read IOHANN·IA]COB·D[EITZ. Comparing it with the Queenhithe specimen showed that the nape of the neck belonged to Queen Anne, and the RE to the word Regina. Without the London parallel, however, it is doubtful that any numismatist could have identified the "coin" from Maine, for as far as I know, the Dietz counter is not illustrated in any book. Until the Pemaquid example was found, the London counter appeared to be the only known specimen. That the two should have been brought together unheralded and unprompted from sites an ocean apart is another of those coincidences which make one wonder whether, with that kind of luck, a research trip to Las Vegas might be in order.

In addition to Queenhithe, another dock used to cut back into the London shoreline, one infinitely better known, even though it was filled up in 1848 to make room for the city's fish market. Billingsgate Dock had existed since the tenth century, and in medieval times tolls and customs duties were collected at an adjacent quay. It is not surprising, therefore, that modern collectors searching there could expect to find all manner of relics from almost every period of London's history. Not only was it the principal loading berth of ocean-going ships, the dock was also close to one of the supposed sites of the Roman bridge. Unfortunately, the building of revetments associated with the fish market left only a minuscule patch of shore that still dried out at low water, and then only at spring tides. Although the exposed area measured barely twenty feet by twenty-five, I was able to recover more early Roman coins there than at any other spot, the most interesting being an as of the emperor Hadrian (an as being the third lowest copper-alloy denomination) having a galley on its reverse of the kind that would have been seen on the Thames in the second century (Fig. 47).

From the same stamp-sized patch of shore, and more pertinent from an American point of view, came three pewter coins

47. The reverse of an as of the emperor Hadrian (A.D. 117–138) depicting a typical Roman galley of that period. Found in the Thames at Billingsgate where such vessels must once have been seen. Diameter 2.5 centimeters.

or tokens minted by authority of James II for use in the New World colonies (Fig. 48). On August 13, 1688, the king's secretary sent a letter to the Royal Mint written on behalf of the English tin miners urging acceptance of a new coin intended "to pass in his Majesty's Plantacons & such parts of his Dominions where they only take Spanish money & value all coynes by that Measure. . . ." The so-called plantation tokens were inscribed as being valued at $\frac{1}{24}$th part of a Spanish real, and the letter noted that "a Ryall being 6d Sterling in value it's alsoe convenient for his Majesty's Europian Dominions."[4] Just which

48. Pewter "plantation token" minted by authority of James II, bearing his equestrian portrait, and intended for use in the American colonies. It was valued at 1/24th of a Spanish real and was briefly issued in 1688. Found at Billingsgate. Diameter 2.8 centimeters.

European dominions the writer had in mind is anybody's guess, but there is no doubt that these pewter coins were intended for use in the West Indies and in Britain's continental American colonies where small change was scarce and where Spanish coins freely circulated.

The questions posed by artifacts or antiques are often more provocative than the objects themselves are interesting, and this is certainly true of the three tokens from Billingsgate. Where had they come from? How did they get there, and where were they going? Had they been to America and back, or were they about to make their first crossing when their owner lost them overboard? If outward bound, were they perhaps on their way to Port Royal in Jamaica, which was then Britain's most important Caribbean base? We know that the tokens were minted no earlier than August, 1688, and presumably no later than December, for on the eleventh James lost his throne. Had they not ended their journey in the Billingsgate mud, the coins could have been consigned to an equally watery grave if they had reached Port Royal before June 7, 1692, when the earthquake broke the town apart and sent half of it sliding and sinking into the sea (Fig. 49).

Archaeologists and divers began serious attempts to salvage the artifactual remains of sunken Port Royal in 1965, and in the on-again off-again operations since conducted there, a tremendous number of objects have been salvaged (Fig. 50). Although I was twice privileged to dive with Robert Marx, who was in charge of the underwater work, the experience was more depressing than enlightening. The once-visible ruins are now buried under feet of silt, the diver can rarely see his hand in front of his face, and the seabed is strewn not with seventeenth-century treasures, but with modern whisky bottles, beer cans, and automobile tires. It is a far cry from the experience of a British diver who went down in 1859 and reported that he "landed among the remains of ten or more houses, the walls of which were from 3 to 10 feet above the sand." A month later the same diver noted that he had found Port Royal's Fort James in a remarkable state of preservation and the water exceedingly clear. "At times," he wrote, "I could see objects 100

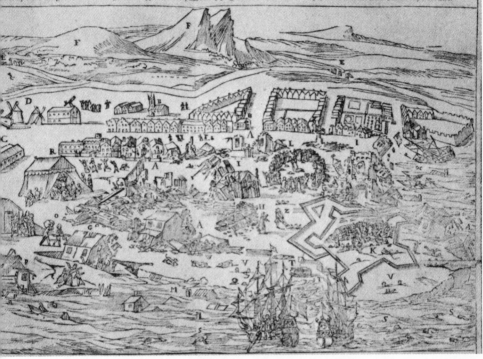

A True and Perfect Relation of that most Sad and Terrible

# ARTHQUAKE, at Port-Royal in JAMAICA,

Which happened on *Tuesday* the 7th. of *June*, 1692.

, in Two Minutes time the Town was Sunk under Ground, and Two Thousand Souls Perished : With the manner of it at Large: in a Letter from
, Written by Captain Crocker : As also of the Earthquake which happen'd in *England, Holland, Flanders, France, Germany, Zealand, &c.* And in most Parts of *Europe* : On *Thursday*
h of *September*. Being a Dreadful Warning to the Sleepy World : Or, God's heavy Judgments shewed on a Sinful People, as a Fore-runner of the Terrible Day of the Lord.

49.  A contemporary artist's imaginative impression of the destruction of Port Royal, Jamaica, in the great earthquake of 1692. Fort James is shown in plan form in the foreground. From a broadsheet in the British Museum.

50.  Port Royal as it was to be seen from the harbor in the mid-nineteenth century. Ships lie at anchor over the submerged part of the town.

115  /  *Billie and Charlie and Margaret North*

feet away from me."[5] Alas, not even the blue Caribbean has been spared man's muddying of the waters.

Among the artifacts brought up from the archaeologists' slices into the silted bottom came a lidded measure or mug (one of many fine pieces of pewter recovered), having an inscription engraved around its girth reading "William Deaven att yᵉ Ship Tavern one St mary hill," and on its lid and handle the initials w.d. and wᴅᴍ respectively (Fig. 51). At first glance one might have been tempted to assume that William Deaven was a Port Royal tavern keeper, but he wasn't, and the subsequent pursuit of him provided a typical example of the marriage of archaeological evidence and historical research,

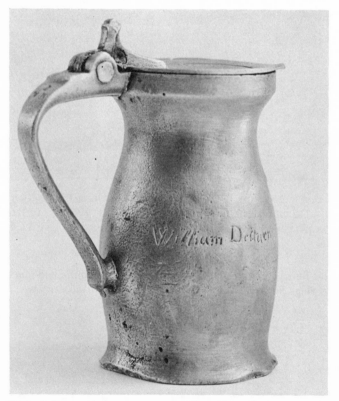

51. William Deaven's pewter measure from his tavern on London's St. Mary Hill, recovered by divers from the sunken city of Port Royal. The mug must have been made no later than 1684. Height 5½ inches.

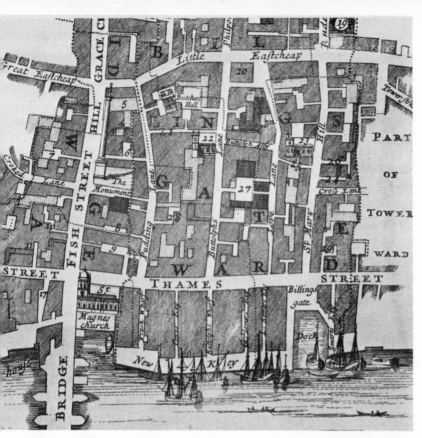

52.   London Bridge, Billingsgate Dock, and St. Mary Hill in 1754.

complete with red herrings and seemingly dead ends. It began when I remembered that there is a parish of St. Mary at Hill in London with a church of that name rebuilt by Sir Christopher Wren after the Great Fire of 1666. I did not immediately recall that the street in front of the church is named St. Mary Hill and leads directly to Billingsgate Dock, but when I saw this on the map (Fig. 52), I was convinced that here was the location of William Deaven's Ship tavern; the trick was to prove it.

In 1889, George C. Williamson published a new and vastly enlarged edition of a catalogue of British seventeenth-century tradesmen's tokens originally compiled by the veteran collector William Boyne. The catalogue which still bears his name (and known simply and familiarly as "Boyne") lists a great many tokens struck on behalf of tavern keepers. This, then, was the obvious first place to look—but, disappointingly, William Deaven was not among them. The next question was whether Boyne listed anyone else living on St. Mary Hill at the sign of the "Ship"—and it did. A token bearing a ship in full sail on one side, with the inscription ON ST. MARY HILL M.N. on the other, was issued by Margaret North in 1668. The inscription read very much like William Deaven's "one St mary hill," and the triple initials on the tankard's handle showed that his wife's first name began with an *M*. Was it possible, therefore, that he acquired the Ship tavern by marrying the widowed Margaret North?

So well did the clues fit together that I was reluctant to spoil it all by taking my reasoning the last clinching miles and to find out whether the union of William Deaven and Margaret North was recorded in the marriage register of St. Mary at Hill. Nevertheless, it had to be done—though when the answer arrived I wished I had left it alone. Deaven's name was not there; instead it was found in the register of the Vicar General of the Archbishop of Canterbury, the entry reading as follows:

1684 Sept 5. William Devon of St. Mary Athill, London, Vintner, Widower, about 45, & Dorcas Walton of St. Magnus the Martyr, London, widow, about 40; at Tooting, Surrey.

So I seemed to be half right. The Port Royal mug had come from William Deaven's London tavern, but he, it seemed, had not married Margaret North. The Guildhall Library's research showed that William Devon (Deaven or Deavon) was paying diocesan tithes in the parish of St. Mary at Hill as early as 1674, but no record could be found of any "Ship" tavern. The final nail in the coffin of my theory was hammered home by the revelation that Margaret North's name did figure in another of the St. Mary at Hill registers. She was buried there on December 6, 1656. So that seemed to be that.

If you (who used to be cloyingly referred to as "dear reader") have a penchant for detective fiction, you will have detected an obvious flaw in the evidence. If Margaret North died in 1656, how did she manage to issue a trade token in

1668? Prompted by this paradox, the librarians looked again and discovered that John and Margaret North of St. Mary at Hill had five children born between 1651 and 1661, one of whom, Margaret, was baptized in 1656. The death record was obviously that of the infant daughter—demonstrating the kind of pitfall that awaits us along the paths of historical research. John North died in 1665, and therefore the evidence of the token shows that his widow carried on his business after rebuilding their premises following the Great Fire which had left nothing standing on St. Mary Hill. No record of Margaret's death has been found, but as William Deaven was a widower when he remarried in 1684 at the age of forty-five, it is entirely possible that he had previously been married to the widow of John North. If we assume that she would have been about seventeen when she bore her first child in 1651, Margaret North would have been an eligible thirty-one in 1665, and the same age as William Deaven.

The final piece of evidence comes again from the St. Mary at Hill register of deaths. On a cold winter's day, December 27, 1692 (six months after William Deaven's pewter mug sank into the blue Caribbean), the register listed the burial of William (?)eavon. The writing is barely legible, and I am advised that the initial letter could be an L, an I, or the first stroke of a D. It is true that I have not been able to *prove* that William Deaven married Margaret North, but her token and his tankard still insist that he did. In any case it is established that he was married, presumably to "M," before he married "D" for Dorcas in 1684, and therefore the wDM mug was in use at the Ship tavern before that date and had no business to be at Port Royal at the time of the earthquake.

Objects that ended their lives far from home are, perhaps, the most intriguing, for they are imbued with the charisma that used to adhere to world travelers, permitting us to share in our imaginations the wonders they have seen and the adventures they have experienced. The Ship tavern mug must score high marks on both counts, yet the bones of its story are relatively easily conjectured: stolen from Deaven's taproom, it was carried aboard a merchantman lying at Billingsgate, then shipped in the thief's locker to Jamaica, where it may have been sold to another tavern keeper. We can wonder what became of him (and of the thief, for that matter) as Port Royal shuddered, the houses crumbled, and the streets broke apart and slid away. But here we are free-flying on a balloon of romance—which is where the serious student of the past must quit the trip. That is not to say that he is eager to do so, but he knows that his academic credibility will deflate if he goes higher.

I recall that the first school essay I was ever required to write was entitled "A Day in the Life of a Penny." So infinite were the possibilities that my small mind boggled, and my first sortie into fiction was received with appropriate scorn. Since then, in many an idle moment, I have looked at coins and have amused myself imagining through whose hands they may have passed and what joys, sorrows, rages, and yearnings they may have engendered along the way. Perhaps because they have passed through so many hands without belonging in a permanent way to any of them, coins do not as a rule speak as clearly to us as does, say, William Deaven's pewter mug. Besides, they are generally predictable in themselves and their discovery is rarely cause for surprise. There is nothing particularly amazing about finding Roman coins on the foreshore near London Bridge—not when we realize how they got there. When, however, they turn up in Maryland, Virginia, and North Carolina, four in the space of six months, that is something else again!

In 1956 I heard that a reportedly Roman copper coin had been found in the coastal Guinea section of Virginia's Gloucester County, but unfortunately my informant could not remember the name of the finder and so I never was able to track it down. Needing a rationale to dismiss so improbable a discovery, I concluded that an English farthing or halfpenny with its classical-style portrait of the monarch and Latin legend had been mistaken for something much older. It was a more acceptable explanation than supposing that a Roman ship had crossed the Atlantic, had been wrecked on the Virginia coast, and its crew and contents carried off by Indians. I should add,

53. Sestertius of the emperor Nero found near Bennett's Point in Maryland. A.D. 64–66. Diameter 3 centimeters.

however, that when I so readily dismissed that proposition, Thor Heyerdahl had not yet demonstrated that it was possible to get here on bundles of papyrus.

The report of the Gloucester coin remained interred in my "idiot" file until, in 1969, I was shown a large collection of artifacts found at Bennett's Point in Queen Anne County, Maryland. Among a group of eighteenth-century odds and ends found near an earlier colonial house site was a sestertius of the Roman emperor Nero, a coin minted between A.D. 64 and 66 (Fig. 53). A few weeks later another visitor to my office brought in a box of colonial artifacts found along the west bank of the Machapunga River in North Carolina, and the site of the eighteenth-century town of Woodstock. Among the pieces was a badly worn copper coin of either Greek or South Italian origin, and dating from some time between 300 and 200 B.C. Neither coin is in a condition that would make it desirable to a numismatist, and as the wear seems to be the product of use rather than burial in a corrosive soil, it is reasonable to assume that if they were brought to America in the eighteenth century, they were already in poor condition. Although there were then many European collectors of coins and classical antiquities, excellent specimens were so readily available to them that it is hard to believe that even colonial collectors would have been satisfied with such inferior specimens.

While I was still pondering the significance of those discoveries, I received photographs of two more, these apparently of silver and found on the south side of the James River, close to the James River Bridge (Fig. 54). One looked to be a denarius of the emperor Augustus and of a type minted between 25 and 22 B.C., while the other was of uncertain denomination and had the head of Octavian on one side and that of Mark Antony on the other—which should have dated it between 40 and 36 B.C. It *should* have; but in fact both coins were forgeries, excellent copies, but plated base-metal fakes nonetheless. I was reminded by Ralph Merrifield, deputy keeper of London's Guildhall Museum and a specialist in classical coins, that many good quality forgeries were minted by eighteenth-century counterfeiters to supply the growing antiquarian market—forebears of Billie and Charlie.

How, one wonders, did these forgeries come to be in the bank of the James River, and are they evidence of colonial American interest in coin collecting?

The one factor common to all these real and faked classical coins has been their discovery close to estuaries, to places where ocean-going ships might have been moored or beached, and where their ballast could have been jettisoned. Because

54.   Forgeries of Roman silver coins of Octavian and Mark Antony found in the bank of the James River, Virginia. Largest 1.9 centimeters.

both Roman and forged coins have often been found on the foreshores of England's river Thames, it might be suggested that fill dug from those shores was sometimes used as ballast and later dumped in American rivers and bays. It seems a most implausible theory, yet it is now evident that on at least one occasion in the third quarter of the nineteenth century a ship bound from London to America did take on Thames riverfront garbage as ballast and eventually unloaded it near the mouth of St. Mary's River near Jacksonville, Florida. It was found there in 1972 by amateur archaeologists who were amazed at discovering a wide range of English pottery and other odds and ends, some of which dated as far back as the fifteenth century. Much more plentiful, however, were pieces of late seventeenth-century pottery and tobacco pipes, as well as similar material from the eighteenth and nineteenth centuries, along with pieces of English brick and ceramic drainpipe of obviously Victorian date. But it was not these that so clearly proclaimed the collection's Thames-side origin. Also included were many fragments of unglazed delftware and kiln equipment dating from the late seventeenth and early eighteenth centuries, pieces of glassmakers' crucibles probably of similar date, and waste products from an early eighteenth-century brown stone-ware factory. As far as I know, there was only one place in England that had both medieval origins, and delftware, stone-ware, and glass manufactures at these dates, and that was in Southwark on the south bank of the Thames at Gravel Lane, just east of Blackfriars' Bridge. But as seagoing ships could not pass above London Bridge, one can only deduce that a barge loaded with foreshore dredgings became the source of ballast for a vessel lying in the Pool of London or at some other dock below the bridge.

Although I have been unable to find any written evidence that riverside rubbish was used as ballast (sand or gravel were most commonly employed), there can be no other explanation for the Florida discovery. Thus, if it can be proved to have happened once, who is to say that other ships at other times did not bring similar rubbish to America and in it Roman coins, Bronze Age swords, Saxon brooches, even, perhaps, the missing head and leg from Charles Roach Smith's figure of Jupiter. The possibilities are endless and appalling, offering hideous opportunities to misread the evidence and turn Leif Eriksson and Christopher Columbus into latter-day tourists.

### SEVEN

# Of Mud, and Pots, and Puppy Dogs, and Mistakes that Come Back in the Night

THERE MAY WELL BE more collectors of pottery and porcelain than of any other antiquarian category—providing you exclude the people who buy antique furniture as furniture and include those who acquire "bits of china" because they are pretty to have around. It is a relatively safe bet that six out of every ten American and European homes contain at least a couple of old and decorative ceramic items that are classed among the family treasures, even if they are no more ancient than a porcelain model of the Eiffel Tower commemorating the Paris Exhibition of 1889 or an 1897 souvenir mug from Queen Victoria's diamond jubilee. Although it may be hard to dredge up words to praise the aesthetic qualities of such mass-produced collectors' items, it would be foolish to deny them their historical interest or their eventual value as antiques. Once over the hurdle of obsolescence and the attrition of careless familiarity, any ceramic object can be expected to aspire to antiquarian respectability and to being described by dealers, auctioneers, and collectors in terms that would astonish the original potters. It is because it is so easy to be beguiled by such laudatory garbage that we must learn to see whatever it is we collect not only in the context of the time in which it was made, but also within the artistic and technological framework of what went before and came afterward. Just as the architectural historian who praises the achievements of colonial American builders should first have seen the temples at Karnak, the Parthenon, and Blenheim Palace, so ceramic collectors who enthuse over the artistry of hand-painted British earthenwares of the eighteenth century should do so in full awareness of the accomplishments of Corinthian, Attic, and Athenian vase decorators more than two thousand years earlier.

Unlike objects fashioned from most metals or from wood and other organic materials, those of baked clay will survive in the ground more or less indefinitely, providing the archaeologist with his most ubiquitous and reliable yardstick by which to gauge the sophistication of past civilizations and cultures. Almost from the birth of pot making (which occurred independently in different parts of the world at different times), regardless of whether the shapers were creating storage jars and cooking pots or modeling likenesses of potbellied mother goddesses, the craftsmen were appealing not only to the needs but to the taste and interests of their customers—just as were the casters and throwers of Eiffel Towers and jubilee mugs.

Once we are able to recognize the artistic taste of our ancestors (which, of course, means comparing it favorably or, more often, unfavorably with our own), we are halfway to understanding them as individuals and, collectively, as tribes, nations, or cultural blocs. The archaeologist's reliance on pottery to help him do this decreases the closer we get to our own times, and as the availability of written sources takes the fun out of educated guessing. Even so, the surviving ceramic tablewares of our grandparents' day are capable of providing a more graphic understanding of then current popular taste than can any assortment of written words.

My own interest in ceramics was initially that of the conventional British archaeologist, by which I mean that I could not see beyond the decline of Roman Britain. I had no broad-based knowledge of earlier Mediterranean cultures, and I was blissfully unaware that just about everything Roman had been done before—and better. Consequently, I naïvely concluded that the pottery used in Britain in the first century A.D. represented the zenith of artistic achievement. I say the *first* century, rather than the Roman period in general, because it was very evident that by the end of the reign of Hadrian in A.D. 138 at the latest, the glory was fading. The term *Roman* is itself misleading, for very little of the Roman period pottery found in England (or elsewhere in the empire) was manufactured in Italy. Most of the wares used in Britain came from France, from the Rhineland, or were homemade—the same sources that were to provide the Englishman with most of his pottery designs and techniques for another fourteen hundred years.

Although the majority of ceramic enthusiasts in North America are collectors of British pottery and porcelain, or of wares introduced into the United States and Canada through British trade, very few have pursued their interests back into ceramic history before the rise of the Staffordshire industry. Romano-British pottery is rarely seen in American shops, in part because there is not enough around to encourage anybody to collect that alone, but partly because most collectors specialize rather than assembling specimens illustrative of the whole story. Nevertheless, most of the firing and decorating techniques for which Staffordshire was renowned in the eighteenth century were known and used in the Roman world, and therefore these early wares should not be ignored.

A *need* to know is the best reason for learning about anything, and to interpret what I was finding on London's bombed sites I needed to know all that could be learned about the evolution of Romano-British pottery. Many of the wares used in Roman London were identical to specimens found on marshland sites on the south shores of Kent's Medway estuary. This allegedly Kentish pottery had been termed Upchurch ware after a village of that name on the edge of the marshes; but it was an identification that had been used by different writers to describe pottery of widely differing styles, shapes, and even colors. To add further confusion, one glossy black type decorated with incised geometric lines which some authorities called Upchurch ware, others classified as "London" or

"Weymouth" ware (Fig. 55). It was evident, therefore, that in the late 1940s no one had a very clear idea of what Upchurch ware really was, and there was even some doubt as to whether it was anything at all. While one school saw the Medway marshes as the site of a once great Romano-British potting industry (a kind of mini-Staffordshire of the first and second centuries), another was contending that the vast quantities of pottery found on the mud flats came not from local factories, but was merely rubbish from extensive domestic occupation. I did not know whom to believe, but it seemed important that somebody should take a crack at sorting it out, for if all these pots, jars, bowls, flagons, and dishes were not made on the marshes, it was time we discovered who had produced them, and where.

The ubiquitous Charles Roach Smith, who had been so lucky in his salvaging of antiquities from the Thames, had been equally successful in his quest for Roman pottery amid the Medway marshes. He and three other nineteenth-century antiquaries, George Payne, the Reverend C. E. Woodruff, and his son, Cumberland H. Woodruff, between them salvaged literally hundreds of more or less complete vessels, many of which are now in the collections of the British Museum and of the Rochester and Maidstone museums in Kent. Although these men were educated antiquarians and well able to catalogue the things they found, their interpretation of archaeological evidence left more to be desired. All too often the mere finding of

55. A Roman period bowl found at Upchurch in England. The black-surfaced pottery with its incised geometric decoration has been misleadingly termed "London" or "Weymouth" ware. This example in the British Museum may have been the one seen in the right foreground of the engraving shown in Figure 56. Early second century A.D. Surviving height 4½ inches.

pots was considered a sufficiently rewarding end product, and I confess that when I began to follow in their footsteps I soon discovered how easy it was to be similarly suborned.

Roach Smith and his antiquarian friends lived in an age of gentle contentment for the gentry, when nothing needed to be pursued to the point of fatigue. The contemporary engraving (Fig. 56) of laborers floundering about in the Upchurch mud in search of specimens is in graphic contrast to George Payne's account of one such research project as seen from his vantage point on the bank. On the morning of July 21, 1882, he and his friends set out to "rough it" on the marshes. The fresh, salty smell of the estuary hung in the air, the sun shone, thrushes sang in the apple orchards, crickets chirruped (or whatever it is crickets do) in the long marsh grass, and the sea gulls soared and glided over the water as it ebbed from the creeks. That it was a Friday, when the world's workers were stacking hay, loading coal, or pushing pens, was of no concern to the Payne expedition. "Our party on this enjoyable day," he would write, "also included Mrs. Payne, Miss Claypole, and Mr. Roach Smith. Luncheon was served at the mouth of the creek upon a

56. Groping for Roman pottery in the mud of Otterham Creek, Kent, in the mid-nineteenth century.

green sward, as the tide was rising, and afterwards our distinguished friend entertained the ladies with anecdotes of past experiences, and sang to them from one of Planché's extravaganzas, while Mr. Dowker and the writer prosecuted further research."[1]

As a result of these forays, both Payne and Roach Smith claimed to have found the actual remains of potters' kilns, Payne going so far as to declare that "in this obscure corner of Kent existed one of the most important industries of Roman Britain."[2] Another contemporary, Thomas Wright, went even further:

> If we go up the little creeks in the Upchurch marshes at low water [he wrote] and observe the sides of the banks, we shall soon discover, at a depth of about three feet, more or less, a stratum, often a foot thick, of broken pottery. . . . This immense layer mixed with plenty of vessels in a perfect, or near perfect state, has been traced at intervals of six or seven miles in length, and two or three in breadth, and there cannot be the least doubt that this is the refuse of very extensive potteries, which existed probably during nearly the whole period of the Roman occupation of Britain, and which not only supplied the whole island with a particular class of earthenware, but which perhaps also furnished an export trade.[3]

Cumberland Woodruff also claimed to have seen the remains of actual manufacturing, stating that most of his collection had come from Otterham Creek, and that it was on the right bank where he had "seen the clearest traces of kilns. . . ."[4]

They may have been clear enough in the 1880s, but there was not a sign of them when we began our search in 1951; the three-quarter-mile stretch of the creek identified by Woodruff yielded only three sherds of Roman pottery and the bronze frame from a sixteenth-century purse. With my wife, who was already an experienced excavator of Romano-British sites, and two friends who worked as volunteers with me on the London salvage projects, we set up our headquarters first in the hamlet at the head of Otterham Creek, and then, when that site proved barren, we moved on to the village of Upchurch itself. It was from there, on and off over the next five years, that we explored the miles of mud flats and marshlands (Fig. 57). It was quickly apparent, however, that they bore small resemblance to the easily accessible sites with their adjacent green swards from which Roach Smith had sung to his admiring Victorian ladies. The Ordnance Survey map of the area put it in a nutshell when it marked "ROMAN POTTERIES (Site of)" in the midst of terrain simply labeled "Mud."

Most of the spots marked as the sites of Roman remains were now unproductive, the pottery either having been washed away or buried deep in the silt. In some areas its place had been taken by literally tons of brickbats and thousands of sherds of Victorian crockery, shattered bottles and other garbage brought down from London in the 1870s and used to build dikes to protect ground then remaining above the tide level. The rubbish was also used to build roads or strayways between the islets where a few stubborn sheep farmers still lived, the last of a line of such inhabitants stretching back nearly a thousand years. Ruined houses, the skeletons of sheep, and the remains of farm equipment half submerged in the mud are all that is left of generations of effort. Here and there the hulls of abandoned wooden barges survive as reminders that clay for brickmaking used to be dug on the marshes, an operation that opened large holes which subsequently filled with mud and remain as traps for the unwary. It was the clay cutters who first began finding the Roman pottery and who brought Roach Smith and his colleagues out onto the marshes in those halcyon Victorian days. Another much more recent hole-digging activity had no archaeological reward, namely the use of the mud flats as artillery and bombing ranges during the Second World War. The mud-filled shell holes and bomb craters added appreciably to the hazards, for none of them could be seen until we sank struggling into them. But we were all sufficiently young to find the dangers stimulating, and when at last we hit pay dirt the rewards were unbelievable.

At a point about a mile and a quarter out across the marsh, in an area about a thousand feet in diameter, broken Romano-British pottery was strewn over the mud as thickly as pebbles on a beach. We began picking up every piece as we approached it, and long before we reached the main concentra-

57.   Crossing a gully on the Upchurch marshes, 1951.

tion our back packs were so laden that we could barely struggle onward. When we got there we dumped out the packs and reassessed our goals. Picking up everything was an impossible task and would accomplish little. We could see that the sherds had a date range of more than a hundred and fifty years and so were not directly related to each other; so I decided to collect representative samples of each type, as well as all the pieces of shapes I had not seen before. In addition, I elected to salvage every fragment of one seemingly common type of shallow gray dish (Fig. 58). This arbitrary decision made on

58. Romano-British pottery found amid the Upchurch marshes; first and second centuries A.D. It is questionable whether the left jug or the center tazza were actually made there, but all the other vessels are now established as being typical Upchurch products. The center black dish was recovered, fragment by fragment, over a period of two years. Height of the small jug 5¼ inches.

the first day of discovery was adhered to over the years, and before long my attic became loaded with fragments of literally hundreds of dishes, disappointingly few of which joined to each other. Nevertheless, three large fragments making up two-thirds of one specimen did go together, and after eighteen months of failure to find the still missing pieces, I restored the dish, substituting plaster for the missing segment. Six months later, the absent sherd turned up. Later yet, all the pieces of another such dish were found lying together.

The vast majority of the potsherds rested on the modern mud surface, but under it lay the uneroded bottoms of Roman rubbish pits into which more pottery had been thrown. By probing through the mud with steel rods it was possible to feel the buried vessels and then to dig slices through the pits before the tide came in and again filled them with mud. Many of the pit bottoms were found to be lined with perfectly preserved sedge and peat, and with the remains of roots extending into the clay below, suggesting that the holes had been dug by the potters to obtain clay and then had been left open while plants grew up in them. Later, domestic pottery and other refuse was tossed in. Amid the usual miscellany of animal bones and bits of shapeless wood, we found part of a writing tablet, a toy boat, and a bronze brooch; but it was the pottery that was important, for at last we were finding associated groups that included waste products from the kilns. However, the best of all the pots were discovered lying together in the mud within a foot of the surface, and were found only because I happened to tread on them (Fig. 59). These wafer-thin and highly burnished carinated beakers epitomize the pure art of the thrower, and for simplicity and fluidity of form they are surely the equal of any pots made anywhere at any time. One is broken at the rim, but the larger and better specimen is unchipped, and I have wondered time and again as to how and why it came to be lying in the Upchurch mud (Fig. 60).

We were eventually able to find enough evidence to confirm the presence of potters on two different sites at dates from the mid-first to the mid-second century, and a review of previous finds made as long ago as 1868 showed that some pottery making had continued in the area as late as the third or fourth century. Although the real success of our years of hard work rested on the recovery of that information, it would be a canard to contend that we were unmoved by the realization that intact vessels were scattered through the mud waiting to be scooped up by anyone lucky enough to put his foot in the right place. The instinct of the treasure hunter and the gambler

59. Two Romano-British beakers as revealed on the Upchurch marshes after discovery through the scientific process of stepping on them in the mud.

60. The carinated beakers (Fig. 59) freed from their mud. These thin and highly polished black vessels represent the British domestic potter's craft at its best, and for simple, geometric elegance have never been excelled. About A.D. 60–80. Height of largest 6½ inches.

is common to most of us, but for those having a professional responsibility toward the past, the pleasures of finding must be subordinated to the discipline of finding out.

That treasure in the popular sense might be found on the marshes remained a real possibility, for the map showed two spots in our sector marked "Roman Jewellery found 1864." So when I found a pot standing vertically in a freshly eroded area, I felt sure that it contained something of importance. The mud filling its mouth was removed with a degree of care that would have earned applause from a surgeons' convention—which, as it happened, would have been appropriate. The pot contained bones, the remains of an embryo puppy mixed with a small quantity of charcoal. Between 1951 and 1956, seven puppy burials were found, six of them by our team and the seventh by the owner of the land. All except one of the pots were of the same type and dated from the latter half of the second century A.D. (Fig. 61). No parallels for these potted puppies had previously been recorded from Roman sites in Britain, nor in Europe as far as I have been able to determine, yet it is certain that these were ritual burials and not merely the whimsy of an early British dog lover.

The association of dogs with the underworld is a well-known feature of classical religions. We know, for example, that young dogs, preferably black puppies, were sacrificed to Hecate, the goddess of darkness, of magic, and of childbirth. She was also believed to have power over fishermen and the sea, which attributes could have had particular relevance to the inhabitants of the low-lying Medway marshes. But were our puppies black? There was no knowing, nor even any certainty as to their breed. Later, however, two rubbish pits were found containing in one the bones of an adult male dog, and in the other the remains of a bitch and two puppies. These bones were examined at the Royal Veterinary College and tentatively identified as those of dogs similar in appearance to the Russian Laika, a small husky with a long history in northern Europe as a hunting, sled-pulling, sheep, and guard dog. Similarities between the bones of the puppies found with the bitch and those in the pots suggested that all were of the same breed.

61. Gray earthenware urns found together on the Upchurch marshes, each containing charcoal and the bones of an infant or unborn dog. Late second century A.D. Tallest 7¼ inches.

The Hecate theory was not the only one put forward by colleagues in the archaeological world; the most convincing alternative was that the puppies were sacrifices to Roman earth spirits in the hope of promoting and protecting the growth of crops. In Devonshire, as late as the nineteenth century, a farmer wanting to keep them free of weeds was advised to "bury three puppies brandwise" or "brandiwise" in the field. Dogs also figured in British folklore as the means by which unpleasantnesses could be drawn away from the physically and mentally sick. Thus, for example, in the counties of Devon, Northampton, Wiltshire, and Gloucestershire it was believed that by taking a hair from the nape of the neck of a patient suffering from measles or whooping cough, placing it between two pieces of buttered bread, and feeding it to a dog one would transfer the evil of the illness to the animal. Presumably, of course, one fed the sandwich to somebody else's dog. In America the Iroquois New Year festival included the hanging of white dogs decorated with feathers and red paint, and to which the tribal sins for last year were transferred.

Although the true significance of the Upchurch puppy cemetery has never been determined, one more clue remained to be added before we were through. On my last visit to the marshes in the winter of 1957, only days before leaving for Virginia, I returned to the puppy area and found that recent storms had further eroded the remaining high ground, leaving a large gray urn protruding from the bank. The pot was of local earthenware, but it was covered by a red, Gaulish, Samian ware dish made at Lezoux in south-central France in the mid-second century, and impressed with the name of Statutus, the potter (Fig. 62). The urn contained cremated bones (unlike the previous puppy burials where the bones had been accompanied by charcoal, but had not themselves been burned), and I deduced that this was a human burial and not just another dog. Although I knew of no others being found in that sector of the marshes, cremation burials were common in Roman Britain in that period, and a number of such cemeteries had been found in east Kent. There being no time to make a careful study of the bones before leaving for America, the urn and its contents were packed for shipment and were not examined again until a year later in Williamsburg when a local physician identified the bones as dog. This certainly made better sense than the idea of burying one human in a doggy cemetery. Two more years elapsed before I finally got around to preparing an account of the discovery for publication, at which time I took the charred bones to a veterinarian pathologist in the hope that he might identify the breed. He did; it was *Homo sapiens.*

The Samian ware dish covering the human ashes was one of the few examples of non-British pottery found on the marshes; another was the fragment seen in Fig. 63. The latter seems to have been part of a thinly potted redware beaker coated with a brown metallic slip and decorated with an applied ornament in high relief, perhaps representing a scene from the legend of Venus and Adonis. Professor Jocelyn Toynbee has described the modeling as "an exceptionally fine piece of work of its kind—graceful, delicate, and sensitive."[5] Indeed, nothing quite like it had previously been found in England, and when first shown to ceramicists at both the British and Victoria and Albert museums, they suggested that it was too accomplished to be of Roman date and must have been made in Staffordshire in the eighteenth or nineteenth century. Subsequently, however, the fragment was examined by nine of the foremost classical scholars in England, all of whom accepted it as Roman. It was an interesting division of opinion that had been

62.  A gray Upchurch urn and the Samian ware dish that covered it.
The pot contained cremated human bones and one small fragment from
the leg of an unidentified bird. Found in the same marsh area as the
puppy burials (Fig. 61). Second half of second century A.D. Height of
urn 9⅝ inches.

63.  Ceramic historians often
think of sophisticated sprig
molding as a sixteenth-century
German development. They are
only half right, as this early-
second-century Rhenish fragment shows. Sprig-molded onto
a thin, metallic-slipped earthenware beaker, the pattern was
probably borrowed from a
Roman silver vessel and depicts
the death of Adonis. Found on
the Upchurch marshes. Height
2¾ inches.

matched a few years earlier when a black pottery lion found in the top of a Roman well near Bristol was hailed by classical archaeologists as a major example of Roman ceramic art. It later turned out to be the finial from the lid of a Wedgwood basaltes teapot.

That experts disagree is well known in academic circles, but when the public hears of two great museums rejecting an object and being off by at least sixteen hundred years, eyebrows are raised and doubts fostered. But in reality there is nothing to be surprised about. The Upchurch sherd was initially shown to ceramic specialists who do not ordinarily have much to do with classical wares. The sophisticated technique of sprig molding exhibited by the sherd reminded them of the work of eighteenth-century potters such as Astbury, Whieldon, Wedgwood, and Turner (Fig. 7). The black basaltes lion, on the other hand, was first examined by classical archaeologists having no experience with Wedgwood teapots. Similarly, the William III halfpenny from Queenhithe was examined by an extremely knowledgeable specialist in English coins, but who had not examined specimens that had acquired their patinas through being buried in the Thames mud.

Inevitably, the amateur collector will want and need to turn to professionals for advice; after all, that is what museum staffs are there for—though I know that some colleagues see their curatorial roles quite differently. The caliber of the advice received depends upon taking one's question to the right person. The lepidopterist who takes a rare butterfly to a professional geologist theoretically deserves as little satisfaction as he gets. In practice, however, this seemingly idiotic example is frequently unwittingly acted out. As I have previously noted, many small-town American and British museums contain a bit of everything from butterflies and rocks to arrowheads and an incredibly ancient waffle iron, and are maintained by a single curator whose own specialty may be botany. Nevertheless, the public expects him to be able to pronounce authoritatively on any object in his custody and, by extension, on any object we may own that is remotely comparable. Rather than admit that waffle irons are not his forte, the embattled curator will protect the credibility of his museum and give the best answer he can based on his limited experience and on whatever books he has to hand. It should be no surprise that the result may, on occasion, be something short of splendid. I speak from experience, having more than once been guilty (and disastrously) of dispensing what is known in the trade as bum information.

After working as the Guildhall Museum's archaeologist for less than a year, I was asked to visit a warehouse near the street called the Minories, where builders underpinning a basement wall had unearthed some fragments of decorated stone. When I got there I was shown what looked like part of a sandstone pillar with scalelike leaves sculpted all around it. The hole whence it came had been back-filled and there were no potsherds or any other artifacts to suggest the stone's date. It did not resemble anything I had seen before (which, in view of my minimal experience, was hardly surprising), and as I adjudged the warehouse to be well outside the limits of early London I decided that the pillar was almost certainly Victorian and not worth keeping. So I said so. Some months later I discovered that there was a similar column fragment in the London Museum, where it was identified as Roman. A closer look at the map showed that the warehouse was near the site of Londinium's city wall into which many important pieces of earlier Roman architectural stone had been built. I am convinced that through ignorance and a distaste for admitting I did not know, I was guilty of causing the rejection and destruction of a major Roman object, and the memory of it has haunted me ever since.

I remember with equal horror the day when a silver collector came into the museum to look at mousetraps—at least that was what I thought he wanted.

"I'm collecting information about pest abatement," he told me.

"About er . . . ?" I countered.

"Pest abatement."

He had to be talking about rodent control. "Ah, yes, well. You're thinking about old rat traps and that sort of thing, I suppose? Right offhand I can't say that we . . ." Whereupon the man snorted and walked out—which I thought was rather overreacting. It being "my Saturday," I was alone in the museum, and it was not until the following week that I mentioned to the keeper (British museum-eze for "curator") that I had had this rather unsatisfactory exchange with the mousetrap man. Only then did I discover that the silver collector had not been asking about pest abatement but about the celebrated female silversmith Hester Bateman.

# Adam and Eve to Caroline,
# with Intermediate Stops

I T IS PROBABLY just as well, from an archaeological point of view, that few collectors are ever likely to come upon eighteen-hundred-year-old ceramic pots by stepping on them, and it may be equally fortunate for the landowner that the sector of the Medway marshes which I found so productive is now reportedly as barren as Roach Smith's Otterham Creek. I am told, however, that one area still yields its treasures—in the shape of the bottles, stoneware jars, pot lids, and broken crockery from the London garbage used to build up the now-eroding Victorian strayways. Although, in the 1950s, I could see no merit in such modern junk, and loudly said so, my wife viewed it differently, and I more than once found her so laden with Victoriana that she could hardly stagger out to the Roman sites. Few people in England were then interested in ordinary domestic ceramics and glassware of the nineteenth century, but today they are, and such "rarities" as Stephen's Ink bottles, the printed lids from pots of "Genuine Russian Bears' Grease," and torpedo-shaped mineral water bottles are to be found in many antique shops at precocious prices. A close friend, now a middle-aged timber broker, who shared many of our early Upchurch adventures has long since given up Roman archaeology and has turned his attention to salvaging Victorian artifacts from the large land-fill dumps that turn up from time to time on the outskirts of London. He is by no means alone in his unusual antiquarian pursuit; indeed, one of his principal concerns is to keep secret the discovery of a new dump for fear that hordes of competitors will descend on it when he is not looking. In England such treasure hunting can be tolerated by professional antiquaries on the grounds that Victorian artifacts are too recent to be worthy of scholarly attention. That is not the case in America, however, where the roots of many towns and states go no deeper than the mid-nineteenth century, and where archaeological sites of that period can be just as significant as are Roman remains in Britain. From Charleston, South Carolina, to San Francisco come hair-curling tales of bottle collectors tearing up private property, mutilating the remains of abandoned mining settlements and frontier ghost towns, all in search of Grandpa's trash, a surprising amount of which turns out have been made in England. It is worth noting, incidentally, that when the object is marked with the country of origin, it was made after 1891 and so identified to comply with the McKinley Tariff Act. When the mark is even more explicit and instead of simply reading "England" it shouts, "Made in England," it is also telling us that the object was made in the present century.

The ever-forward-shifting focus in the collecting of small antiques is occasioned primarily by availability, but specialization (like the fellow who collects everything ceramic in the shape of a pickle) often stems from reasons other than practicality. Some do so to become part of a fraternity, while others find their satisfaction in being different from everybody else. One would not expect, for example, to find many people who would be trying to create the largest collection of cow-shaped creamers in captivity. Not long ago, however, two such English collections were put out to pasture at about the same time, each thought to be the largest herd on record. One was auctioned off and the other was presented to a famous museum whose curator accepted it shortly before retiring, leaving it to his successor to find space for four hundred spotted, speckled, striped, and splotched Staffordshire creamers. For my money, two or even three can be interesting and mildly amusing, but half a dozen are altogether too many. My own ceramic interests are more catholic, for I have tried to acquire examples that illustrate the evolution of British domestic pottery from Roman times to the mid-nineteenth century. It is hardly possible to embrace a wider range, but at the same time it has a serious purpose, providing an opportunity to compare the craftsmanship of different periods and places and thus to single out the trees within the woods.

For the American collector there is much to be said for buying those wares that were in use at one time or another in his own town or state. Thus, for example, one can profitably pursue (as I do) examples of all types of ceramics to be found in Virginia in the seventeenth and eighteenth centuries. This takes us far beyond the confines of British production to encompass porcelain from the Orient, stoneware from the Rhineland, faïence from France, earthenware from Spain and the Netherlands, and an occasional piece of pseudo-porcelain from seventeenth-century Persia. In the process we become armchair travelers in both time and space, following the trade routes of East Indiamen plowing their way through the Indian Ocean toward Madras or Batavia, checking their homecoming cargoes through customs and merchants' records, pursuing their wares into the china shops of Boston or Philadelphia, and finally into the inventories of deceased householders in county court records. To people with no love for history, this vicarious voyaging will have little appeal; for my part, however, the romance of the past, however distorted and fanciful, can be a paregoric for the soul. Besides, one meets a surprising number of fascinating people along the way—many of them remarkably like ourselves.

Of all man's creations, pottery is, as I have noted, among his most enduring legacies. It is also the scion of one of his oldest crafts stemming from one of his greatest inventions, the potter's wheel. Thereafter, thanks to the cunning of the Chinese, the dedication of the Children of Islam, the artistry of the Italians, the regimentation of the Rhinelanders, and the celebrated

shopkeeper reputation of the British, anything was possible—
and marketable even unto the four corners of the earth. Just as
the influence of Rome is recalled by its pottery found in the
ground all the way from Scotland to India, so Britain left her
ceramic mark around the world from northern Canada to
southern Tasmania by way of Poona and Pretoria. But although Britain captured the utilitarian ceramic market in the
eighteenth century (she never made much of an impression on
the Oriental and European porcelain trades) and has hung
onto it into the present century, very few of the technological
achievements for which England is so often given credit were
actually born there. Slipware techniques were borrowed from
medieval France; English delftware was first made by emi-
grants from Antwerp; salt-glazed stoneware was developed in
the Rhineland more than three centuries before its "mysteries"
were unraveled by John Dwight, and the secrets of hard-paste
porcelain were unlocked in Saxony while British potters were
still hunting for magic ingredients. The fine red English stoneware so often attributed to the Elers brothers in the late seventeenth century (Fig. 7) was only a copy of the similar Chinese
ware that had already been successfully duplicated in the
Netherlands; even the Elers brothers themselves were less than
true blue. They came from Amsterdam, David Elers having
learned the potting trade in Cologne. Nevertheless, and due in
large measure to a handful of Staffordshire potting families
(not the least of them named Wedgwood), British business
acumen, in step with some nifty potting and a good deal of
political and military clout, gave England an edge which the
Industrial Revolution honed to a sharpness that cut out the
competition with surgical efficiency.

By the mid-eighteenth century British domestic earthenwares and stonewares were as well made and better priced
than most of those to be bought in Europe, a fact not lost on
the American housewife, who deplored the temporary short-
ages of Staffordshire ware during the American Revolution,
and who stood ready and waiting to "Buy British" as soon as
the shooting stopped. In the meantime she could hope for
occasional shipments to America by cynical British merchants

through the neutral Dutch. Then, as in the past, Staffordshire potters were willing to put pots before principle, and in their efforts to recapture old markets they were not beyond decorating their wares with near treasonable antigovernment and pro-American prints. Later unpleasantnesses like the War of 1812 were taken in an equally buoyant stride, and the cause of American freedom was espoused by English engravers whose burins created appropriately cringing British lions and spelled out words that even a modern radical might think disloyal. Much earlier, Lord Thurlow (afterward Lord High Chancellor of Great Britain) roundly condemned Josiah Wedgwood for printing portraits of William Pitt in the bottoms of "spitting pots and other vile utensils," voicing his displeasure in verse:

> Lo! Wedgwood, too, waves his Pitt-pots on high!
> Lo! the points where the bottoms, yet dry,
> The visage immaculate bear!
> Be Wedgwood d——d, and double d——d his ware.[1]

Throughout the nineteenth century British potteries made and decorated wares specifically for the American market, first with direct political or patriotic appeal, and then in the 1820s with transfer-printed American views on pearlware and on the white wares that followed it. Long sought after by American collectors, those prints included towns, bridges, state houses, and natural wonders and are most often seen on plates and serving dishes, though they also occur on pitchers, mugs, and chamber pots. The fact that they are still to be seen in so many antique shops is occasioned in part by the enormous original popularity of these wares and in part by the fact that the patterns have been reissued from time to time, many of them quite recently.

For the collector of memorabilia, commemorative ceramics provide an ideal field for specialization, and as a rule pieces recalling people and events of secondary significance are rarely faked or reproduced. Centennials and bicentennials are, alas, principal sources of trouble, for at such times anything remotely relevant becomes available in replica, "heirloom quality" souvenirs to sicken us now and sucker us later.

In England, Admiral Nelson and the Battle of Trafalgar are

64. Press- or bat-molded, this cream-colored earthenware plate is relief-decorated around the rim with the slogan SUCCESS TO THE KING OF PRUSSIA AND HIS FORCES. The plate is underglaze colored in green, yellow, gray, and purple, and commemorates Frederick the Great's contributions to allied victory in the Seven Years' War. About 1758. Diameter 9 inches.

the perennial favorites, while even greater heroes of a few decades earlier are barely remembered. The British public is not in the least interested in recalling the contributions of Frederick of Prussia in the Seven Years' War. Frederick who? What Seven Years' War? Nevertheless, in the late 1750s, Frederick the Great was Britain's premier hero and ceramically remembered on wares from cheap white saltglaze to costly Worcester porcelain. Rim fragments of plates bearing his name, his portrait, and the trophies of his battles have been found on tavern sites in Virginia and on plantations in the West Indies (Fig. 64).

Better known in America as the French and Indian War, the long conflict of the Seven Years' War resulted in the manufacture of a wide range of commemorative and souvenir items in other materials besides ceramics. Part of a copper-alloy shoe buckle decorated with the words SUCCESS TO THE KING OF PRUSSIA has been picked up from amid dirt disturbed during utility laying in New York. Another buckle inscribed LOUIS-BOURG TAKEN BY ADMIRAL BOSCAWEN JULY THE 26 1758 has been found in Williamsburg, recalling the capture of the fortress of Louisbourg in Nova Scotia from the French. Other commemorative metal items included "King of Prussia" sleeve buttons and German-made tobacco boxes with cast brass tops and bottoms recalling specific allied victories. The example illustrated in Figure 65 depicts the British assault on Fort Royal that led to the surrender of Martinique in February, 1762, and is marked as being the product of J. H. Hamer of Iserlohn who was working there by 1760. In reviewing the history and scope of these boxes, Katharine McClinton has contended that "The battle scenes are similar and without their inscriptions one could not be distinguished from the other."[2] In this example, however, we can clearly see flaming mortar shells being lobbed from the British bomb ships into the heavily fortified town, and it so happens that Sir George Rodney, who commanded the attack, had brought three bomb vessels, the *Basilisk, Granado,* and *Thunder,* with him from England, and it was their presence that speeded the French capitulation. Thus the battle scene shown on this box would appear to have been drawn with the Fort Royal engagement in mind.

Souvenir tobacco boxes were inexpensive and were intended for a none-too-discerning mass market; for the same reason it is probably no accident that most of the "King of Prussia" salt-glaze plate fragments found in Williamsburg came from a tavern site. The same is true of clay tobacco pipes decorated with the Hanoverian royal arms, and of Rhenish stoneware mugs and jugs adorned with the GR initials of the Georges Rex. Throughout history, the lower social classes could be

65. A German brass and copper tobacco box commemorating on its bottom the capture of Martinique by Sir George Rodney in 1762. The lid shows a spirited stag hunt of no historical importance. From the workshop of J. H. Hamer of Iserlohn. Length 6 inches.

relied upon to be the most unabashed in their expressions of patriotism and hero worship. Few workers' homes in Victorian England were without their framed lithographs or engravings of "The Queen—God Bless Her"; similarly, one is today more likely to see Old Glory decals and "America, Love It or Leave It" stickers on the bumpers of blue-collar workers than on the cars of management. Mercurial though these open expressions of affection may often be, they generally represent honest emotion—something that political and social expediency (disguised as good manners) has taught top dogs to conceal. Thus the street sellers who were the principal purveyors of commemorative wares sought their customers amid the crowds who waved the flags and cheered the heroes. Their wares, therefore, were not only cheap, but usually hurriedly produced to capture a short-lived market for which quality was less important than availability.

The bowl illustrated in Figure 66 is a good example of an eighteenth-century, quick-sale, commemorative item and recalls the British Admiral Vernon's seizure of Porto Bello in 1739 during the War of Jenkins's Ear. The thin, lead-glazed earthenware (known as Astbury ware) is decorated with applied reliefs depicting the admiral, his ships and cannon, the city of Porto Bello on the Panamanian coast, and the following inscription: Ye PRID: OF SPAIN HUMBLeD BY ADMIRAL VERNON He TOOK PORTO BeLLO WITH SIX SHIPS ONLY. Besides leaving the "e" out of pride and putting the rest in lower case, all the Ns are retrograde, and the first and last letters of many of the words have been left behind in the molds. It is, in short, a very sloppy piece of work, produced in great haste to exploit popular enthusiasm for the admiral while it lasted. As it happened, Admiral Vernon was to remain a popular hero until his death in 1757, although his cantankerous nature, his outspoken attitude toward his superiors, and his tiresome talent for being right made him unpopular in government and caused him to retire before his time. Nevertheless, his memory lives on in four English villages named Portobello, two more in Scotland and Ireland (not to mention London's celebrated Portobello Road antiques market), and on the sign-

66. This red-bodied Astbury ware bowl exhibits sprig molding at its worst. Nevertheless, it is rare and historically interesting in that it commemorates the British sacking of Porto Bello in 1739. Diameter 5⅝ inches.

boards of countless English public houses called the Admiral Vernon. The Scottish village of Portobello would later become a pottery-making center producing wares that bear that name, as also do Staffordshire products commemorating the battle. It is just another of those quirks of ceramic terminology designed to unhorse the novice collector. To be correct, however, the commemorative wares should be spelled "Porto Bello" and the late eighteenth- and nineteenth-century Scottish products should be written as "Portobello ware," a small difference but enough—just as tin-enameled earthenwares made at Delft in Holland are dubbed Delftware with a capital "D," while similar wares made in the British Isles are called delftware.

The Porto Bello bowl (Fig. 66) is a good example of one of the three ways in which relief decoration is created. In this case the technique is called sprigging; the wet clay is pressed into the individual molds and transferred to the already shaped bowl. Alternatively, the entire bowl can be pressed into a mold set on the potter's wheel, as were the Roman Samian wares (Fig. 5). The third method, illustrated in Figure 67 by another Porto Bello commemorative piece, is known as slip casting, and here liquid clay is poured into a porous mold through which the water soaks, leaving the clay particles clinging to the wall. When left to dry, this clay skin shrinks sufficiently for the vessel to be lifted out of the mold. The "Venus and Adonis" fragment from the Upchurch marshes discussed in the previous chapter (Fig. 63) is a marvelous example of sprig molding, and by comparison the Porto Bello bowl regresses rather than advances by sixteen hundred years. Of the three techniques, only slip casting was new to eighteenth-century British potters

67. This slip-cast white salt-glazed stoneware mug also commemorates the capture of Porto Bello and provides a potter's portrait of the victor, Admiral Vernon. About 1740. Height 9%16 inches.

and marked a major step toward quality mass production. Thus scores of salt-glaze Porto Bello mugs could be produced from a single matrix calling for no artistic judgment on the part of the potter nor any great degree of manual dexterity. The Astbury ware bowl called for both, in the placement of the reliefs and in the skill with which they were applied. The need for speed production being paramount, it got neither.

Neophyte collectors often have difficulty telling the difference between relief-decorated wares that were press molded and those that were slip cast. The answer is usually to be found on the interiors, for in slip casting the even buildup of clay particles against the mold wall results in external convexities being mirrored by modified internal concavities, and vice versa. Press molding, on the other hand, calls for the clay to be smeared and smoothed into the incuse-walled mold with the potter's fingers and who subsequently leaves the interior even surfaced, or, if it will not be seen, he may be content to let the marks of his finger manipulation remain. As the potter's hands do not touch a slip-cast piece until it is dry enough to be lifted from the mold, he generally has little opportunity for interior manual finishing.

White salt-glazed stoneware, which was the principal beneficiary of the new slip-casting technology in the mid-eighteenth century, was on its way out when Lord Rodney followed in the footsteps of Admiral Vernon and Frederick the Great as the potters' best-selling hero. It was a distinction that came not with his capture of Martinique in the Seven Years' War but with the defeat of the French fleet at the Battle of the Saints at the end of the American Revolution. By that time, the cream-colored earthenware made universally popular by Josiah Wedgwood had become the medium through which the adulatory message would be imparted. The good word then was that Rodney had seized the French flagship the *Ville de Paris* and had taken the French admiral, the Comte de Grasse, prisoner.

There had been precious little for the British public to wax enthusiastic about during the long land war with the Americans; even the victories had a sour taste when it was remembered that the losers had been relatives and customers. But defeating the French was something else again, and British jubilation was magnified out of proportion to the value of the victory. The battle was fought on April 12, 1782, and in May Sir George Bridges Rodney became a baron and, like Admiral Vernon before him, aspired to pub-sign immortality. He, too, became the subject for souvenir mugs, but this time the sprigged decoration was more accomplished (Fig. 68). On the front, in an oval medallion, sailed the captured French flagship under a streamer reading VILLA DE PARIS (spelling was nobody's strong suit in the eighteenth century), and flanked by standing figures in naval uniform, holding a telescope, and behind a flag inscribed LORD RODNEY. These creamware mugs were painted in a variety of underglaze colors, commonly with bands of green at top and bottom, and with plain brown or leopard-spotted brown on yellow backgrounds to the white pipeclay reliefs. One might suppose that these mugs would be of interest only to the British—but one would be wrong. A fragment has been found in a privy pit in downtown Alexan-

68. More accomplished sprig molding greeted Admiral Rodney's 1782 victory over the French at the Battle of the Saints. This cream-colored earthenware mug is decorated on the exterior with a brown-mottled orange slip and with green bands at top and bottom. A central medallion depicts the captured French flagship the *Ville de Paris* and on either side stand figures of Lord Rodney holding a blue banner bearing his name and his newly bestowed title. Height 4¾ inches.

dria, Virginia, having been thrown there in the early nineteenth century and another has been unearthed at Louisbourg in Nova Scotia, its presence puzzling because the fortress site had long since been abandoned. By 1782 the township is thought to have been occupied only by impoverished fisherfolk who would hardly have been interested in Rodney souvenirs.

The next moment for British souvenir-promoting elation was tempered with sorrow, which, if anything, was better for business. The date was November 21, 1805, the victory Trafalgar, and Admiral Horatio Nelson the dead hero. Creamware was by then being replaced as the common household earthenware by a whitened glazed fabric today known as pearlware, and it was this, decorated with underglaze blue transfer prints, that provided the cheapest and most popular of commemorative mugs and jugs. Hastily engraved copper plates provided transfers that could be cut and trimmed to fit vessels of different sizes. That the cutting resulted in the almost nonsensical cobbling of elaborate inscriptions mattered little, for the women who applied the transfers could read no better than could most of the customers. Thus the small jug shown in Figure 69 has had its print trimmed to such an extent that Nelson's flagship *Victory* is labeled VICORY and even the admiral himself has lost so

69. Poorly transfer-printed in underglaze blue, this pitcher recalls the death of Lord Nelson at the Battle of Trafalgar in 1805. His ship, the *Victory*, is illustrated on one side and his portrait on the other, with a list of his titles, honors, and battles in between. The rim and handle are sloppily outlined in overglaze brown. Probably made at Swansea. Height 4¾ inches.

much of his "L" that his name almost reads NESON. As for his famous signal to the fleet before the battle, that is reduced to ENGLAN PECTS EVRY MAI TO DO HIS DUTY. There were, of course, many more accomplished memorials to the great man, from ceramic busts and plaques to marble effigies and sculptured snuffboxes, but for my money the once common souvenirs for common people are the most interesting. Not only are they associated with a historic figure and a momentous event but they also recall the popular emotion of a nation, an unparalleled blend of elation, pride, sorrow, and patriotism that has left Trafalgar as the best remembered British victory of any war.

In ceramic terms, love of king and country were sometimes rather curiously expressed, as in the case of slipware chamber pots made near London in the third quarter of the seventeenth century after the restoration of Charles II and inscribed PRAISE GOD AND HONOUR THE KING. A century later, Staffordshire salt-glaze potters applied medallions to the fronts of chamber pots bearing the initials and even the portrait of George III. It has been suggested that these were intended to amuse customers who did not like the king, but that explanation can hardly explain a pearlware specimen found in Jamaica decorated in the same way with a coronation portrait of the popular and virginal Queen Victoria.

In Britain, ceramic coronation souvenirs date back at least as far as the seventeenth century, when they were produced both in slipware and delftware, but it was not until the introduction of transfer printing that it became possible to mass-produce them. The long reign of Queen Victoria was marked by a string of souvenirs, though, surprisingly, those of her coronation are among the rarest of commemorative ceramics (Fig. 70). Her jubilee souvenirs, however, are still readily available at modest prices. Artistically, there is not much to be said for the Messrs. Doultons' tribute to Victoria's diamond jubilee in 1897 (Fig. 71), yet there is a piquancy in its prayer ENDUE HER PLENTE-OUSLY WITH HEAVENLY GIFTS, GRANT HER IN HEALTH, WEALTH, LONG TO LIVE. GOD SAVE THE QUEEN, and in its resonant styling VICTORIA THE BELOVED QUEEN OF GREAT BRITAIN, IRELAND & THE COLONIES, EMPRESS OF INDIA the words roll from the tongue like waves before the bow of a British dreadnought. To modern Englishmen such mugs are a glimpse of lost glory, but for their original owners they were a tangible reminder of a glorious summer day and the greatest free show of the age. Chauncey Depew, a distinguished American who was there, declared that the reality of the spectacle far exceeded anyone's expectation. "To have in one hour," he said, "the representation of the

70. A brown stoneware gin flask decorated in mold relief on both sides with a figure of Queen Victoria at the time of her coronation. The pose is actually borrowed from Sir George Hayter's 1833 portrait of the then Princess Victoria. Probably made at Lambeth. About 1837. Height 7 inches.

peoples of one quarter of the habitable globe, representing every race and religion, marching under one flag, and expressing in the most emphatic way their loyalty to Queen and Empress, was the most superb exhibition of world-wide Empire and loyalty to a sovereign witnessed in modern times."

71. A typical and rather horrible souvenir of Queen Victoria's diamond jubilee in 1897, this mug made by Doulton of Burslem is transfer-printed in orange brown. A piece of now-black ribbon is attached to the handle, perhaps put there to identify ownership in a large family that had the misfortune to possess a number of such mugs. Height 3½ inches.

Then, politician that he was, Depew quickly covered his tracks, adding, "As an American I ascribe much to the lesson of the American revolution changing the colonial policy of Great Britain, so that she now keeps her colonies instead of losing them."[3]

I hope somebody gave him a free mug.

In my own collecting of commemorative ceramics I began in the eighteenth century, without any clearly defined goals, and gradually worked my way forward. There is much to be said, however, for starting with the silver wedding of Elizabeth II and working backward. Just as in philately, ceramic errors and anomalies provide added interest, so, for example, mugs, cups, and beakers made in the expectation of Edward VIII's coronation have a special appeal. Large numbers of them were shipped to the West Indies when manufacturers found that they had put their money on the wrong man, presumably hoping that the colonials might have difficulty distinguishing between abdicated Edward and his brother George.

Most of these souvenirs are quite horrible examples of the pot-decorator's art, but now and again ugliness was no accident. Thus the jug seen in Figure 72, with its scowling face and

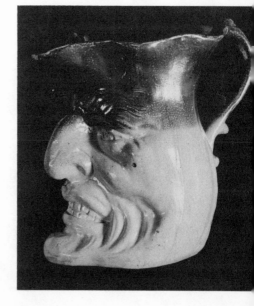

72.  Press-molded into a caricature of the Duke of Wellington,
this brown stoneware jug was
probably made after he became
Prime Minister in 1828. At that
time the Iron Duke's popularity
was waning and unkind car-
toons proliferating. However,
there is said to be a companion
jug portraying Napoleon, in
which case a manufacture date
around 1815 would be reasonable. Probably made at Lambeth. Height 6⅞ inches.

hooked nose, is a deliberate caricature of another hero of the Napoleonic Wars, the Duke of Wellington, who, alas, was later to become less popular as a politician than he had been as the victor of Waterloo. "Old Nosey," as he was called by the notoriously irreverent British public, was lampooned on beer mugs for his temperance and on tobacco pipes for his banning of smoking in soldiers' barracks. A London street seller of tobacco boxes and pipes found the latter particularly profitable. "The best sale of the comic heads," he said, "was when the Duke put the soldiers' pipes out at the barracks; wouldn't allow them to smoke there. It was a Wellington's head with his thumb to his nose, taking a sight, you know, sir. They went off capital. Lots of people that liked their pipe bought 'em, in the public-houses especial, 'cause, as I heard one man say, 'it made the old boy a-ridiculing of hisself.' "[4]

Just as ceramic souvenirs could be used to praise or discredit, so, on occasion, they could be employed to express public sympathy. A good example is provided by the pearlware jug shown in Figure 73a and bearing on its side a printed portrait of Caroline of Brunswick, niece of George III and the wife of George IV. It is not a particularly becoming pose, but the engraver has made up for that by adding a loudly loyal GOD SAVE QUEEN CAROLINE! It is an innocent enough picture—if one does not remember what happened in 1820. It was in that year that the king tried to be rid of his wife, saying that he would never allow her to become queen. On his accession he had offered Caroline an annuity of £50,000 if she would renounce her rights and stay out of England. She refused to do so and persisted all the way to the coronation when the doors of Westminster Abbey were closed against her. Meanwhile, the government (at the king's urging) had instituted divorce proceedings in the House of Lords, alleging her adultery with an Italian, Count Bartolomeo Bergami; but the unsavory business was handled with such ineptitude that no matter how guilty Caroline may have been, it offended the British workingman's sense of fair play. Unfortunately it did her little good, for less than three weeks after she had been denied the crown, she died.

In 1818, while still Prince Regent, her husband (whose own morals left everything to be desired) had sent a commission to Milan to collect evidence against Caroline, and it was the report of that commission, backed by an imported troop of seedy Italian witnesses, that led to the introduction of the infamous Bill of Pains and Penalties and the Lords' attempt to sit in judgment. The other side of the Caroline jug relates to this hearing, which began on August 17 and went juicily on until November 10 when the House narrowly ruled against her. Printed in purple on the pitcher is a parody on lines from the national anthem framed by a wreath containing the names of Caroline's principal supporters, among them Henry Brougham and Thomas Denman, her attorneys, and Alderman Wood, who had accompanied her to England in January and in whose London house she had first stayed. The verse begins with the lines "As for the Green-Bag crew,/ Justice will have its due," a reference to the green baize bag in which the Milan Commission's evidence was carried in and out of the House of Lords.

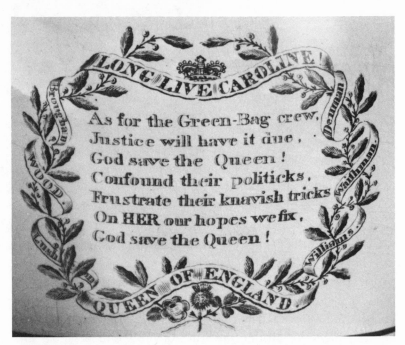

As for the Green-Bag crew,
Justice will have it due,
God save the Queen!
Confound their politicks,
Frustrate their knavish tricks
On HER our hopes we fix,
God save the Queen!

73a & b. Memorial to one of Britain's most embarrassing moments. A pearlware jug decorated in copper luster and with purple transfer prints showing on one side Caroline, the estranged wife of George IV, with the not entirely accurate inscription GOD SAVE QUEEN CAROLINE!, and on the other (Fig. 73b) a parody on lines from the British national anthem. 1820. Height 5¾ inches.

Thus this now innocuous jug (and many more mugs, plates, and vases like it) was once the propaganda instrument of a nation's rage against an unpopular monarch and a discredited government—as well as being the memorial to one of the nastiest and most tragic scandals in British royal history.

The story behind the Caroline jug is infinitely more interesting than is the object itself, yet, as in the case of most commemorative artifacts, the two are inseparably wedded. The jug preserves the history and the history dates the jug. Sometimes the incidents and people are relatively obscure and might not be remembered at all were it not for the survival of a ceramic cenotaph which, ironically, was never intended as such. This is certainly true of George Pocock and Jeffreys Allen, whose names, and the date 1802, adorn the neck of a blue-printed,

74. How to get the message to the voters. This large pearlware jug was almost certainly used to dispense free beer to the voters of Bridgewater in Somerset when Pocock and Allen were standing for re-election to Parliament in 1802. Probably made at Swansea. Height 8⅛ inches.

pearlware pitcher (Fig. 74). Ironically, too, the jug was intended to draw attention to an event yet to come, and not to one that had passed. The two men had been elected Members of Parliament for Bridgewater in Somersetshire in 1798, and four years later were running for re-election. This jug, and others like it, filled with free beer and given away to potential supporters, may have been instrumental in sending Pocock and Allen back to Westminster for four more years. They do not appear to have been particularly notable parliamentarians, but their jug serves as a reminder that the balloon and bumper-sticker ballyhoo of the American electoral process has been around for a long time—as has a little honest graft.

I found the Pocock and Allen jug on the top shelf of a stall in London's Portobello Road market, and as the dealer specialized in Chinese export porcelain he had little knowledge of English wares and put a price on the pitcher that was almost contemptuous. Much more significant than its value as an "election" jug is the fact that it may be the earliest dated example of "willow-style" chinoiserie on transfer-printed pearlware. Although the "moth" pattern around the neck occurs on Staffordshire pieces, it is also found on examples made at Swansea in South Wales, and that fact coupled with the style of the handle had already prompted me to lean toward Swansea before I discovered that Pocock and Allen came from Somerset, a county in easy reach of the Swansea Pottery across the Bristol Channel. In short, there is more to be learned from a pot than first meets the eye, but much else is forever lost—and if that sounds like a cue for another flight of fancy, it is. It is not one of my own, however; it was written nearly 250 years ago, and published in the *Pennsylvania Gazette* under the heading "A Meditation on a Quart Mug," and this, in part, is what it said:

How often have I seen him [the mug] compell'd to hold up his Handle at the Bar, for no other Crime than that of being empty; then snatch'd away by a surly Officer, and plung'd suddenly into a Tub of cold Water. . . . How often is he hurry'd down into a dismal Vault, sent up fully laden in a cold Sweat, and by a rude Hand thrust into the Fire! How often have I seen it obliged to undergo the Indignities of a dirty Wench; to have melting Candles dropt on its naked Sides, and sometimes in its Mouth; to risque being broken into a thousand Pieces, for Actions which itself was not guilty of! How often is he forced into the Company of boisterous Sots, who lay all their Nonsense, Noise, profane Swearing, Cursing, and Quarreling, on the harmless Mug, which speaks not a Word! They overset him, maim him, and sometimes turn him to Arms offensive or defensive, as they please; when of himself he would not be of either Party, but would as willingly stand, still. . . . And yet, O Mug! If these Dangers thou escapist, with little injury, thou must at last untimely fall, be broken to Pieces, and cast away, never more to be recollected and form'd into a Quart Mug. Whether by the Fire, or in a Battle, or choak'd with a Dishclout, or by a Stroke against a Stone, thy Dissolution happens; 'tis all alike to thy avaricious Owner; he grieves not for thee, but for the Shilling with which he purchased thee![5]

This remarkable portrait of the life and death of a colonial artifact was composed by the owner of the *Pennsylvania Gazette*, the twenty-seven-year-old Benjamin Franklin, and having read it, I can no longer look at an eighteenth-century tavern mug without thinking of the indignities it has endured (Fig. 75). Franklin went on to describe the fate of the mug's sherds after it was broken and they were tossed away, following them into the field where they snagged a mower's scythe and were "with bitter Curses" tossed over the hedge, later to be used by boys to throw at birds and dogs "until by Length

75. Rhenish stoneware mugs like this were common in British and American taverns through much of the eighteenth century. About 1740. Height 7 inches, and two-quart capacity.

of Time and numerous Casualties, they shall be press'd into their Mother Earth, and be converted to their original Principles."

The average collector will not, as a rule, be acquiring his specimens from the earth, and his tavern mugs will have escaped the final humiliations so graphically imagined by Franklin. Nevertheless, the accident of survival is equally intriguing, for one wonders how it is that a common mug with no intrinsic value managed to avoid the hazards of usage and to surmount the usually towering obstacle of obsolescence. Where has it been from then until now, can be a question quite as interesting as what happened to the object during the span of its normal life expectancy. The latter question was brought home to me through another of those coincidences to which I seem prone, and which cheating playwrights employ to tie up the loose ends of mysteries that otherwise defy solution.

On a visit to England in 1961, I encountered an important and early English delftware dish in a Dorchester antique shop. Belonging to the class known as "blue dash chargers" and dating from about 1640, the dish was decorated in polychrome with the figures of Adam and Eve. Although cracked and riveted, it was a tremendous find—and a bargain to boot (Fig. 6). To its back was glued a faded paper label reading as follows: "The figures on this dish are drawn in the main with anatomical truth, and have been vigorously conceived by the painter. The trees are shown as detached clusters of leaves joined by bare branches, a method which perhaps distinguishes the Lambeth versions of this theme from those of Bristol. Rackham & Read, p. 48." Two days after I found the Dorchester dish, I came upon another in the Portobello Road; though later in date and much cruder, this, too, bore a label on the back written in the same hand as the first and again quoting Rackham and Read. Both references were to the same page in Bernard Rackham and Herbert Read's classic, *English Pottery*, first published in 1924. A trip to the book revealed that both dishes were illustrated in it as type specimens showing the evolution of the Adam and Eve design on English delftware.

The captions added that the chargers were then in the collection of W. M. Beaumont.

Because most well-known collections eventually end up on the auction block, and because Sotheby's of London is the best-known British firm specializing in the sale of ceramics, I wrote asking whether the Beaumont Collection had passed through its rooms. It was my guess that as two pieces from it had turned up simultaneously in different parts of England, the collection must recently have been sold. I was right—or partly right. Sotheby's had indeed auctioned the Beaumont Collection, but that was in 1931! The records showed that sixteen items had not been sold, having failed to command bids higher than the reserves, and the two Adam and Eve dishes were among them. Where they went for the ensuing twenty-nine years, and why they surfaced again at points 120 miles apart, I shall probably never know. But I do know that the odds against my finding them both were long enough to choke a computer.

The dice are so heavily loaded against the survival of any aging object (be it of fragile pottery or of sturdy oak), that it is miraculous that only nine-tenths of everything manufactured in the last three hundred years has been destroyed. Works of art generally stand the best chance of survival, for being intended for admiration rather than use, they will endure as long as they are liked. Pictures, furthermore, are more readily recognized as the product of creative talent than are utilitarian objects, and consequently one thinks twice before destroying them. The artistry of the cabinetmaker, the potter, or the glass-blower, on the other hand, enjoyed that kind of protective respect only when its products bore a date sufficiently far removed for them to be recognized as old by anyone with the ability to read four digits. A classic example was provided a few years ago by a resident of Williamsburg who had no interest in antiques, but who owned a Bow porcelain tea bowl with the name "A Target" and the date 1754 painted on the bottom in red enamel (Figs. 76a, 76b). She did not know where it came from, beyond recalling that it had been in her family as long as she could remember, a family that originally

76a & b.   This Bow porcelain tea bowl of the first importance saw service as an ashtray in a Virginia home until it was dropped and broken. Decorated in underglaze blue in a chinoiserie bamboo and peony design, it was then enameled in green, yellow, purple, and red, the same red used to mark the base (Fig. 76b, *below*) with the date and the name of the purchaser. 1754. Diameter 3 inches.

came from England. To her the bowl was simply something to have around, and it made a nice ashtray—until it was knocked off a table and broken in half.

There are, as far as I know, only ten earlier pieces of dated Bow porcelain on record, most of which were brought together for a special exhibition at the British Museum in 1959. It also included three examples dated 1754; one of them, a bowl, was inscribed "Thos: Target 1754," while an ornamental flowerpot was marked "Thos. & Ann Target July 2$^{th}$ 1754." Clearly, therefore, the tea bowl was made for Mrs. Ann Target; furthermore, its enameled chinoiserie decoration is similar to that of the third 1754 example in the British Museum exhibition, a cream pitcher inscribed "W Pether May 10, 1754." Although nothing is known about Thomas and Ann Target, that in no way detracts from the little bowl's importance as a rare, documentary addition to the chronicle of early English porcelain. Had its existence been known in 1959 there is no doubt that it would have been offered an honored place in the exhibition. But it was not known, and it is unlikely that it would have survived even in its ignominious role as an ashtray (let alone being glued together after it was broken) had it not been for the date on the bottom that cried "Keep me!"

The reasons why some things survive and others do not are of paramount interest to the archaeologist, and in seeking the answers he is likely to unearth some improbable villains. It is no secret that the church deserves to be roundly hissed as his archenemy. The victory of Christianity has left a multitude of losers in its wake, an alphabetical roster beginning with Aztec and ending at Zulu, and which includes archaeologists among the "A's." Most non-Christian cultures thought it necessary to send their dead into the next world properly equipped for the journey, and so the graves contained whatever the survivors thought appropriate; the wine in bottles and the food in metal or ceramic vessels. Thus the mourners were inadvertently providing future archaeologists with cultural time capsules and a source of intact objects which, under any other circumstances, would have been unlikely to survive. It is no overestimation to claim that two-thirds of all the intact ceramic and glass vessels that have come back to us from the pre-Christian world have been retrieved from graves. Fortunately for the art and anti-quarian fraternity, the looting of non-Christian graves has long been recognized as a legitimate cultural pursuit to which nineteenth-century Anglican clerics took like Burke to Hare. Paradoxically, however, disturbing the Christian dead is called desecration and can land you in jail. Fortunately the tempta-tion is not great, for the vast majority of such burials contain nothing of archaeological interest. This is less true today than it was in earlier generations, for beginning in the nineteenth century it became fashionable to transform the corpse into an exhibit, attiring it in its best clothes. It is a practice that was specifically barred by English law in the reign of Charles II, when an Act of Parliament required that the dead should be buried only in woolen shrouds, with the possible addition of woolen caps and gloves. No linen was permitted nor any use of thread. The statute's purpose was not religious but was in-tended as a stimulus to the English wool industry—just as fish on Fridays had been cooked up centuries before to help a floundering French fishing trade.

One of my least enviable duties while archaeologist for the Guildhall Museum in London was to record details of burials removed from bombed city churches in the course of their restoration. Although I examined the contents of hundreds of coffins dating from the seventeenth and eighteenth centuries, only one of them contained anything that might remotely be described in archaeological parlance as "grave goods"—not counting a man with a wooden leg. The exception was found in the churchyard of St. Martin Vintry, one of the churches not rebuilt after the Great Fire of 1666 but whose burying ground continued to serve the parish. The coffin contained a skeleton with a delftware plate inverted on its pelvis, the hands resting modestly over it. The plate proved to be one of the best examples of late-seventeenth-century delftware unearthed in London and is decorated with the characteristic "Chinaman and rocks" motif borrowed from Ming porcelain (Fig. 77). I had half expected to find the plate covering some precious object, but when I turned it over, all that was revealed was a

77. A London delftware plate decorated in blue with a pseudo-Ming motif typical of the 1670s; what was not typical was its discovery in a coffin inverted over the pelvis of the occupant. Diameter 9 inches.

tuft of hair clinging to the underside and indicating that the plate had rested directly on the corpse rather than having been placed on top of the shroud.

I could discover no immediate explanation for the plate's presence, but later a colleague drew my attention to an exchange of correspondence published in the *Gentleman's Magazine* in 1785 following the finding of a similarly entombed plate in St. Mary's churchyard at Leicester. The first correspondent sought an explanation for "the custom of putting a plate of salt on the belly of a deceased corpse."[6] The scholarly response (politely ignoring the redundancy) was not particularly revealing, but it did state that in the late eighteenth century it still remained a Leicestershire custom "to place a dish or plate of salt on a corpse, to prevent its swelling and purging."[7] John Brand in his *Observations on the Popular Antiquities of Great Britain* (1849) went further, explaining that the salt was intended to discourage the swelling which in turn caused "a difficulty in closing the coffin." He also quoted other statements suggesting that the salt represented the incorruptible human soul. Thus, in Scotland, relatives laid on the deceased's breast "a wooden platter, containing a small quantity of salt and earth, separate and unmixed: the earth an emblem of the corruptible body, the salt an emblem of the immortal spirit." There was also the possibility that the salt helped to keep

Satan at bay, for, as Brand pointed out, "the devil loveth no salt in his meat, for that is a sign of eternity, and used by God's commandment in all sacrifices."[8]

In May, 1972, sixteen years after I found the London plate, another was discovered, this time in Wedgwood-style cream-ware, interred beside the left thigh of a man buried at Green Park in Jamaica. A newspaper report of the find described another discovered in 1967 in a partially robbed eighteenth-century burial vault. In that instance the container was a white saltglaze saucer. Groping for an explanation, the newspaper suggested that the occupants of the coffins "might have over-eaten, and the contents of those two dishes being the last straw that caused their demise, they were buried with them. Or," the writer went on, "in each case the dish might have held the owner's favourite treat, eaten at the last repast he or she enjoyed on earth." The paper added that the consensus of popular opinion was that the plate and saucer had contained food to accompany the dead on the journey into the next world in case "he arrived after hours, and the pearly gates were locked for the night, there was the handy snack."[9] This last observation carries us back to the pre-Christian era (or side-ways into the non-Christian world), and one wonders whether it may stem from the blending in Jamaica of African and Anglican funerary traditions. The evidence, however, does not support that explanation. Both burials were unquestionably those of white colonials and date from the second half of the eighteenth century before black and white cultures began to merge. Much more reasonable is the conclusion that the de-ceased came from parts of Britain or Scotland where the salt tradition persisted.

I should add that I am not promoting assaults on cemeteries in pursuit of collectable goodies; I mention these discoveries only as another example of those chains of coincidences whose links fit together to tell us something about the past—something which might so easily have been lost. Had not the Jamaican discoveries been made by a careful amateur archae-ologist, and had the London plate been found by a builder's laborer, the plates would have been destroyed or would have entered the antiques market robbed of their significance. As for the coincidence, I cannot help but be uneasy at the prospect that some unknown arbiter prompted the Jamaican archaeologist to write to me about his strange discoveries and that they should so closely match my hitherto unparalleled London discovery—unparalleled or unrecorded, that is, since the Leicester plate was unearthed in 1784. Had I not been in St. Martin Vintry's churchyard at the right moment on the right day, the delftware dish would not have told its story, and without it I would never have learned about the salt custom, and the Jamaican plate and saucer would have been dismissed as the residue of handy snack packs for after-hours arrivals at the pearly gates.

# NINE

# History in a Green Bottle

M<small>Y INTEREST</small> in collecting glass grew accidentally out of my work on the London bomb sites. As I have earlier admitted, my original concern was for the preservation of the history and relics of the Roman period, and had it remained so neither my career nor this book would look at all as it does. But once I began my battle with the bulldozers I found myself in the presence not only of Londinium but all those other Londons that came after it. Furthermore, and as I mentioned in the last chapter, I was to have more difficulty finding museum specialists able to help me date the artifacts of the more recent periods than I would those of the classical centuries. I knew at once that I needed the same kind of closely datable artifactual signposts for the sixteenth, seventeenth, and eighteenth centuries as I had for the Roman remains. As the most common artifact of the later centuries seemed to be broken bottle glass, I decided that I had better try to establish a viable chronology of shapes. I was not the first to attempt it; that credit belonged to E. T. Leeds of the Ashmolean Museum, who in 1914 had made studies of tavern bottles excavated in Oxford. I may, however, have been among the first to see wine bottles as a major archaeological tool, but if so, it was through no genius on my part; it was simply that few archaeologists were then paying any attention to the post-medieval centuries.

The history of the glass wine bottle as we know it today began in the mid-seventeenth century, and right from the start a small percentage of them were embellished with a glass seal attached to their shoulders and impressed with the sign of a tavern, the arms of a nobleman, the mark of a merchant, or the name or initials of anyone wanting the prestige of "personalized" bottles. More important, though least commonly, some of the seals also bore a date, usually that of the year in which the bottle was made or filled. Just as dated ceramics stood a better chance of surviving, so dated bottles were more likely to be retained as curiosities than were those whose age could be recognized only by specialists. Consequently the number of dated specimens now in private and museum collections gives a totally false impression of the numbers that were so marked. Second only to the survival chances of bottles with dated seals were those having seals of any sort. Together they formed a minuscule percentage of the total British bottle output in the seventeenth and eighteenth centuries, the vast majority of which lived and died as bottles, functional to the last. Nevertheless, it was the sealed specimens that survived to be studied, and it was they that provided the means of dating the silent majority.

Valuble assistance in determining who owned what, and where, had been provided by Sheelah Ruggles-Brise in her book *Sealed Bottles* (1948), including as it did a listing of the specimens in the most important British and American collections. Today we know that the list was woefully incomplete; but it was a good start, even though it was much more concerned with genealogy than with the all-important evolution of bottle shapes. In those days so little was known about shapes that a dealer sent me a price list for a collection of unmarked specimens in which he put the highest value on examples dating in the 1780s and the lowest on another of about 1660—needless to say, the latter is now in my collection. Nowadays, however, the majority of dealers have a working knowledge of bottle evolution and ask prices for unsealed examples that a decade ago could have been commanded only by dated specimens.

Naturally enough, the highest prices are generally obtained by bottles having the earliest dated seals, followed by those bearing names that are well known or are of shapes and sizes that are unusual. One's chances of landing such prizes without paying through the nose for them are slim at best—but it does happen. In 1954 a large collection was auctioned at Sotheby's in London, among them some obviously high-bid specimens. As is common when a large collection of comparable objects is sold, many of them were put up in lots of from two to seven items, with only the prime pieces being described in the catalogue, the rest lumped together as "and five others" or whatever the number might be. It was in one such anonymous group that I spotted what, to me, seemed to be the most desirable specimen in the entire sale; dating from about 1660 and in immaculate condition, it was of an almost unique half-bottle size and adorned with the seal of a Rose Tavern and the WHM initials of the landlord and his wife. On the bottom was a paper label reading "Dug up in Mrs. Anstey-Perks garden, Breaston, Derbyshire" (Fig. 78). I attended the sale ready to secure the bottle at almost any price, hoping to get my money back by reselling the more obviously desirable specimens. But something went wrong. I had assumed that all the bottles in each lot would be carried round the auction room before the bidding opened, but only those described in the catalogue were paraded, and I waited in vain for "my" bottle to appear. Having failed to bid on the lot, I stayed until the sale's end and tried to learn the name of the buyer, but by the time I found out, he had left. I did learn, however, that he was bidding for an American client. So that seemed to be that.

The next day I received a phone call from another dealer reminding me that two years earlier I had visited his shop in Kent (though he, himself, had been away at the time) and had left my card, asking to be advised of any bottles that might come his way. He had subsequently moved his shop to London and had brought my card with him, and now he had some bottles to show me. Had they come from Sotheby's sale? I asked. He did not think so. But when I got to the shop, there was "my" bottle, and I could have it for three pounds—a frac-

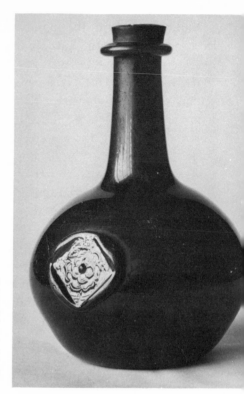

78. Wine bottle of the rare half-bottle size and decorated with the seal of an unidentified Rose Tavern and the owners' initials W.M.H. Found at Breaston, Derbyshire, and dating from about 1660. Height 6¾ inches.

tion of what I had expected to pay for it at the auction. The explanation for the bottle's reappearance was as simple as it was improbable: the American customer was only interested in dated specimens and had instructed his agent to dispose of those that were not, never realizing that there might be a cygnet among his undated ducklings.

Another "Rose Tavern" bottle came to light at about the same time that the Breaston specimen was sold, but unlike the latter, which steadfastly refused to surrender any more of its history, this one was shamelessly ready to tell all—and there was plenty to tell. It came from the notorious Rose Tavern in London's Covent Garden, the setting for William Hogarth's famous orgy scene in his *A Rake's Progress* series. Now in the collection of Henekey's, the London vintners, the bottle's eroded surface indicates that it had been buried and presumably unearthed on a construction site, but just where or when, no one knows (Fig. 79). It is the bottle's early history, how-

79. Another Rose Tavern bottle, this one identified as belonging to William and Mary Long, operators of the notorious establishment in London's Covent Garden. Before 1661. Height 9½ inches.

ever, that makes it interesting. The seal on its side bears a Tudor rose and in its center the initials wʟᴍ for William and Mary Long who, besides producing twenty-two children, found time to be the landlords of the tavern that stood at the mouth of the passage leading to the King's House theater.

Like my pursuit of William Deaven's pewter tankard, the trail began amid the pages of Boyne's catalogue of seventeenth-century tokens, but with results that were immediately more successful. Although William was unlisted, Mary Long appeared on her own at the sign of the rose and with an inscription which established her as living in Russell Street, onto which the Rose Tavern faced. Not all seventeenth-century tokens are listed in Boyne, and as Figure 80 shows, a token issued by William and Mary Long ᴀᴛ ᴛʜᴇ ʀᴏsᴇ ᴛᴀᴠᴇʀɴ ɪɴ ᴄᴏᴠᴇɴᴛ ɢᴀʀᴅᴇɴ was one of them, its triple initials identical to those on the bottle seal. Neither token is dated, but subsequent

80. William and Mary Long's
Rose Tavern trade token. Brass,
and pre-1661.

research revealed that William Long died in 1661, proving,
therefore, that the bottle was in use before that date. Like
Margaret North of the Ship Tavern on St. Mary Hill, the
widow Long continued in business on her own, issuing a token,
and probably continuing to serve from her husband's old bottles until her own death in 1673. It is entirely possible that
these same bottles were put before Samuel Pepys, whose diary
records three visits to the Rose, the first on the night before
Christmas in 1667.

And so took my coach, which waited; and drank some burnt wine
at the Rose Tavern door while the constables came, and two or
three bellmen went by, it being a fine light moon-shine morning:
and so home round the City.[1]

Few passages in the diary are as evocative as these few lines.
One can almost hear the clop of the horses' hooves as the coach
rumbles away from the tavern through the sleeping Christmas
streets.

Pepys's next visit was in May, 1668, in broad daylight and in
quite different weather, when he drank a tankard of some
unspecified cool drink before going into the playhouse to see
what turned out to be a particularly dismal play. Four days
later, he was back again to see another play, *The Mulberry
Garden*, by Sir Charles Sedley, "of whom, being so reputed a
wit," wrote Pepys, "all the world do expect great matters. I

having sat here awhile and eat nothing today, did slip out, getting a boy to keep my place; and to the Rose Tavern, and there got half a breast of mutton off of the spit, and dined all alone."[2] He did not comment on the quality of the meal, possibly because the play stuck so deep in his craw. "I have not been less pleased at a new play in my life," Pepys concluded. He should have stayed at the Rose!

By the end of the seventeenth century, Covent Garden had earned itself the kind of reputation now enjoyed by New York's Central Park. "In those days a man could not go from the Rose Tavern to the Piazzi once but he must venture his life twice," wrote playwright Thomas Shadwell.[3] Sixteen years later George Farquhar in *The Recruiting Officer* had one of his characters declare, "If I had you in the Rose Tavern, Covent Garden, with three or four hearty rakes or four smart napkins, I would tell you another story, my dear."[4] It is evident from Hogarth's engraving that at the Rose just about anything went (Fig. 81). Thus, the patch-prettied doxie in the foreground in the process of disrobing, long ago outdid (or undid) the topless go-go dancers of our own time. Capping the talents of the pregnant singer of bawdy ballads, and with the aid of the candle and Rose Tavern serving dish held by Leather-coat the waiter, Aretine, the "posture woman," did her celebrated thing. Behind her the liquor freely flows from bottles much like those found on the Sandwich beach but eighty years later than that of William Long (Fig. 79). To those who see bottles simply as glass, that is all the Rose Tavern bottle is, an antique desirable because of its early date. To others it is a hundred years of wine, women, and song, a link with Samuel Pepys, Edward Gibbon, David Garrick, and most of the great names in the eighteenth-century British theater—including the now forgotten but once immensely popular young actor Hilderbrand Hordern, who was murdered in a room at the Rose in 1712.

Of much the same date as the Rose bottle, but with a recent history as remarkable as its past, was another that nearly met its end for the second time, in a London street called Aldermanbury. Unearthed by workmen digging test holes to determine the subsoil's bearing capacity before erecting a new office

81. The Rose in Covent Garden was renowned for its divertissements. Here, in a detail from William Hogarth's 1735 engraving of a room at that tavern in his *A Rake's Progress* series, Aretine, the "posture woman," prepares to entertain.

building, this bottle, and an undetermined number of others like it, was thrown against a wall for the pleasure of hearing glass break. It proved to be a blessing most cunningly disguised, for the rude shattering of the city's Saturday-afternoon silence drew an antiquary colleague to the scene. Knowing that I was interested in wine bottles, he rounded up a miscellany of the fragments and some weeks later gave them to me, saying that he thought they came from a cellar sealed over after the Great Fire of 1666 and breached by the test-hole diggers. My informant died very soon after, and I was never able to determine exactly where the cellar lay, but I was able to put the best part of two bottles together, both of them bearing a seal impressed with the initials R. W. (Fig. 82).

Throughout the second half of the seventeenth century it was common practice for bottle factories to provide separate letter stamps which could be set up in combinations of two or three initials to "personalize" the bottles of people who could not afford, or be bothered, to have their own dies made. The R. W. seals were of this type, and it is reasonable to suppose that if other customers with those initials ordered bottles from the same factory, the chances of the letters being set up again in precisely the same juxtaposition would be very slim. Nevertheless, more than four thousand miles away as the brigantine sailed, at Jamestown, Virginia, there was another R. W. seal, identical even in its flaws.

In the summer of 1956 I was invited to visit the United States for the first time and to spend four months in Williamsburg making a study of the wine bottles found there in nearly thirty years of archaeological excavations. At the same time I examined the bottle fragments in the National Park Service collections at Jamestown and so encountered the other R. W. seal. It had been found in excavations on a lot once owned by Captain Ralph Wormeley, who died in 1651. Some historians have placed his death rather later (1655 and 1669), but the argument in favor of 1651 is the most convincing. If correct, it follows that the R. W. bottles were made before that date and thus would be the oldest documented specimens of their type on record. The earliest actually dated seal is in the London

82a, b, & c.  A wine bottle made for Ralph Wormeley of Jamestown in Virginia, but found in London; shown with it are a detail of its R W seal (Fig. 82b) and a matching fragment found on Wormeley's house site at Jamestown (Fig. 82c). Before 1652. Height of bottle 9¼ inches.

Museum and bears the name John Jefferson and the year 1652, while the oldest intact, dated bottle bears a seal decorated with a Carolean royal profile (presumably the sign of a King's Head tavern), along with the initials R. M. and 1657. This is in the collection of the Northampton Museum.

Although the pre-1651 date for the Wormeley bottles is only inferred, they can claim other distinctions: They are the only objects made for a seventeenth-century Virginian yet found in England, and they are among the oldest objects associated with a known American family. That my enforced interest in wine bottles should have been instrumental in bringing the bottles to me (they would otherwise have been left where the workmen threw them), and that I, in turn, should have been brought to Jamestown and to the R. W. seal stored there is another of those coincidences that, for me, recurrence renders commonplace. I readily admit that any reader who suspects that they are too numerous to be true has a right to be skeptical. The fact remains, however, that the morning after the foregoing paragraph was written I received a parcel of artifacts recovered by divers from wrecks off the coast of Maine. Among them was an earthenware pipkin, lead-glazed on the inside, and with traces of paint on the rim. It looked French, but I had no idea of its date, and I had never seen anything quite like it. In the afternoon I was visited by an archaeologist who had been excavating on the home site of John Watson, the early American portrait painter, at Perth Amboy in New Jersey. My caller brought with him only a few of the many artifacts he had recovered, but among them was an inch-long rim fragment bearing traces of paint. He set it down on the same table on which stood the Maine wreck material; the sherd matched the pipkin exactly, and thus the latter revealed the shape of the Perth Amboy vessel, while that, in turn, provided the Maine pipkin with a date in the late seventeenth or early eighteenth century. Over the years I have examined hundreds of thousands, perhaps millions, of pots and potsherds and have no recollection of having seen one of these before—until two turned up on the same day, each needing the other and a catalyst to make them meaningful. On such occasions it is hard not to hear the secret laughter of Macbeth's weird sisters and to give credence to their supernatural soliciting.

Both in archaeology and in antique collecting we are constantly groping into the unknown and more often than not we quickly find ourselves with nowhere to go. It is only natural, therefore, that American collectors should be most interested in objects that can be proved to have belonged to individuals whose names are familiar in colonial and later American history. Consequently, a wine bottle bearing the seal of Bernie Schwartz of Poughkeepsie is unlikely to be as desirable as another that belonged to a Signer or a Founding Father. It is by no means a latter-day prejudice, as a bottle in the collection of Colonial Williamsburg can testify. On its seal it bears the name JOHN CUSTIS and the date 1713, and on its shoulder has been affixed a silver plaque engraved with the following inscription:

Found 1810 in the Cellar on the "Six Chimney Lot" the old residence of the Custis Family in Williamsburg Vᵃ and Presented by Mʳˢ E Galt to Jaˢ W. Custis. 1852.

One might reasonably suggest that had not John Custis become the reluctant father-in-law of Martha Dandridge-Custis-Washington, the bottle would have had considerably less historical interest and certainly a far smaller chance of aspiring to a silver talisman (Fig. 83). In truth, however, John Custis was a much more interesting individual than his daughter-in-law would ever be—as I slowly learned as we began excavating his house site in 1964.

John Custis was the fourth of that name and the son of John Custis of "Wilsonia" on the Eastern Shore of Virginia (Fig. 84). At some date between 1712 and 1717, after marrying Frances Parke, the daughter of another wealthy plantation owner, John the Fourth built or acquired a brick house on the outskirts of Williamsburg. His wife died in 1715, leaving him wealthy and relieved, so much so that forty-four years later his will instructed that his tombstone should record that he died "Aged 71 Years, and yet liv'd but Seven Years, Which was the space of time He kept a Bachelors house on the Eastern Shore of Virginia." He never remarried; instead he took up gardening, and being the man that he was, he carried his enthusiasm to obsessive lengths. Not content with flowers in the garden, we find him ordering fire screens from England ornamented with painted blooms, and for those times when live flowers could fill his fireplaces he ordered green-painted urns. His tremendous and increasingly scholarly interest in horticulture caused him to embark on a voluminous correspondence with the famed London botanist Peter Collinson, and, fortunately, copies of most of the letters survive. One of them, believed to have been written in August, 1737, is concerned with the dispatch to Col-

83. Dated 1713, this wine bottle was made for John Custis of Virginia,
but it was not its age or Custis's fame that earned the bottle its silver label
and stopper. They were added because he happened to have been the
sometime and reluctant father-in-law of America's first First Lady. Height
7 inches.

84. John Custis at the age of forty-five, a painting believed to be by John Wollaston and now in the collection of Washington and Lee University. About 1726.

linson of a collection of fossils. The pertinent passage reads as follows:

As you are a very curious gentleman I send you some things which I took out of the bottom of A well 40 feet deep; the one seems to bee a cockle petrefyd [,] one a bone petrefyd; [this] seems to have been the under beak of some large antediluvian fowl. Wish they may bee acceptable.[5]

We found the well and discovered it to be forty feet and one inch to the bottom—seated in a bed of Miocene marl rich in fossils. Although no antediluvian fowl beaks were forthcoming, there were fragments of whale bone amid the shells. According to Earl G. Swem, who published the Custis-Collinson letters in his book *Brothers of the Spade,* the fossils sent by Custis were seen in the 1930s in the collection of the Mill Hill School in north London which now occupies the site of Peter Collinson's home. Today, however, the school disclaims any knowledge of them, stating that the only surviving link between Collinson and America are some of the trees standing in the grounds. Although this has something to say about the fate of private collections, it was not the fossils from the well that were important. Much more interesting was the discovery in its filling of examples of no fewer than seventeen different types of plant, shrub, and tree described in the Custis letters as being in the garden during his lifetime, among them the leaves of American holly and Dutch box still green after being buried for nearly two centuries.

It was evident that the well had been filled over a protracted period ending at the close of the eighteenth century, but it was the lower levels that were the most productive. From the bottom four feet came two intact bottles bearing the John Custis 1713 seal, and the seals and fragments of sixty more. Other broken and intact bottles were of shapes attributable to the 1730s, and were simply marked I CUSTIS, the "I" being the common form of capital "J" until the late eighteenth century. These may well have been some of the bottles that Custis ordered through Messrs. Loyd and Cooper of London in 1737:

I sent for 3 gross of quart bottles by Rumsey mark$^t$ I. Custis; I hope you will see y$^t$ they hold full quarts since y$^e$ price you say is y$^e$ same; and desire you will likewise send me all I desired by Rumsey; let y$^e$ bottles bee carefully pack$^t$. . . .[6]

This, however, cannot have been his only order of I CUSTIS sealed bottles, for the collection in the well included examples of half-bottle size which are not mentioned in the 1737 instructions to Loyd and Cooper. One of the quart bottles had had its seal deliberately defaced, the letters being ground down until they almost disappeared (Fig. 85). Could this have been done by someone with a deep and abiding malice toward John Custis? It was a question jokingly asked and lightly dismissed, but it would surface again when the character of Martha Washington became an element in the story.

Among many other items found near the bottom of the well (which included the finest group of early-eighteenth-century drinking glasses yet found in America) was a group of iron keys of various sizes, suggesting, perhaps, that they and the rest of the material in the well had been cleared up and thrown out when the Custis house changed hands. As neither the bottles nor the glasses were dated later than the 1730s, it at first seemed reasonable to conclude that they were discarded at John Custis's death in 1749. We would probably have gone on

85. Wine bottles from John Custis's well at his house site in Williamsburg. The seals are undated and are marked simply I Custis, though not simply enough for someone's taste, and the center example has had the name carefully defaced. About 1735. Tallest 8½ inches.

believing that had we not found a salt-glaze mug and a cream-colored earthenware cup of types introduced in the 1750s but lying under some of the earlier objects. It was more likely, therefore, that the well began to be used as a rubbish dump five or ten years after John's death, and the documentary records pointed to another major upheaval on the property in 1757.

John Custis's brief and stormy marriage had yielded four children; two died in infancy, the third and oldest died in 1744, leaving him but one son, Daniel Parke. Just how close was the young man's relationship with his mercurial father is unclear, but there is evidence that John Custis had another and favored natural son by his slave "young Alice," a boy named John, known as "Jack," and for whom Custis signed a deed of manumission in 1747. A month later he prepared a deed of gift giving the boy a tract of land on the estate inherited from Frances Parke Custis, and at the same time presenting him with his own mother and four other Negro boys. Custis also gave Jack a bond of £500 besides making various annual provisions for him until he should reach the age of twenty. Seeing that Jack was all right appears to have been one of John Custis's latter-day obsessions, and in his will he required that his executor should build and furnish a house for the lad and that he should continue to live in the household of Daniel Parke and there be "handsomely maintained" from the profits of the estate until he came of age.

It is possible that Daniel Parke was unamused by all this and that he said so, for John Custis subsequently reneged on the deed of gift which had left Jack his land in perpetuity. It was now to revert to Daniel Parke and his heirs upon Jack's death, and as it turned out Custis could thereby have been signing the boy's death warrant. Among other provisions in John Custis's will was the bequest of a painting of Jack to Mrs. Anne Moody, the wife of a tavern keeper on Williamsburg's Capitol Landing Road. It was the only picture specifically identified in the will, and one might therefore conclude that Custis feared for its safety and could no longer rely on Daniel Parke (and particularly his wife) to love Jack like a brother. John did not trust anybody very much; so suspicious was he that he even expressed concern lest someone might do something tricky with his own corpse. The will gave explicit instructions about obtaining a tombstone, specifying the already-quoted inscription, and ordering his heirs to send for another should the first stone fail to arrive. He was to be buried beside his grandfather at Arlington, his Eastern Shore family home, and the executors were to be certain that his body really got there and that they were not burying "a sham coffin."

When Daniel Parke married Martha Dandridge, his father was soon unhappy. He thought it a poor match and disliked the girl's father, and, characteristically, Custis put such life into his passion that it outlived him. Before his death Anne Moody had been given a number of pieces of the Custis family plate and pewter, and she openly displayed them in the public room of her husband's tavern. Daniel Parke and Martha subsequently went to court to get them back, and the incomplete record of the resulting lawsuit throws fascinating light into the shadows. Mrs. Moody testified that she had been given the plate because John Custis did not want it to fall into the hands of "any Dandridge's daughter." She revealed, too, that Custis had given her numerous other gifts including a pair of gold shoe buckles engraved "In Memory of John Custis Esq$^r$." She was, of course, the same Anne Moody who had inherited the portrait of "John otherwise called Jack" and an endowment of £20 for life. What, one might wonder, was the relationship between the powerful John Custis and the tavern keeper's wife?

It is not known how much time Daniel and Martha Custis spent at the Williamsburg house, but it seems to have been used only occasionally. Who, then, was looking after Jack? It was not a question that had to concern anyone for very long. The diary of John Blair of Williamsburg contained the following entry for September 19, 1751:

ab$^t$ 1 or 2 in y$^e$ morn$^g$. Col. Custis's Favourite Boy Jack died in ab$^t$ 21 hours illness being taken ill a little before day the 18$^{th}$ w$^{th}$ a Pain in the back of his Neck for w$^{ch}$ he was blooded.[7]

As quickly as Jack was rid of his pain in the neck, Daniel and Martha were relieved of theirs. So convenient a death should have been enough to make any coroner suspicious and to send even the most dim-witted detective reaching for his quizzing glass, but under the circumstances it is hardly likely that Daniel Parke Custis's peers had anything but unquestioning compassion for the nice young couple who, by the Grace of God, had been relieved of an intolerable burden. There is, in fact, a convincing medical explanation for Jack's sudden death. His neck pain may have been a symptom of meningitis, and if the boy was also suffering from sickle-cell anemia, bleeding could easily have killed him.

Daniel Parke Custis died in 1757 leaving Martha in control of the entire Custis estate, transforming her, at the age of twenty-six, into the wealthiest and most desirable widow in Virginia. So, when George Washington married her two years later, he was on to a very good thing. As befits the memory of the wife of the Father of the Nation, Martha is usually described in terms that would do justice to a White House press secretary. She exuded an "infectious gentleness," we are told; she possessed superlative tact and had beautiful teeth; she called herself "a fine, healthy girl," and only an oaf would confuse her agreeable plumpness with fat. In the face of all this charm, it is a little surprising to find her, in 1757, selling off the Custis possessions—even to the family's pictures (more than 135 of them) and items that had been in Custis homes since the days of John the Emigrant. Although these heirlooms may have meant nothing to her, they nonetheless were the lineal inheritance of her two surviving children. It might be construed, therefore, that in stripping the Williamsburg house, Martha was deliberately eradicating the memory of John Custis—though not, of course, the Custis estate, which was worth in excess of £23,500. Then, after remarrying, and in a move of almost Ashmolean irony, she rented his house and precious garden to another Dandridge, her brother Bartholomew.

If, indeed, Martha was trying to be rid of John Custis, the

presence of so many of his wine bottles at the bottom of the well makes a good deal of sense. Consequently, whenever I hear Martha Washington's virtues extolled, I am reminded of the bottle with its Custis seal defaced and wonder whether the damage could have been the work of a gentle, pleasantly plump young lady who hid her beautiful teeth behind a tight-lipped angry mouth as she ground away at the name and memory of the man who had described her as "much inferior to his son."

As one reads the lengthy inventory of the Custis goods auctioned off on Martha's instructions, and sees the relatively modest prices that they fetched, one wonders what became of them and what they might be worth today. Unlike his bottles, few of John Custis's possessions would have borne his name, and once absorbed into another household they would have become nothing more than second-hand furniture and used pots and pans. Not knowing that a hundred years later these things could be promoted as precious relics from the family of the first First Lady, the buyers could have had no reason to be seeking memorials to the cantankerous eccentric whose relationship with Mrs. Moody and his flaunting of "Negro Jack" must have been an embarrassment to Williamsburg society.

The bottle salvaged from the cellar of the House of the Six Chimneys in 1810 is the only relic of John Custis known to have remained there throughout the history of the home, and how it escaped Martha's 1759 clearance and survived later tenancies and ownerships will never be known, but like William Long's Rose Tavern bottle, it must have been privy to some extraordinary goings-on. It has seen the comings and goings of botanists and naturalists like John Bartram and Mark Catesby, and the visits of great Virginians such as William Byrd, James Blair and, of course, George Washington. It may have been touched by Anne Moody and have known the truth about the luckless Jack.

The contents of the Custis well showed that his cellar had contained many other bottles having no identifying seals, and if nineteenth-century collectors had carried those off, there might now be no knowing (and certainly no proof) that they came from the cellar and are just as historically evocative as the 1713 example. Indeed, it is possible that were it not for the silver label identifying the source of that bottle, it might never have returned from its last home in Philadelphia to the safety of the Colonial Williamsburg collection. Although I am not suggesting that every bottle collector should have the source of each specimen engraved in silver on its side, there is much to be said for keeping a careful record of everything he knows about it.

Sometimes, of course, the sellers find it to their advantage to pretend ignorance of the origins of their wares. Thus, for example, the sudden arrival on the American market of hundreds of eighteenth- and nineteenth-century Dutch wine bottles found on colonial sites in Surinam and the Guianas prompted some traders to label them English and to display them on the same shelves as others bought in Britain. Until 1971 little or nothing was known about Dutch bottles, except that most of them were not appreciably different from their English counterparts. Nobody in the Netherlands had paid much attention to them, and apart from the few picked up along the Florida Keys very few were seen in the United States. Then, with the sudden influx from South America, the picture changed. Sold singly and in groups to East Coast dealers, museums, and collectors, they brought prices that had at first run as high as $125 for examples from the second quarter of the eighteenth century, then had fallen a year later to as little as $20. At the same time a nervousness developed about the value of eighteenth-century bottles in general, discouraging investment in even the normally desirable English specimens. Meanwhile, another collector in the West Indies was busily buying up more eighteenth- and nineteenth-century Dutch bottles in South America with a view to injecting them into the American market after the first wave had been absorbed and prices recovered.

As soon as magazines and antiquarian journals began to discuss Dutch bottles and to describe their identifiable characteristics, uncertainty among both dealers and collectors would be replaced by a new expertise making them desirable antiques. Then, as the supply dwindled, prices would rise again. That this does happen was brought home to me when, some years ago, I published an article on French faïence from Rouen imported into America during the Revolution. Comparable pieces which I had previously been able to pick up for less than $10 were subsequently offered to me for as much as $200—an excellent argument for keeping quiet!

The illustrated group of Dutch bottles (Fig. 86) shows their basic evolution through the eighteenth century. Those of the first half are generally thinner than are the British, are more olive green in color, and possess more conical basal kicks and mouths with distinctive W-sectioned string-rims (Fig. 87). Later in the century, straight-walled cylindrical bodies in association with curiously elongated and bulbous necks were common. Molded, square-sectioned bottles have long been recognized as Dutch and loosely classified as being for gin, though they were actually used for a variety of liquors from rum to claret. Bottles of this type were made both in Europe and in England in the first half of the seventeenth century and were often closed with pewter caps rather than corks, but by the eighteenth century they do seem to have been predomi-

86. A group of Dutch wine and gin bottles found in Guyana, South America. From left to right these examples are tentatively attributed to about 1730, 1770, 1750, 1790, and the mid-nineteenth century. The tall-necked specimen measures 11 inches and has a molded anchor on its base.

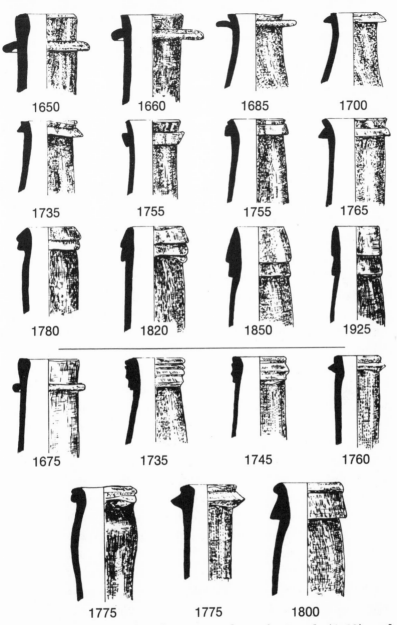

87. Comparative mouth and string-rim shapes for British (1–12), and Dutch wine bottles. Alas, like most simplistic criteria, there are enough exceptions to obscure the rule.

nantly Dutch—and corked. They were transported and stored in partitioned boxes known as cellars and are usually described as "case bottles" by those who flinch from associating them only with gin. The bottoms of the molds used in shaping the bodies were often crudely decorated with crosses, stars, rosettes, and anchors, and occasionally with initials, any of which would thus be embossed on the bases of the bottles. Similar mold marks are occasionally found on the bases of the later eighteenth-century cylindrical Dutch wine bottles, and it is to be expected that these will eventually be sought as desirable anomalies.

The Dutch and Anglo-Dutch colonial sites in South America are not the only rich sources of bottles still available to the adventurous collector or entrepreneur. Although the West Indian islands that are easily reached have either been fairly thoroughly milked or have been put off limits by prudent government conservation controls, there are no doubt others that will remain productive for some time to come. Virtually untouched, however, are India and the continent of Africa, both of which received tremendous quantities of bottles through the eighteenth and nineteenth centuries. In addition, there are the globe-spattered dots on the map, minute island outposts of empire where bottled palliatives were the only solace. One of them, the thirty-eight-square-mile Ascension Island in the south Atlantic, which was uninhabited until Napoleon was imprisoned on neighboring St. Helena in 1815, has begun to see its bottle assets emigrating to America. The two specimens illustrated in Figure 88 are typical of British bottles of the mid-nineteenth century. Both were shaped in molds, that on the left having the word PATENT embossed on the shoulder and P.R.BRISTOL on the bottom, the latter identifying it as a product of Powell and Ricketts of Bristol, a partnership established in 1856. The factory had earlier traded under the name of Henry Ricketts & Co., and in 1823 had secured the first patent for manufacturing liquor bottles in molds that shaped not only the body but also the shoulders and neck. All bottles made by this process can be identified by the mold

88. Empty bottles are invariably the legacy of Western culture. These were found on Ascension Island in the South Atlantic. *Left,* a light-repelling "black" bottle commonly used for beer in the mid-nineteenth century, and *right,* a much thinner pale green specimen made under the Ricketts Patent of 1823 but dating no earlier than 1856. Height of the latter 11¼ inches.

marks encircling the shoulders and thence extending vertically to the string-rim.

The other Ascension Island bottle possesses the mold marks, but they are less pronounced, due in part to the density of the glass. It was this kind of bottle that was meant when hostile London crowds shouted "Black bottle!" at the Seventh Earl of Cardigan (later of Crimean War fame) following an 1840 incident in the officers' mess of the 11th Hussars. Cardigan had censured a junior officer for bringing a common black bottle into the mess in the belief that it contained porter. Although the culprit, Captain Reynolds, assured his commanding officer that the bottle held Moselle, Cardigan retorted that a gentleman decanted his wine and ordered Reynolds expelled from the mess. The black bottles commonly did contain porter, a dark and bitter beer deriving its name from "porters' beer" normally drunk by laborers. Belonging to the same class is the example to the right of Figure 89 which was made for the use of the common room at All Souls College at Oxford. Dating from the

89. English wine bottles made for the common room of All Souls College, Oxford. *Left,* free-blown in about 1760, and *right,* mold-blown and dating from about 1820, its height 10¾ inches.

1830s, it is one of the most recent bottles to be marked with an applied seal. The shape is in distinct contrast to that of its companion, made for the same Oxford college about seventy years earlier. Both originally held wine, for as Captain Reynolds had the misfortune to prove, British bottles of the eighteenth and most of the nineteenth century were not made in different shapes to distinguish between types of wine or between wine and porters' beer.

It is dangerously easy to generalize out of truth, and in the last paragraph I may have been guilty of doing just that. Although I have yet to see a nineteenth-century British bottle bearing a seal dated later than 1837, it does not follow that sealed bottles (without dates) were not made after the 1830s. Dutch and French sealed bottles were common through much of the century, and I have seen a French olive oil bottle with a seal dated 1910. Then again there are the commemorative anomalies like those made to honor the coronation of George VI in 1937, and, most recently, a gross reproduction of an early eighteenth-century shape (Fig. 29) with a 1972 seal commemorating the silver wedding of Queen Elizabeth and Prince Philip. I would be doing a further disservice were it to be supposed that no wine bottles were made in molds prior to the Ricketts patent of 1823. Both square and cylindrical glass wine bottles were widely used during the Roman centuries, and, as I have already noted, case bottles were shaped in the same way in the seventeenth century. Even the early globular wine bottles were partially shaped in a mold to ensure that the bubble was of the right size for the bottle's intended capacity; then, by the mid-eighteenth century the body was allowed to remain long enough in the mold to hold the shape, and by 1792 London glass-sellers were selling quart bottles specifically identified in their invoices as "moulded" bottles. There are earlier references to molds, such as the 1752 newspaper announcement of the theft of "one Brass Bottle-Mould," though it is possible that the mold was intended for shaping patent medicine phials rather than common green wine bottles.[8]

Patent medicine bottles are becoming as collectable as wine bottles and are a lot easier to store. Unlike the free-blown green phials of the seventeenth and eighteenth centuries, others dating from the 1720s onward were of clear or "white" glass, essentially rectangular in section and blown into two-piece brass molds that opened diagonally so that the marks ran up opposite corners of the bottles. The oldest dated example yet recorded was found at Wetherburn's Tavern in Williamsburg, but was made in England to contain Robert Turlington's Balsam of Life and is embossed with the date March 25, 1750. Four years later Turlington began using a new bottle designed to prevent, so he said, "the villainy of some persons, who buying up my empty bottles, have basely and wickedly put therein a vile spurious counterfeit sort."[9] Ironically, the new bottles became the most widely pirated and copied of any used for eighteenth- and nineteenth-century patent medicines and were reproduced in both England and America where the magic ingredients (twenty-six of them) of Turlington's Balsam were considered a universal cure-all (Fig. 90). Although there were numerous other patent medicines in the eighteenth century, and advertisements indicate that they were dispensed in characteristic bottles, few are known, and it seems likely that the identifying features were fancy labels and impressed wax

90. Pirated versions of Robert Turlington's bottles originally designed for his Balsam of Life in 1754. All were found in Williamsburg, Virginia. The left example may have been made in the latter part of the eighteenth century, but the others date from the first half of the nineteenth century though they were not discarded until 1856. The right specimen is 2⁹⁄₁₆ inches in height and is pale blue in color; the others are clear.

seals over the mouths. If this was so, then it is probable that the elixirs and potions, purgatives and carminatives, were usually sold in bottles and phials like those shown in Figure 91. They are, incidentally, part of a collection of forty (most of them having faded paper labels bearing London street names) that turned up in a shop specializing in ethnography and Egyptian antiquities!

The United States is often, but incorrectly, thought of as the instigator of the patent-medicine boom in the nineteenth century, but in fact the majority of the proprietary, nonprescription medicines sold in nineteenth-century America were not patented but were protected by the registration of their brand names. The first truly patented medicines came from England, the oldest of them being Stoughton's Elixir, which acquired its royal license in 1712. Little attention has yet been paid to nineteenth-century medicine bottles in England, and the molded bitters and historical liquor flasks so widely collected in America lack their English counterparts, possibly because

91.  British pharmaceutical phials and bottles dating from the seventeenth to the early nineteenth century. From left to right they can be
given the following median dates: about 1815, 1650, 1740, 1700, 1680,
1740, 1790, and 1750. All are green save for the 1650 example, which
is amber, and that of 1790, which is clear and 6⅛ inches tall.

the British were more firmly wedded to beer, wine, and gin and
did not have to contend with the American temperance move-
ments (first promoted by Benjamin Rush in 1785) that turned
medicinal bitters into a socially acceptable substitute for
honest liquor.

In 1968, excavations on the site of an eighteenth-century
Williamsburg store revealed two abandoned well shafts, and
with the Custis treasures still in mind, hopes were high that
equally exciting discoveries were about to be made. It soon
became apparent, however, that both wells had been filled in
the present century, the first around 1910 and the second in
about 1930. Each had been in use when the property was
occupied by a barber's shop and drugstore—as the artifacts
lucidly reminded us. Mixed with the bottles for cologne, Ayer's
Hair Vigor, Swamp Root, and Mexican Mustang Liniment
found in the 1910 well were bottles for bitters, beer, and
various brands of whisky. The second shaft, on the other hand,
yielded no liquor bottles and, instead, contained a surprising
number of broken Mason jars—surprising only until an elderly
Williamsburg resident recalled that during Prohibition local
moonshine was dispensed in these jars. The same well sur-

92. The best of the new rubbish. A group of soft-drink and other bottles found in a Williamsburg well abandoned in about 1929. From left to right, a Ball "Mason" jar; a bottle made for the Williamsburg Bottling Works, and others for Taka-Kola, Hayo-Kola, Indian Rock Ginger Ale, and Great Radium Spring Water, this last 10 inches in height.

rendered a medicine-type bottle embossed with the name of a neighborhood bottling company whose history should have been easy enough to trace, yet Colonial Williamsburg's research staff reported that no record could be found of a company under the proprietorship named on the bottle. Later, however, another old resident remembered it, recalling that the business closed around 1928 when one partner was said to have gone off with the other's wife.

There were two lessons to be learned from these drugstore bottles: first, that the people and events of our own time slip into oblivion much more quickly than we complacently suppose, and second, that relatively recent artifacts, unable yet to be officially called *antiques,* already attract the attention of serious collectors (Fig. 92). This last point was demonstrated when the contents of the two wells were shown in a tongue-in-cheek display at a Williamsburg Antiques Forum, and to our dismay drew as much interest as did the newly discovered colonial objects that we considered to be the cream of the exhibition. Tennyson made the same point more succinctly and certainly more eloquently when he wrote:

> Let us alone. Time driveth onward fast,
> And in a little while our lips are dumb.
> Let us alone. What is it that will last?
> All things are taken from us, and become
> Portions and parcels of the dreadful Past.[10]

# "All the Best Rubbish Is Gone"

IT WAS COMMON in the nineteenth century for gentleman-travelers to stop and draw the scenes and buildings that pleased or interested them, and their journals and sketchbooks were filled with pen-and-ink renderings of minarets, fallen columns, fountains, and architectural details. Today the mindless camera has become the tourist's substitute for the talented hand and the educated eye; nevertheless, a few artist-travelers linger on as anachronistic scions of a more leisurely age. One of them, an American resident of the Caribbean island of Saint Eustatius, has made a hobby of drawing the fretwork designs characteristic of West Indian architecture in the nineteenth and early twentieth centuries, jigsaw work that is rapidly disappearing as wooden buildings are replaced by cinderblock construction and mail-order ornament. While sketching the fretwork on a dilapidated frame house on the island of St. Kitts, the artist saw a small black girl emerge from the garbage-strewn alley beside the building. She shook her head sadly, and then to nobody in particular sighed, "Oh, dear, all de bes' rubbish is gone." Had she been referring to the state of antique collecting in the later twentieth century, it would surely have been one of the most honest and naïvely profound observations on record.

The lament might equally well have been that of the despairing archaeologist who must stand impotently by as the detritus of the past is bulldozed away. The world's lesser museums have long drawn their treasures from what once was considered rubbish, things worn out and no longer wanted, things out of fashion and obsolete, things relegated to rot in the cellar or to shrivel and fade in the attic. But now most of the cellars and attics are gone or have been cleared out as the houses have changed hands or been pulled down. The old family home is a thing of the past, made outmoded by shifting fortunes, by death duties, and above all by twentieth-century mobility and the need to go where the jobs are. Relocation has become an accepted punctuator of modern working life, and where, less than a century ago, moving to a town fifty miles away was a relatively serious undertaking, job-seeking on another continent is now as commonplace. It is true, of course, that British fortune-seekers went off to America in the eighteenth century and to Australia in the nineteenth, but having got there they generally put down roots, as did the majority of Americans who moved westward across the continent. The difference today is that few people stay anywhere very long, certainly no more than two generations, and their houses are built with that in mind, so shoddily constructed that most have a life expectancy of barely twenty-five years.

The attrition resulting from kitchen fires and portable flame lighting decreased with the introduction of municipal gas and was further reduced with the advent of electricity in the 1880s, but these advances, coupled with the increasing availability of indoor plumbing, did much to promote new construction, and thus hurried the demise of the old. In England, villages and towns that had changed little in two or three hundred years were drastically transformed in the late Victorian era. In America and the Caribbean, a greater reliance on wood-covered frame construction, coupled with the voracious appetites of termites and a high degree of inflammability, did much to dictate the life-span of the average nineteenth-century home —and as the house went, so went its furnishings and the "almost antiques" stored in its darker recesses.

It would be foolish to suppose that seventeenth- and eighteenth-century houses invariably remained jammed from attic to basement with aged furniture and old crockery, just because they had a better chance of survival in their own time than did the less strongly constructed homes that came later. It is true, however, that the absence of municipal garbage disposal services made getting rid of the rubbish more difficult, but at the same time the presence of large and ever hungry hearths for both cooking and heating made sure that old furniture served one last turn. Strictly utilitarian, country kitchen joinery was the first to go, for having neither aesthetic merit nor value as scrap, no one pleaded for its reprieve. Like the undated and unmarked ceramics and glassware discussed in previous chapters, its simplicity made it dateless, and even if by accident it escaped to live beyond its time, it remained an *old* table or chair and never a desirable antique. It is for these reasons that the simple kitchen, wash-house, and buttery furniture of the eighteenth century is now more rare than are quality pieces. Admittedly they are not losses loudly bemoaned, and the collector of Queen Anne or Chippendale is unlikely to have a good word to say for a butcher's oak bench. To me, however, the example shown in Figure 93 is tremendously interesting—

93. An oak butcher's bench, typical of the common, utilitarian furniture that has rarely survived to become antique. Length 5 feet.

quite apart from the fact that it makes a splendid coffee table. Although impossible to date with accuracy, the bench is typical of countless work tables, boat trestles, and rustic benches seen in any number of paintings and engravings from Bruegel to Hogarth, and rightfully belongs in any museum, period room, or historic restoration that purports to show how the other half lived. But being part of all that rubbish which, alas, is gone, such furniture is conspicuous by its absence.

The conversion of furniture into firewood was a natural enough step, particularly if it did not happen to be *your* furniture (Fig. 94a). In time of war the occupying enemy—be he British regular, Sherman's Yankee, or Wehrmacht Nazi—made no distinction between good and indifferent furniture, any more than he considered the cultural consequences of ripping out the balusters from elegant staircases. In all fairness (if that is the appropriate word) one must admit that the vandalism of necessity has never been confined to one's enemies. Liberators can be equally destructive, and when it comes to staying warm, even friends and scholars will eschew the cold comfort of antiquarian scruples. The point was well made shortly after the Second World War when, living in a London apartment house, I descended to the basement to pay my rent and found my landlady busily tearing up old books and stuffing them into the furnace. She explained that the fuel shortage was such that she was using anything that would burn—including a trunkful of books left behind by a Polish officer. Loose pages and ripped covers littered the floor, evidence enough that the majority of the books had been of considerable age and possibly of some importance. I was able to salvage only one volume, and that only after it had been shorn of its vellum covers. It was a dictionary of law, *Vocabularius Pro Communi Utilitate* printed in Paris by Philip Pigouchet in 1510, and a note on the final page written in a sixteenth-century hand stated that the book was the property of Stephen Long, who had bought it from Gerard for one pound and twelve pence (Fig. 95). The title sheet had gone with the covers and many of the fragile pages had suffered from being thrown on the floor, and therefore in spite of the fact that this copy was thirty-seven years older

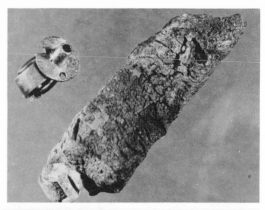

94a & b.  The back leg of an eighteenth-century chair burned almost down to its brass caster, a reminder of the fate shared by most old furniture. Had this example survived it might have resembled the Philadelphia example shown in Figure 94b. About 1770. The fragment is seen with a cleaned brass caster found on the same archaeological site, that of cabinetmaker Anthony Hay in Williamsburg.

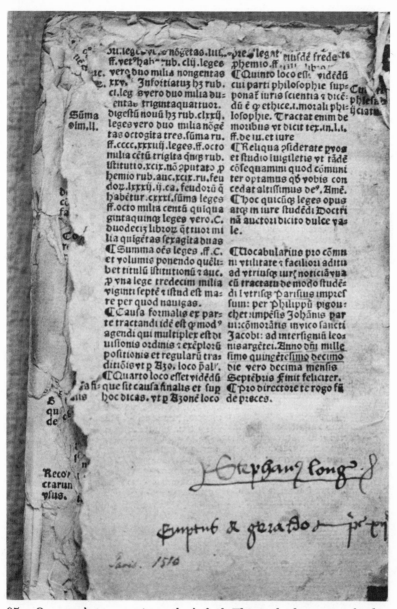

95. One man's treasure is another's fuel. This is the last page of a law dictionary printed in Paris in 1510, a book barely saved from a domestic furnace in 1947.

than the earliest edition in the British Museum, its parlous condition made it of little monetary value. This, then, was one occasion when my supernatural solicitors let me down, for had they sent me down to pay the rent an hour earlier, many other books might have been saved.

One can find some sympathy for the unfortunate landlady and her houseful of chilly and complaining tenants; at least her vandalism was the product of ignorance and necessity. It is far harder to condone the destruction of books by antiquarian dealers, yet they have often been guilty of taking fine seventeenth-, eighteenth-, and nineteenth-century volumes apart to remove the engraved and hand-colored maps and illustrations to sell them separately for greater profit. Atlases, books on travel, natural history, and archaeology have been prime targets. The culprits would doubtless defend themselves by claiming that the destroyed books had already lost frontispieces, had broken spines and foxed pages, and therefore they were doing us a service by saving illustrations that would otherwise have been lost. They might add, too, that many of the books were so uninteresting that no one would want them. It is, however, such value judgments as these that represent the greatest dangers to the survival of the past's material remains. They are made every day, and at every level of society. They send the wrecker's ball crashing through the walls of an ugly Gothic Revival city hall, route a highway through an unimportant village, and flood a valley containing nothing of architectural merit—"ugly," "unimportant," "of no architectural merit," all conclusions based on opinion, and much too often a monetarily-biased, minority opinion. The destruction of anything can be guaranteed to be to the financial advantage of someone, and thus to the prosperity of cities, counties, states, and nations. Conversely, retaining something of antiquarian interest generally *costs* money rather than earns it, and preservationists tend to be wealthy only in words. Furthermore, they are likely to belong to the "older generation" and to be predominantly female, while those in their ranks who are younger and male are unlikely to offer to wrist-wrestle horny-handed land developers. In short, as far as the progressive businessman is concerned, preservationists belong to a lunatic fringe standing in the path of commerce and prosperity. They might even be politically subversive.

Even when the preservationists prevail, the future of the past can rest in singularly capricious hands. Buildings that have grown and changed over the years, acquiring a weathered if portly dignity, can find themselves the recipients of a Devil's deal that will restore their youth at the price of their integrity. What they have become is sacrificed for what they might have been, in the hands of saviors who do not remember the advice of John Dryden:

> If ancient fabrics nod, and threat to fall,
> To patch the flaws, and buttress up the wall,
> Thus far 't is duty; but here fix the mark:
> For all beyond it is to touch our ark.[1]

The lines are as valid today as when they were written in 1681. There is not the slightest doubt that all is done with the best of intentions, just as the conquest of Peru and Mexico by the Spaniards was a high-minded and godly endeavor—unless one happened to be an Inca or an Aztec. Thus, if we happen to be enthusiastic about Georgian architecture, the "back to colonial times" movement gets our vote. At the same time, however, the Victoriana aficionado and the Civil War buff may deplore the stripping away of nineteenth-century wings from eighteenth-century houses or the removal of ante-bellum buildings to permit the reconstruction of others of earlier date.

In short, the preservation or destruction of the past all too frequently rests in the hands of people with relatively narrow points of view. That also means a singleness of purpose, and without it very few of the major triumphs of historical preservation would ever have been undertaken. The trick is to be sure that this dedication benefits more than the first person singular.

In the 1930s the popularity in England and the United States of things faintly Elizabethan and the architecture that Osbert Lancaster dubbed "stockbrokers' Tudor," brought with it a taste for parchment lamp and sconce shades. As a consequence, thousands of muniments of the sixteenth, seventeenth, and eighteenth centuries were bought by lampshade makers from town clerks, lawyers, and families anxious to be rid of "old papers" that were no longer legally relevant. As the best lampshades invariably included a panel featuring a decorative commencing capital letter, and as you got only one to a deed, the attrition was not unlike the slaughtering of elephants to take only their tusks. Then, too, there has long been a small but lucrative business in wax seals, particularly those in metal boxes attached to royal, ecclesiastical, and municipal charters, freedoms, commissions, and the like, all cut from their documents and sold to collectors. Seals of all types were particularly popular collectors' items in the late nineteenth century, and one might suppose that professional archivists would have shrieked for protective legislation to burn publicly the destroyers of historical documents. But no fires were lit and no flesh melted. The majority of British archivists were medievalists, and their attitude was generally that if it was not in Latin, it wasn't worth bothering about. Consequently, masses of seventeenth- and eighteenth-century records were dismissed in the same cavalier way that we still toss out late-Victorian and early-twentieth-century papers.

When, in 1951, the bombed ruins behind the City of London's Guildhall were to be cleared away, I happened to be the only person around to record the medieval foundations before they were bulldozed. While doing so, I came upon an iron-doored basement room, shelved along two walls, and on the shelves stacks of documents bundled in all shapes and sizes. The door had rested partially open, and although the shelves were protected from the rain, they had not escaped the damp, nor had they been spared the effects of the fire that raged above them when the great building burned in 1940. The pages had stuck together, turning the bundles into solid blocks, while the searing effect of the heat had first buckled the door and then reduced the exposed edges of the documents to black ashes. Nevertheless, it was evident from prying a few of the slabs apart that here were countless papers relating to City legal business dating back at least into the eighteenth century.

Efforts to get the library staff to salvage the contents of the cellar before it was bulldozed away got me nowhere—and bulldozed it was. But not before I had salvaged one slab of papers from a shelf just inside the door.

I took them home with the intent of slowly drying them out and then trying to pry the sheets apart to determine whether they were of any real significance. Fifteen years slipped by before I got around to it, by which time (needless to say) the papers were tinder dry and ready to fall to pieces. Among them were records of repairs to the Lord Mayor's coach in 1791, bills for the guards' wages at Newgate prison in the 1780s, for coverlets for the "poor prisoners," and for the purchase of a "stout plunging bath tub [with] 6 strong iron hoops." Five groups of the papers related to the transfer of felons from Newgate to prison hulks (Fig. 96) or to the ships aboard which they would be "transported beyond the Seas" to Botany

96. Hulks at Portsmouth aboard which felons from English jails and prisoners from British wars were confined. From a colored print of about 1800 drawn by a French inhabitant.

Bay in Australia. The earliest of these lists contained 210 names delivered to the vessels between December, 1785 and November, 1789, and of whom the first 112 almost certainly sailed aboard the "First Fleet" of nine transports and men-of-war that left for New South Wales in March of 1787. The second list amounted to a further 138 names, among them those of thirty-four women deposited aboard the *Lady Juliana* transport between March and April, 1789, the vessel then lying in the Thames waiting to make its second trip to Australia (Fig. 97). There is no doubting that the reluctant passengers would remember the ship and their long voyage for the rest of their lives, but the memory would have died with them had it not been for the presence of a young cooper, John Nicol of Edinburgh, whose first duty was to remove the shackles from the prisoners' ankles as they came aboard. Years later, toward the end of his days, Nicol wrote a long and colorful account of this and other voyages, in a book first published in 1822. In it he mentioned the names of nine of the women from the total of 245 put aboard the *Lady Juliana*. Three of them figure in the salvaged lists: Elizabeth Davis, described by Nicol as "a noted swindler"; Mary or Sarah Dorset, who "had not been protected by the villain that ruined her"; and Eleanor Kerwin (alias Karravurn), to whom he referred as "Mrs. Nelly Kerwin, a female of daring habits." At once these faceless names spring to life, and the convict ship creaks and groans at her moorings ready to sail again on the next tide. But, in fact, she was in no hurry and remained in the Thames for six months, "all the gaols in England [being] emptied to complete the cargo." When at last she was ready, the *Lady Juliana* was setting out on one of the most unconventional voyages ever sponsored by a British government.

Like the rest of the crew, John Nicol soon chose himself a shipmate—in the pleasing shape of Sarah Whitelam, "a girl of modest reserved turn, as kind and true a creature as ever lived." Her crime had been the mere "borrowing" of a mantle, and the punishment a seven-year stint in the penal settlement at Port Jackson, Australia. She would bear John Nicol a son before she got there, but though he would later return in search of her, he would never see either of them again. But there was little thought of the future as the *Lady Juliana* cut across the Atlantic in fine weather and with morale as high as a milkmaid's petticoat. The prisoners proved more noisy than dangerous, said Nicol, and when the ship put in for water at Tenerife, St. Jago, and Rio, she was warmly received—as she had been by two slavers from Santa Cruz that heard the call of the sirens and "sailed thus far out of their course for the sake of the ladies."[2] The *Lady Juliana* had become an erotic Pied Piper of the high seas, and it is tempting even now to hoist sail in her further pursuit. Alas, however, she is a digression whose purpose has already been served, a demonstration that even a list of forgotten names may conceal the stuff of drama, in this case an unexpectedly comic interlude in an otherwise grim chapter of British colonial history.

The salvaged prison papers were signed by Newgate's jailer and governor, Richard Akerman, a man whom James Boswell described as exhibiting "a tenderness and a liberal charity which entitles him to be recorded with distinguished honour"[3] (Fig. 98). Similar assessments were made by Edmund Burke and Samuel Johnson, and during his governorship Newgate came to be known as "Akerman's Hotel." He was twice commended by another celebrated figure of his day, John Wilkes, who was Chamberlain of the City of London during the period covered by the documents. The present deputy keeper of records has stated that the papers probably were "Chamber vouchers" relating to payments authorized by the Chamberlain on behalf of the City, and that other extant records show that the Court of Aldermen authorized the payments to Akerman described in the salvaged bundle. Furthermore, Dr. L. L. Robson, senior lecturer in history at the University of Melbourne (and author of *The Convict Settlers of Australia*), has noted that other lists of the prisoners shipped to Australia are preserved in the Home Office archives, and that it is unlikely that these papers contain information not preserved in another form elsewhere.[4] But can the same be said for the rest of that roomful of documents? If the top shelf on the right-hand side contained data on convicts shipped to Australia in the 1780s

Delivered on Board the Ship Lady
Juliana Transport Ship on the 12th
of March 1789

118  Elizabeth Johnson alias Jee
119  Mary Jones
120  Ann Hager
121  Jane Forbes
122  Elizabeth Jones

97.   Part of a list of female felons delivered aboard ships lying in the
Thames in 1787 and 1789, the latter being the *Lady Juliana* transport
ship destined to be part of the Second Fleet bound for Australia. The
blitz- and weather-damaged documents were saved when the London
cellar in which they were stored was demolished during postwar rebuilding.

and '90s, is it possible that bundles on the bottom shelf in the
far left-hand corner recorded the names of other convicts
transported to America and the West Indies in the seventeenth
century? If so, that would be information not now available to
American historians.

The decision to let the cellarful of London records be destroyed may have been justified on the grounds that the papers
would have cost a great deal to transcribe before they fell
apart, and even more to preserve. Besides, the City had a very
real space problem resulting from the extensive wartime damage to its offices, library, art gallery, and museum. Lack of
space is perhaps the commonest reason used to explain the

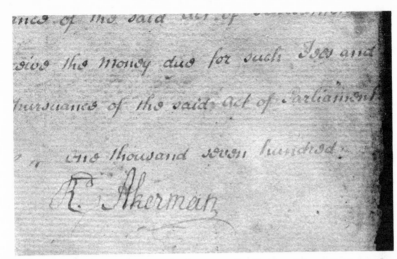

98. The signature of Richard Akerman, the famous humanitarian jailer of Newgate Prison, as it appears on one of the salvaged documents. 1790.

disposal of records that do not interest the person charged with their retention, and today consciences are quietened by first microfilming the material to be destroyed. States, cities, and institutions of all kinds take this easy way out, little realizing that unless the papers are grouped by subject and placed in chronological order, the microfilm is useless without the subsequent compilation of indexes that may take years to complete. In truth, with the film out of sight and out of mind, the chances of either funds or scholarly indexers being found to do the job are as remote as finding a palm tree pruner in Alaska. Nevertheless, organized or not, the future of the records of our own age must inevitably depend on microfilming, in part because the volume is so great, but more importantly because modern paper is not nearly as stable as were the rag-based papers of previous centuries. Documents less than twenty years old are already falling apart without any assistance from fires or floods, reproduction processes have proved to be unstable, and many photocopies made a decade ago have faded into illegibility. One has only to leave the daily newspaper out in the sun for a few hours to see the exposed pages turn brown and brittle. Consequently, in spite of modern technology, the future of our own past is very much in doubt, and we can expect that nine-tenths of everything written about us will go out with the trash.

The best of documentary rubbish is that which was not intended for our eyes; it has the piquancy of a secret discovered; it stimulates the imagination and creates a bond between writer and reader no matter how great the time or distance dividing them. I recall finding an unfinished page of a letter shut inside a Gideon Bible in a New York hotel room, a letter written on the hotel's stationery by an unnamed girl ending an affair with a married man back home. I tried to imagine what she looked like and speculated as to why the letter was never finished. Did she decide to call him and say on the phone what she so clearly had difficulty writing? Did she decide, instead, to let the affair go on, or did she plan to step out of the man's life without a word? The letter was undated, but this sad and solitary little drama had been played out in the room not too long before I occupied it, yet it posed the same questions that I would have been asking (and failing to answer) had the letter been written centuries ago.

The same intriguing possibilities were posed by a small leather-bound notebook found by a laborer demolishing a house in Great Smith Street, Westminster, in the 1920s (Fig. 99). He told me about his discovery thirty years later, saying that the book had fallen from behind a fireplace mantel, and that he had taken it home and put it in a closet where it had remained until found by his children, who tore out some of the pages. When he discovered the loose sheets and found that they contained "bits of writing" unsuitable for children, he had locked the book in a drawer where, as far as he could remember, it still resided. I pressed him to be more explicit about the "bits of writing," but he would say only that they were very old and "a mite too 'ow's-yer-father to leave lyin' around." Some weeks later he brought me the book and offered to sell it for twenty-five shillings (Fig. 100). The leather binding was in shabby shape, many of the pages had indeed been ripped out, and those that remained were heavily damp-stained; but there was enough of the book surviving to be worth the price.

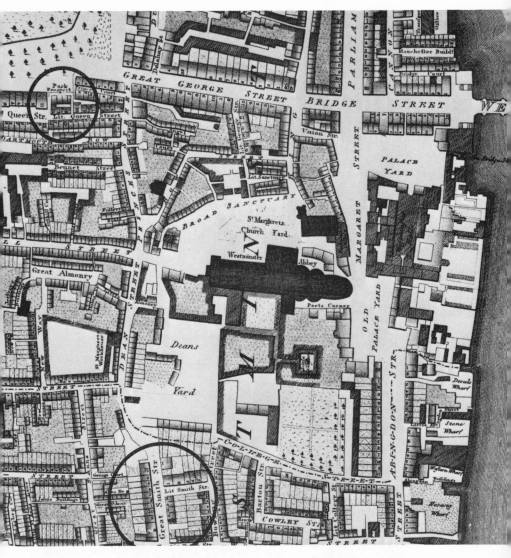

99. Westminster in the eighteenth century. The manuscript notebook (Fig. 100) was found in a house in Great Smith Street at the bottom left of this detail (*lower circle*). Park Prospect, which figures in the book, is to be seen close to the top left edge where the houses give way to St. James's Park (*upper circle*). From Richard Horwood's Map of London, 1792–99.

One page was dated November 12, 1718, and other entries related simply to three November days:

Nov 8th    A Bill for Otes
Nov 8th    _____ 3 strike
Nov 10Rump _____ 1 strike
Nov 13    _____ 3 strike

The reference to a rump and strikes had a magisterial look—until I discovered that a strike or strickle was a corn measure. The injection of "Rump" was not so easily explained, but its presence was no more peculiar than was a great deal more of the book's contents. There was a scattering of names, often repeated and differently spelled, though seemingly in the same hand; thus, for example, "Mr Willoughby at Aspley near Nottingham," and on the same page, "To Mr Willoghy at . . ." There is still a country mansion near Nottingham named Aspley Hall, and it is probable that this Mr. Willoughby was the grandfather of Sir Nesbit Josiah Willoughby of Notting-

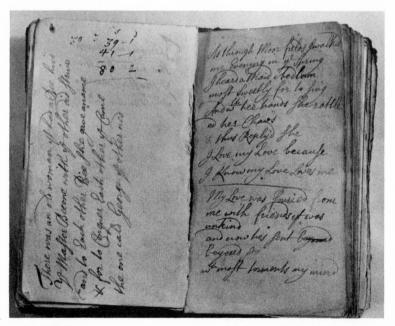

100.   The notebook of an untalented poet found during the demolition of a Westminster house in the 1920s. An entry in the book is dated 1718. Page length 5⅛ inches.

hamshire who distinguished himself in the Napoleonic Wars. Also named was "Sir John Stathams in Queen's Street, Park Prospect, Westminister [sic], London," the address twice repeated and correctly spelled the second time around. Contemporary maps of London did not identify "Park Prospect," but it is shown on Richard Horwood's map of 1792 as a block of houses at the junction of Great and Little Queen streets and facing St. James's Park (Fig. 99). So it is reasonable to conclude that Sir John Stathams lived in or was staying at one of the houses with a park view or prospect. So far so good. But as the book was found in Westminster and almost certainly was written in London, why were both so carefully included in Sir John's address? He, however, is easier to pin down. With his country home at Wigwell in Derbyshire, Sir John Stathams was recorded in 1714 as being deputy lieutenant of the county and a justice of the peace. Later he was to become Member of Parliament for St. Michael's in Cornwall, First Gentleman of the Privy Chamber, and just before his death in 1759 he had been chosen British envoy to Turin. What, then, was the relationship between Sir John and the semiliterate notebook scribbler, most of whose attention seems to have been directed toward the creation of seemingly maniacal poetry, some of it mildly obscene and some strongly Tory and rejoicing in a July election victory:

> Last night as I musing
> Did sit by yᵉ fire
> Yᵉ true hearted Tories
> Now now yᵉ may See
> The wiggs and Fanaticks
> cant have their desire
> Sing tantararah boys
> up go we.

Many of the verses occur two or three times on scattered pages and in different versions and degrees of completion, yet there is no obvious creative progression. Thus, for example, the complete version of something entitled "A Paradox" comes before another seemingly preliminary version. For what it is worth, it reads as follows:

Before my father was begot
I'm sure I was begotten
And Born before my Mother
Ye Both are dead & Rotten
And now I'm Lying in y$^e$ be[d]
Where I got my Grand
mothers Maiden head.

Other verses dwell on death, on whores, copulation, and the gods of mythology, sometimes incomprehensibly omitting key words at the line's end.

I'l Range all round y$^e$ Shady
and Gather of all y$^e$
I'l streap y$^e$ Garden and
to make a Garland for my
And y$^n$ at night to rest
I'l make my Love a Grassy
And w$^{th}$ Green Boughs
y$^t$ nothing may her rest
But if this nimph whom
Should Ever false and
I'l seek some Dismall
And never think on woman

FINIS an End

Of all the antiquarian puzzles that have come my way, this book and the identity of its author have been the most baffling. I have searched for cryptographic meanings, codes based on the upper-case letters, and messages in the letters omitted, but all to no avail. The political lines seemed to be the most useful clues, in that they were written at a time when political clubs were common in London. At their meetings it was usual for the members to entertain their fellows with newly composed songs and verses. Jonathan Swift was a member of the Brothers' Club, and on publishing *The Fable of Midas,* he described it as "a poem printed on a loose half sheet of paper. I know not how it will take," he added, "but it passed wonderfully at our Society to-night."[5] A year later "T.B.," a fictitious contributor to *The Spectator* satirizing club practices described the activities of the Amorous Club at Oxford, declaring that "A Mistress, and a Poem in her Praise, will introduce any Candidate:

Without the latter no one can be admitted; for he that is not in love enough to rhime, is unqualified for our Society."[6]

It might be argued that the owner of the notebook was a clubman who found versifying rather beyond him; yet so many of the compositions are not only bad but utterly senseless that it is hard to accept them as the products of any rational mind, and perhaps this is the real clue. It seems fair to assume that the writer was male, for most of the lines are written from a masculine point of view, and in the early eighteenth century relatively few women were even remotely interested in politics. Nevertheless, a few of the verses are distaff-oriented, as is one beginning "I'l marry w^th a Person if Ever I marry man." Just to confuse the issue further, the most effective (and perhaps revealing) poem in the book begins in what one assumes to be a masculine first person singular and then quickly shifts to the female:

> As through Moor fields I walked
> one Evening in y^e Spring
> I heard a Maid i'bedlam
> most Sweetly for to sing
> And w^th her hands she rattle
> ed her Chains
> & thus Reply'd she
> I Love my Love because
> I Know my Love Loves me
>
> My Love was fouried from
> me with friends y^t was
> unkind
> and now hes sent
> beyond sea
> w^h most torments my mind
> Although I'm
> Ruind yet constant
> will I be I Love my
> love because I know
> my Love Loves me

The idea of love being close to lunacy was a common joke even in those days, and in an otherwise forgettable play produced at the Theatre Royal (of Rose Tavern fame) in 1674, the author had one of his characters say "Taken by my short experience, I find a man is in Love and in *Bedlam* both at one minute."[7] The Bethlehem Hospital for the Insane had been moved to Moorfields, north of the old city wall, in 1676, and it was a common divertissement to walk in Moorfields as in a public park and then to visit the lunatics and engage them in amusing conversation. One begins to wonder, however, on which side of the bars the Westminster poet belonged, and it is frustrating to realize that we know the names of people who could have given us the answer. Even if Sir John Stathams and Mr. Willoughby were unaware that they had any contact with him, Rebecca Bassert knew his face for she sold him "6 Loaf 2 white Loafs," as must John Bomford from whom he was to obtain "A pair of riding gloves" and a "barbers razor." So, too, must Dr. Gells who sold him "halfe an Ounce of Coffey." The small quantity of the coffee is itself curious. By the 1730s approximately seventy tons of coffee beans (then called berries) at a value of £300 a ton were annually imported into England. The fact that the poet was getting his small supply from a doctor (of something or other) might suggest that the half ounce was for medicinal purposes, and it might therefore be pertinent to note that "clysters" of coffee were sometimes used to cure apoplexy. However, according to Chambers's *Cyclopaedia* (1738) coffee's principal medicinal use was pretty much as it remains today: "It carries off fumes and disorders of the head arising from too much moisture, dissipates megrims, and absorbs acrimonies of the stomach, whence its use after a debauch of strong liquors."

The mantelpiece which had concealed the notebook for the best part of two hundred years was located on the second floor (in England called the first floor), and the fireplace was a large one, but the exact location of the house or who had lived there will never be known. Impoverished poets traditionally lived from hand to mouth in garrets and not on the second floor, but it is equally true that gentlemen of substance would hardly have been buying their own bread or "halfe an Ounce of Coffey." So there the trail ends, the mystery just as tantalizing as it was when I first attempted to unravel it; yet, in its way, it remains no more intriguing than does the untold story behind that unfinished letter shut in a Bible in a modern New York hotel room. It is true, of course, that in both cases there is a real danger that if the full truth were known, neither the London poet nor the lady lover might really merit our attention. But that is an accepted hazard of the game; it is the speculation that titillates—like a whisper in the dark.

# ELEVEN

# A Word in Your Eye

I'M A MOVER. I get it in and I get it out. I don't have time to research the stuff!"

Such was the response of a successful British antique dealer to a collector's question about the history of an item in his shop. Although one might argue that by being able to tell a customer more about his wares, the dealer could make them more attractive and "pricey," there is no denying the importance of a quick turnover in today's highly competitive world of antique trading. Only in that way does the small dealer secure time and capital for the ever more arduous pursuit of increasingly scarce merchandise. The collector, on the other hand, is under no such pressure and, in theory at least, he has the residue of a lifetime for research and the acquisition of keys to doors beyond which lie journeys, adventures, and dramas that are uniquely his own. However, the metaphorical key does not, itself, open the door; it must first fit the lock, which in turn needs to be oiled. Thus, for example, there can be numerous interrelated steps (interlocking, if you will) between acquiring a Victorian spittoon and knowing the men who spat into it. Both must be placed in a setting; the spittoon needs a floor, and the floor needs a room—but what kind of room? Right away we are brought up short. Is this a genteelly domestic cuspidor or one that would have been used in public places, in a barroom, a courthouse, a jail, even an insane asylum? Clearly we have to establish the locale before we can furnish or people it. Alas, the majority of antiques defy us to take that first identifying step.

The spittoon illustrated in Figure 8 is of a type that could have seen service in any of the public places I have mentioned; it is only because it was dug from the rubble and ashes of an American "Bedlam" that we can associate it with an asylum. The same is true of the pair of ceramic papboats found in the debris of the hospital's burned dispensary (Fig. 101). Left to speak for themselves on an antique dealer's shelf, the feeding bottles would have little appeal other than as examples of pharmaceutical ceramics, yet, in truth, they are links not only with the first state-supported mental institution in North America, but also with a moment of high drama on a June night in 1885 when the inhabitants of Williamsburg turned out to watch the biggest blaze in the town's history (Fig. 102). With their story safely on record, however, the papboats can provide the catalyst to set us off in a quest for information about fire fighting in nineteenth-century America, about the feeding of the elderly and infirm, or about the treatment of the mentally ill.

No matter what kind of antique one collects, the first steps along the research road relate directly to that object, learning how it was made, how it was used, and its relative importance to the people who owned it. Because most antique collectors

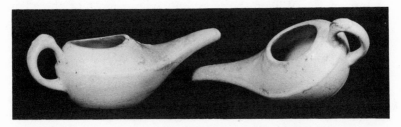

101. A pair of ironstone china papboats whose appearance is as uninteresting as their purpose. They are, however, the stuff of drama, for they were found in the debris of America's first public hospital for the insane, a building opened in 1773 at Williamsburg and burned in 1885. Length of papboats 7⅝ inches.

102. The basement below the dispensary of Williamsburg's "Bedlam" in the process of archaeological excavation. Bottles by the hundred lie in boxes on the floor.

are interested in the relics of the eighteenth and nineteenth centuries, I propose to confine my examples and sources to the Georgian and Victorian periods. That these blanket terms are as well understood in the United States as in England is not due to the influence of latter-day Anglophiles, for British taste, design, and products continued to be as much a part of American life in the eighty years after the Revolution as they had been in the centuries before it—as was demonstrated amid the debris of the Williamsburg asylum where most of the plain institutional plates, bowls, and bedroom ceramics bore the marks of Staffordshire potters.

British trade catalogues, pattern books, and merchants' advertisements remain legitimate sources of information about the goods sold in American stores and used in American homes at least as late as the 1860s, though British influence declined in the post-Civil War years. Thereafter, the possessions of the average American family have been recorded for us through one of America's greatest contributions to Western culture— the mail-order catalogue. Beginning with Montgomery Ward in the 1870s, and Sears, Roebuck in the 1890s, the story of rural American taste and need was recorded in microscopic detail, and the recent bout of nostalgia has usefully resulted in the facsimile reprinting of some of those early catalogues. A few comparable British catalogues (e.g., that of the Army and Navy Stores) have been reprinted, but the vast majority have not, and for the earlier catalogue sources one must go to libraries and museums. The Henry Francis du Pont Museum at Winterthur, Delaware, probably has the best research library of this kind in the United States, while in England the British and the Victoria and Albert museums have important catalogue collections.

Although catalogues were carried by salesmen in the eighteenth century, many of them were hand-drawn and written rather than printed, meaning that few were issued and consequently are extremely rare. It is hardly surprising, therefore, that the survivors are kept in the humidity and humanity-controlled rare-book dungeons of libraries, guarded by frigid-faced jailers who see would-be readers as potential biblio-rapists. Thanks, however, to the emergence of publishers specializing in modestly priced facsimile editions of rare pictorial books, today's antique collector has many more sources available to him than did his predecessors of twenty or thirty years ago. Furthermore, these same publishers provide the added service of reissuing out-of-print books about antiques and dying crafts which, though their texts may be of questionable value, frequently contain valuable illustrations of objects that no longer survive.

Often more useful than books *on* antiques are those written about the same objects when they were new. Fortunately for the general collector there are a number of encyclopedic sources to provide points of departure, and because of their original popularity and large editions, these are still fairly readily available today. The first major encyclopedia prepared and published in England was Ephraim Chambers's *Cyclopaedia or, an Universal Dictionary of Arts and Sciences,* which was printed in 1728, with a second edition ten years later, and a two-volume supplement in 1753. Although most of its engravings relate to such uncollectable subjects as military defenses, ships, heraldry, and mathematics, the text provides tremendously valuable data on the manufacture of all manner of objects from pins to cannon. A French version was completed in 1745, but problems over rights and credits brought Denis Diderot into the picture as an editor and led him to undertake an entirely new *Encyclopédie* which was to run to ten volumes of text (the first published in 1751) and more than six hundred plates comprising a further six volumes. The latter are unquestionably the most valuable pictorial record of eighteenth-century manufacturing processes, as well as being an astonishing picture gallery of topics ranging from classical antiquities to the anatomy of hermaphrodites. Fortunately, the volumes of plates and their descriptions were reprinted in Paris in 1964, thus making this essential source more widely available.

It is hard to find in Diderot's achievement anything but a staggering contribution to knowledge, but in its day the *Encyclopédie* was received with outrage by church and government, both of which saw the seeds of their own destruction in the text's preference for facts over dogma. In the dedication to a supplement for the third edition of the British *Encyclopaedia Britannica* in 1800, the editor declared that "The French *Encyclopédie* had been accused, and justly accused, of having disseminated far and wide the seeds of anarchy and atheism. If," he went on, "the *Encyclopaedia Britannica* shall in any degree counteract the tendency of that pestiferous work, even these two volumes will not be wholly unworthy of your Majesty's attention." First published in weekly segments beginning in 1768, the *Encyclopaedia Britannica* followed more closely in the footsteps of Chambers than of Diderot, and lacked the wealth of illustrations that made the latter's work so valuable.

In addition to these most famous of encyclopedias, there were others elsewhere which can, on occasion, be equally helpful. In France there was *Le Grand Dictionnaire universel du XIX^e siècle* compiled by Pierre Larousse (1865–76), in Italy the *Nuova Enciclopedia Italiana* (1841–51), in Germany the *Conversations-Lexikon . . . &c.*, which began to be published in 1796, and in the United States, first the *Encyclo-*

*paedia Americana* (1839–47) and then the *New American Cyclopaedia* (1858–63). Unfortunately, however, the illustrations in most of these works are more likely to help you build a bridge or a steam engine than identify a cockle pot or an Irish decanter.

The earliest English compendia that described or illustrated common household objects in a semi-encyclopedic way were heraldic dictionaries which described the objects used on crests or in coats of arms. Thus, for example, in James Boswell's *Workes of Armorie* (1597), the arms of the Urinal family are shown to incorporate three pear-shaped flasks of a type described earlier (and rather surprisingly) as "a little vessell with a broade bottom, and a small necke. . . . Such tokens may be given to servitours of kings and princes, which beginne and take assay of all drinks before their soveraigne." In the second half of the seventeenth century, Randle Holme of Chester wrote, and profusely illustrated, a rather similar but much larger work which he called his *Academy of Armory.* Holme, like the encyclopedists who came after him, was interested not only in objects as such, but also in the way they were made, named, and used. Consequently, the *Armory* is a primary source for information concerning the manufacture and terminology for such things as bone combs, tobacco pipes, and pewter ware, for the appropriate furnishings "to a dineing Rome," and dozens of other topics having little to do with heraldry. One volume of Holme's work was reprinted by the Roxburghe Society in 1905, but the rest remains in manuscript among the Harlean papers in the British Museum. Even so, the *Academy of Armory* remains a most useful and entertaining entrée into a century that is sadly short of such sources.

Building a library is just as important a part of antique collecting as pursuing the objects of one's affections. Naturally enough, it is best to begin by reading what other collectors, curators, and professional writers are saying about that particular class of object. From there one can go back to seek older "classic" works on the subject. But for the time traveler there are other less trodden paths, such as acquiring a range of dictionaries and early gazetteers. In their brief descriptions of words and place names, the lexicographers tell us how they were most commonly used, and one frequently discovers that the meanings have changed considerably over the years. Today, for example, a blunderbuss is thought of as a short-barreled weapon flaring at the muzzle and capable of firing iron garbage for relatively short distances, but Edward Phillips in *The New World of Words* (1671) described it as a "long Gun that will carry 20 Pistol Bullets, and do execution at some distance." However, the term "long Gun" was probably used to distinguish the blunderbuss from pistols. The unfamiliar phrasing often makes the reading of such dictionaries amusing as well as instructive. It is gratifying to know, for example, that Phillips considered Florence to be "a proper name of a woman: also the chief City of Tuscany in Italy, so called." He was the nephew of John Milton and his dictionary (first published in 1658) did not pretend to be complete but merely tried to bring together the tricky words derived from other languages.

The first dictionary that attempted to assemble all the words in the English language was published by Nathanial Bailey in 1721, and thereafter went through many subsequent revisions and editions. The *New World of Words* is nice to have (particularly when you pick it up, as I did, for about twelve cents in a street market), but Bailey is indispensable, though admittedly not such fun for the browser as is Samuel Johnson's *English Dictionary* (1755) with its pithy definitions and whimsical words. Bailey makes up for that, however, by appending to the 1737 edition "A Collection of the Canting Words and Terms, both ancient and modern, used by Beggars, Gypsies, Cheats, House-Breakers, Shop-Lifters, Foot-Pads, Highwaymen, &c.," which opens to our astonished twentieth-century ears the voices behind the faces in the taverns, the brothels, and the city slums that we otherwise know only through the brush and burin of Hogarth.

For the collector of earthenwares, wine bottles, drinking glasses, country furniture, pewter, and many another category of everyday objects, it is not the past of kings and courtiers or of palaces and salons that beckons, but rather it is the world of the common folk and the commonplace that must be explored.

Unfortunately, it is the hardest gate to crash, for the people who lived behind it were less eloquent than their social superiors, less given to letter writing or diary keeping, and less attractive to biographers, portrait painters, and lily gilders. Instead, their loves and hates, their physical descriptions, and their personal achievements are best revealed to us through their brushes with the law and their resulting immortality upon the pages of court records. Thus there is no better introduction to eighteenth-century London than through the often verbatim records of the Old Bailey Sessions Papers. If we want to know what ladies carried in the cloth pockets that served them as purses, the trial transcript of a pocket-snatcher has the answer: "37 shillings, and some half-pence, a silver snuff-box gilt, a pocket bottle of geneva [gin], and a tortoise-shell tobacco-box"[1]—all then worth stealing and now eminently collectable. The pocket-picker, Joseph Blake, was hanged at Tyburn on November 11, 1724.

Another London thief was more fortunate; Arthur Gray was tried in December, 1721, convicted, condemned to die, and then, like John Gay's MacHeath, was reprieved. His trial is of interest in that it tells us something about brass door locks (Fig. 103), a crucial piece of evidence which Gray was to use in his defense against the charge of breaking into the "house of George Baillie, Esq; with an intent to ravish Mrs. Murray." She was Baillie's daughter, and among her other misfortunes had the ill luck to be named Grizel. A maid, Elizabeth Trimmel, appeared as a prosecution witness and was cross-examined by the prisoner on whether or not her mistress's door was locked.

"What kind of lock was it?"

"A brass spring lock."

"Was there a key in it?"

"No, it opened and shut with a brass knob."

"But don't you know that the lock was faulty, was difficult to be made fast, and would after slip back and open itself?"

"The spring indeed was bad."

"And might not that be the occasion of the door's being open, when you came to it a second time?"

Brass locks were expensive and were generally used only on

103. A man's life once hung on whether a lock like this did its job. The brass rim lock has a spring latch, a main bolt operated only by a key, and a dead bolt below. It differs from the one described in the trial of Arthur Gray in 1721 in that it cannot be locked from outside the room without using the key. Probably mid-eighteenth-century but with some modern replacement parts. Length 9½ inches.

street doors or on those of reception rooms in relatively wealthy households. Mr. Baillie's wealth is not revealed, but he lived in the parish of St. James, Westminster, which was then, as it still remains, one of London's more exclusive areas. Nevertheless, the presumably costly lock lacked a key and relied only on a knob-operated bolt, and one might be forgiven for wondering whether the term "lock" might then have been synonymous with "latch." But if we could call Ephraim Chambers to give evidence, he would quote from his *Cyclopaedia,* saying that a lock was "a little instrument for the shutting and fastening of doors, chests, &c, only to be opened by a key." He would have gone on, too, to add something else of consequence, telling us that "From the various structures of *locks,* accommodated to their different intentions, they acquire various names—Those placed on outer doors are called *stock-locks,* those on chamber doors, *spring-locks.* . . . Of these the *spring-lock* is the most considerable, both for its frequency, and the curiosity of its structure." Like all pedants he would have gone on to bore us to death, naming its twenty-one different parts, none of which had any bearing on the ravishing of Grizel Murray.

The bed chamber door had lost its key, and as the lock would have been on the room side, there could have been no way for the maid to secure it from outside. Indeed, without the key, the average brass rim- or box-lock could be more than latched only by using the dead bolt which could be shot by no one but the person remaining in the room. Therefore the maid's subsequent evidence that she went to her mistress's bedroom at three in the morning, found the door open, shut it, and was "pretty sure that she locked it fast the second time"[2] leaves the antiquarian Sherlock Holmes wondering how this was accomplished—and why. After all, it is not normal for people in the safety of their own homes either to lock their bedroom doors or to be locked in. Indeed, in another Old Bailey case when house locks were at issue, a witness stated that none of the doors was kept locked because there was only one key for all the locks in the building.

My point in all this is not to retry a case that went to its jury two hundred and fifty years ago, but to show that such transcripts are capable of telling us something about eighteenth-century locks, and at the same time turning an inanimate object into a thing of such dramatic import that a man's life hung on whether or not the lock's spring did its job.

In America, early court records were rarely published and when testimony survives it is not easily available. On the other hand, there is much colorful information to be obtained from contemporary newspapers whose advertisements provide graphic descriptions of the physical appearances and clothing worn by fleeing felons and by runaway slaves and servants. The same colonial and later papers contain equally useful ads for merchandise, telling us what was available and when, though rarely describing the articles as fully as we would like. The same is true of the household inventories filed along with wills in county court records. There, however, even when the objects were poorly described, they were valued, and, more important, we know to whom they belonged and often where they were kept in the house. Information like this is invaluable to the archaeologist who, if he is lucky, may dig up the very items listed in the inventories, but it is also important to the collector interested in imagining or re-creating the associations and surroundings that his objects once enjoyed—or endured.

In our enthusiasm for learning about the names and lives of makers and owners, we readily overlook the middleman who brought the two together, the vendor, the shopkeeper, the dealer; yet he was often the most colorful link in the chain. Henry Mayhew, the Victorian journalist and social reformer, has left us a finely-etched portrait of the 1850 version of today's Portobello Road stallholder and his stock of "second-hand curiosities."

The principal things on his barrow [wrote Mayhew] were *coins*, *shells*, and *old buckles*, with a pair of the very high and wooden-heeled *shoes*, worn in the earlier part of the last century. The coins were all of copper, and certainly did not lack variety. . . . Of the current coin of the realm, I saw none older than Charles II., and but one of his reign, and little legible. Indeed the reverse had been ground quite smooth, and some one had engraved upon it "Charles Dryland Tunbridg." A small "e" over the "g" of Tunbridg perfected the orthography. This, the street-seller said, was a "love-token" as well as an old coin, and "them love-tokens was getting scarce." . . . The colonial coins were more numerous than the foreign. There was the "One Penny token" of Lower Canada; the "one quarter anna" of the East India Company; the "half stiver of the colonies of Essequibo and Demarara"; the "halfpenny token of the province of Nova Scotia," &c. &c. There were also counterfeit halfcrowns and bank tokens worn from their simulated silver to rank copper.

These are precisely the kinds of coins that are to be found on the muddy foreshores of the Thames, and it is quite possible that Mayhew's dealer obtained at least some of his stock from the mudlarks.

"The principle on which this man 'priced' his coins," Mayhew went on, "was simple enough. What was the size of a halfpenny he asked a penny for; the size of a penny coin was 2*d*. 'It's a difficult trade is mine, sir,' he said, 'to carry on properly, for you may be so easily taken in, if you're not a judge of coins and other curiosities," and the curiosities "got scarcer and scarcer."[3] More than a century later one continues to hear precisely the same cry from the dealers, but miraculously the rarities continue to turn up.

Mayhew's coin dealer was but one in a cast of hundreds of remarkable characters who peopled the pages of his famous study of the *London Labour and the London Poor;* others ranged from crossing sweepers and hawkers of gutta-percha dolls' heads, to prostitutes and crumpet sellers, a gallery of ghosts to haunt the memory of starched and complacent scrapbook Victorians. In short, no collector of Victoriana should fail to read Mayhew, any more than he should overlook Flora Thompson, whose writing painted a portrait of rural England every bit as lifelike as Mayhew's faces from the city slums. Her trilogy, *Lark Rise, Over to Candleford,* and *Candleford Green* (happily, reprinted as one volume), records in photographic detail the belated retreat of medieval village life in the face of the Industrial Revolution. Born into the poorest social class in Victorian England, Flora Thompson was the daughter of a farm worker, but through her own industry acquired an education that prepared her for a long career in the Post Office. It was during her later years that she wrote these remarkable books which have so exquisitely and tenderly captured the image of a world that is now beyond our comprehension. They are gems both as literature and as historical documents, and the reading of them cannot fail to enrich any collector of nineteenth-century antiques, and if students of sociology were to be deprived of all but a single volume, this would be the one to keep. Although this wide-eyed recommendation is likely to be viewed as an Englishman's bias, I was introduced to the books not in England, but in Bloomington, Indiana. From American friends who have since become acquainted with the people of Lark Rise, I have discovered that close parallels for some of the rural domestic traditions described by Flora Thompson have been noted in the mountain country of North Carolina, while games and verses played and chanted by Lark Rise children are remembered by a lady editor who grew up in New York City. It is a fair bet, too, that many a nineteenth-century American farm woman reacted in much the same way to a traveling salesman as did the proudly poor wives of Flora Thompson's English hamlet.

One such salesman was a cheap-jack, a seller of ceramic bargains running a gamut from single plates and chamber pots to a twenty-one-piece tea service, identical, so the man said, to another that Queen Victoria had bought for Buckingham Palace. The service was the envy of the women who gathered around to watch the man unload his wares from his cart and lay them out beside the road, but bargain though it was, no one could afford it.

"Never let it be said," the peddler implored, "that this is the poverty-strickenist place on God's earth. Buy something, if only for your own credit's sake. Here!" snatching up a pile of odd plates. "Good dinner-plates for you. Every one a left-over from a first class service. Buy one of these and you'll have the satisfaction of knowing you're eating off the same ware as lords and dukes. Only three-halfpence each. Who'll buy? Who'll buy?" . . . The man had brought the pink rose tea-service forward again and was handing one of the cups round. "You just look at the light through it—and you, ma'am—and you. Ain't it lovely china, thin as an eggshell, practically transparent, and with every one of them roses hand-painted with a brush? You can't let a set like that go out of the place, now can you? I can see all your mouths a-watering. You run home, my dears, and bring out them stockings from under the mattress and the first one to get back shall have it for twelve bob."

Each woman in turn handled the cup lovingly, then shook her head and passed it on. None of them had stockings of savings hidden away. But just as the man was receiving back the cup, a little roughly, for he was getting discouraged, a voice spoke up in the background.

"How much did you say, mister? Twelve bob? I'll give you ten." It was John Price, who, only the night before, had returned from his soldiering in India.[4]

A little drama, to be sure, but like the lock from the Old Bailey records, the tea service comes to life. It may have been no more than five-and-dime porcelain, yet for the ladies of Lark Rise its possession meant dignity and status—as it might still do today now that it would be a hundred years old. Flora Thompson knew her women well, but the traveling salesman was a fleeting figure, and like the villagers, we hear his voice but do not get to know him. We do not know where he came from, how old he was, how he packaged his wares, or what hopes and fears lay hidden behind his glib patter and showmanship. To see the face of a less ambitious china seller we can turn to John Burr's 1865 painting *The Pedlar* (Fig. 104), which shows the man with his basket, knapsack, and dog, and his countrywoman customer coveting a flowered porcelain teapot just as Flora Thompson knew she would.

Paintings, engravings, and drawings are, of course, every bit as important to the collector as are documentary records. To the novice and the lazy-minded they are more so, for they are specific, showing us faces from the past, furnishing rooms, building houses, yet leaving little to the imagination, and discouraging us from looking beyond the flatness of the canvas or the paper. So, to my mind, John Burr's peddler is less alive and provoking than is Miss Thompson's English Barnum with his cartload of crockery and tinware, and his basins—"exact repli-

104. *The Pedlar* (1865) by the British artist John Burr. The salesman is trying to sell a teapot to a country woman, and beside her a broken, transfer-printed pitcher stands on a seat akin to the workbench illustrated in Figure 93.

cas of the one the Princess of Wales supped her gruel from when Prince George was born."[5] Burr would have shown us the basins, removing any speculation as to whether they were white, yellow, banded, or willow-patterned, or whether they were large, small, broad, or tall. To that extent he would be of more practical help.

Contemporary genre paintings show us not only where and how objects were used, but also how long they remained in service. Figure 105 illustrates another painting rather similar in style to John Burr's, at least insofar as it relates to rural aspirations. Called *Early Attempts*, it was painted in 1861 by William Henry Knight and shows a country family encouraging its smallest member in what appears to be the slightly constipated act of creation. For the collector, the picture's interest lies less

105. *Early Attempts* (1861) by William Henry Knight. This view of English rustic life is thought to be more cute than accurate in its portrayal of household furnishings. Detail.

in its subject than in its set dressing, for here in a mid-Victorian cottage we find a late-seventeenth-century gateleg table, a press cupboard at least half a century older, on top of it a wine bottle of about 1780 and a Rhenish stoneware jug of a type made around 1690. More surprising is the broken jug in the left foreground which might be French, Spanish, or Italian, but certainly not English. The occupants of the room clearly are not collectors, and so must have around them possessions that have been there a very long time—at least that is the obvious conclusion. But is it the correct one? Seventeenth-century oak furniture has a fine rustic appearance, a proper setting for the Shakespearean concept of the faithful servant:

> O good old man! How well in thee appears
> The constant service of the antique world,
> When service sweat for duty, not for meed!
> Thou art not for the fashion of these times. . . .[6]

The room, the furniture, the props, all are theatrical in their effect and perhaps, therefore, in their origin, making the picture just another of those artistic clichés for which Victorian painters are renowned. If so, *Early Attempts* has no historical value—and there's the rub. How do we tell the document from the pastiche?

The answer is that all too often we cannot, unless we know the style and scope of the artist's work. If the same objects turn up in two or more paintings, it is clear enough that he was not painting "from the life." The Flemish genre painters David Teniers the Elder (1582–1649) and his son, David Teniers the Younger (1610–1690), both favored tavern and alchemical scenes, the latter frequently being used to illustrate books on glass; but as the same bottles and flasks were repeatedly used, one can use the pictures only to show that the objects were available when the painters were at work, and not that these were the actual vessels used by the alchemist whose workshop is shown. One must also beware of the possibility that common objects that the artist learned to paint in his youth will continue to turn up in his later works, in spite of the fact that those things were by then obsolete or old-fashioned.

The paintings and engravings of William Hogarth are unquestionably the most used and useful windows into English life in the middle decades of the eighteenth century. His portrayals of the people and trappings of high and low life are drawn as much with the scalpel of the social reformer as with the soft brush of the man who conceived the "line of beauty," and thus the objects and furnishings seen in the pictures may be more symbolic than natural to the scenes. Then, too, some of the objects favored by Hogarth were never common. His table knives, for example, are more reminiscent of scimitars than of ordinary eighteenth-century cutlery (Fig. 106). Indeed, so peculiar are they that his best-known biographer, John Ireland, writing in the 1780s, mistook the knife brandished by one of the Drury Lane lovelies in the Rose Tavern caper as "a razor, which, in a posture of threatening defiance, she grasps in her hand"[7] (Fig. 107). Had Ireland better grasped Hogarth's way with cutlery, he would have known that this was how the artist chose to draw his table knives. In his tailpiece to Ebe-

106.  Typical bone-handled cutlery of the mid-eighteenth century. The knife, with its round-ended blade, is marked with the cutler's initials I.P. and his rebus, a tobacco pipe, and measures 10½ inches in length.

107. A detail from William Hogarth's Rose Tavern scene showing a harlot making her point with the aid of a peculiarly-bladed table knife. 1735.

nezer Forrest's account of their peregrination to Rochester and Gravesend in 1732, Hogarth symbolized the temper and elements of the trip by means of its artifacts, drawing a smiling face over a wine bottle, a glass, and a ribbon-tied tobacco pipe, spoon, fork, and knife with its Saracen blade (Fig. 108).

Although caution is always needed in using Hogarth's ob-

108. Hogarth drew this "tailpiece" to illustrate an account of his trip to Gravesend in 1732. Among the artist's symbols of travel and conviviality are a pipe, spoon, fork, and another scimitar-bladed table knife.

109. Dated 1699, this Rhenish stoneware bottle is typical of the quality of such wares as they faded from British favor in the late seventeenth century. Height 10½ inches.

jects as historical documents, it sometimes happens that had we believed him, we might have avoided perpetuating some long-accepted fallacies. In my own writing I have often been guilty of stating, for example, that German stoneware bellarmine bottles ceased to be imported into England and her colonies around 1700, and that any found in later archaeological contexts had to be survivals (Fig. 109). I went on to claim that 1699 was the latest known date on such a bottle. I was aware that Hogarth's sixth picture in his *A Harlot's Progress* series showed a bottle that looked remarkably like a poor drawing of a bellarmine, but I dismissed it as the artist's embellishment of an otherwise uninterestingly ordinary bottle (Fig. 110). It was labeled NANTS and so contained brandy from Nantes in France, and as the picture included a glassy-eyed parson spilling his liquor in his lap, I deduced that the grinning face on the bottle was more comment than correct. I have since

110. A detail from scene VI of William Hogarth's *A Harlot's Progress* showing a stoneware bottle with a bellarmine-style mask at its neck and a label on its side identifying the contents as NANTS brandy. 1732.

111. A further detail from the same engraving, depicting the results of too much Nants. The lady seated beside the cleric was Elizabeth Adams, who would later be convicted of robbery and executed in 1737.

learned that Rhenish potters went on making mask-decorated stoneware bottles well through the eighteenth century, and the latest dated example now known to me is marked 1769. There is therefore no reason why such bottles should not have been present in a 1730 London household, and Hogarth's engraving (the paintings were burned at Fonthill in 1755) can be accepted as proof that they were—though the weight of other negative evidence still indicates that they were far from common.

One of the most entertaining aspects of research of this kind is determining how the people of the past looked at, and thought about, the commonplace things around them. In my search for information that might reveal some subtle second meaning to the word NANTS (alas, none was forthcoming) I learned something about brandy—besides the simple, if impressive statistic that in the 1730s Nantes produced in excess of 174,000 gallons a year. Chambers's *Cyclopaedia* informed me that "The chief use of *brandy* is as a drink: especially in the cold northern countries; among the negroes in Guinea, who fell over one another for a few bottles of *brandy;* and among the savages of Canada, and other parts of north America, who are infinitely fond of it." What at first seems to be nothing more than an amusing choice of words becomes rather sinister, and the brandy that painted a vacant smirk across the face of a drunken cleric (Fig. 111) becomes the fuel that fired the slave trade and robbed the American Indian of a continent.

The brandy bottle's contribution to the history of slavery and so to the racial troubles of our own time is very real and thoroughly documented. Thus, for example, a tradesman's directory published in 1753, after condemning the English, Dutch, Spaniards, and Portuguese for their leadership in the trade, had this to say:

> The Negro's [sic] make a frequent practice of surprising one another, while the European vessels are at anchor, and dragging those they have caught to them, and selling them in spite of themselves; and it is no extraordinary thing to see the son sell, after this manner, his father or mother, and the father his own children, for a few bottles of brandy, and a bar of iron.[8]

From amid the dry pages of what was described by its publisher as a "Necessary Compendium to lie upon the Counter of every Shopkeeper," emerges the bones of a horror story, a skeleton that today's masochistic penitents would prefer to see thrown back into the closet, secured by a spring lock that really works.

The archaeologist labors with broken pots and the historian with half-truths, and from these fragments both try to put the past back together again, and all the while they are beguiled by scores of deliciously aromatic red herrings. Anyone who has ever tried to turn out an attic or even an old trunk knows how a small job inevitably stretches into a mammoth project as memories are stirred and curiosity is titillated. It would be hard, for example, to come upon the front page of the British *Daily Sketch* and not be hooked by the headline "DEATH AMID THE JU-JU MASKS—Woman murdered in theatre-land curio shop—STABBED BY ORIENTAL DAGGER—Pictures on Middle Pages." Even if one did not know either the shop or its proprietor (as I did), it would be disappointing to smooth out the rest of the sheets only to find that the middle pages were missing. Who was the killer? Were the police right in their belief that he was "a curio lover whom [the victim] discovered rummaging through the shop for a rare antique he could not afford"?[9]

It makes no difference whether we are reading a paper from 1961 or 1761, they are still the most lively chronicles of their times available to us. They reflect the concerns, the interests, the mores, the economics, fears, and humors of both journalists and readers, unencumbered by the hindsight of historians who reveal the past to us through the distorting mirror of their own biases. Eighteenth- and nineteenth-century newspapers are to be found in many libraries, and from time to time turn up in antiquarian bookshops at surprisingly modest prices. Whether it is the *Virginia Gazette,* the *Pennsylvania Evening Post,* the *Massachusetts Spy* or the *London Journal,* they are all windows on the past and are well worth opening. Who could fail to be intrigued by the *London Journal's* freshest advice for September 23, 1732:

On Monday Evening, about Six o'Clock, the Lady Dolin and her Daughter returning in her Chariot from Newington to Hackney, was attacked between Dorlaston and Church-street, by a single Highwayman, well mounted on a Black Horse, with a Rug Great Coat, and the Cape about his Face; upon presenting his Pistol, with a Volley of Oaths, they gave him what he wanted, their Money; and he returned back, and committed another Robbery near the Turnpike at Kingsland. A Countryman in the next Field, stood looking over a Gate over-against them, all the time the Ladies were robbed, but never offered to stir to their Assistance.

The last lines could just as well have come from the columns of today's paper in any country, demonstrating that although technology advances and fashions change, human nature obstinately remains the same. Hardly a week went by in the 1730s without the London newspapers reporting one or more attacks on travelers by footpads and highwaymen. Nowadays they would be sufficient to send editorial writers rushing to their typewriters and TV commentators to their microphones to condemn society in general (and the party in power in particular) for the moral decay of our generation, and to augur the imminent collapse of the nation.

In recalling Lady Dolin's stimulating experience, I am less concerned with contemporary parallels than with the reporting of the incident itself. The attack occurred at a point about two miles northeast of London in an area that was part of the turf of the most celebrated of all English highwaymen—Dick Turpin. Every British boy of my generation has thrilled to the cry "Stand and deliver!" and has vicariously galloped away over heath and dale on Turpin's famous Black Bess. Lady Dolin may have met them both, for it was in the 1730s that Turpin was about his business, and doing it north and east of London. But the Dick Turpin that I knew would have doffed his hat, stolen a kiss, leaving a mocking smile beneath a pencil-thin Errol Flynn mustache lingering in the swooning ladies' eyes as he disappeared into the night. An hour or a filmic dissolve later we would find him gaming at White's or causing fans to flutter in the salon of an unidentified dowager duchess. But the brigand who pointed his pistol and fired a volley of oaths at Lady Dolin was obviously no romantic knight of the road—and that is the point. From John Gay's *Beggar's Opera* (1728) to Harrison Ainsworth's fictional account of Turpin's amazing ride to York in his novel *Rookwood* (1834), the public has been conditioned to seeing the highwayman as a hero. The truth was quite otherwise, and well fits the *London Journal's* report.

Richard Turpin was born in 1706 and was apprenticed to a butcher until he was caught stealing. He then joined a gang of deer thieves and smugglers, remaining with them until he went into the traveler-robbing business with a notorious practitioner, Tom King. In the mid-1730s, to escape arrest, Turpin fled to Lincolnshire, where he was later convicted of horse stealing and hanged at York in 1739. It is hard to imagine how such an ordinary fellow who made such a wretchedly antisocial mess of his life could wind up a hundred years later as a popular hero—at least it is until we remember that people fitting the same description today need not wait a century to aspire to similar adulation.

Despite the distortions and misconceptions that tiptoe in their footsteps, modern screenwriters, playwrights, and novelists are largely responsible for keeping alive the public's interest in the past, and we must forgive them for making us believe that all eighteenth-century women wore ball gowns or nothing. If, however, it is the truth we want, then we can usefully look to those writers of fiction who were part of that past but who were writing about the present. There was Daniel Defoe's *The Fortunes and Misfortunes of the Famous Moll Flanders* (1722) and his contemporary *History of Colonel Jack*, then, twenty years later, Henry Fielding's *Joseph Andrews* (1742) and *Tom Jones, a Foundling* (1794), all rich in both rural and urban detail. In the nineteenth century the stuff of English life was recorded by a veritable blaze of luminaries from Jane Austen to Thomas Hardy.

America, unfortunately, was less well served, and her best authors, like James Fenimore Cooper, tended to look either to the past or to the frontier for their inspiration. The concertinaing of time that inevitably takes place as we look backward can lead the unwary into supposing, for example, that Cooper's accounts of the "noble savage" in the French and Indian Wars were drawn from life. After all, wasn't he writing back about there someplace? In fact Cooper was not born until 1789 and did most of his writing in the second quarter of the nineteenth century. Similarly, Daniel Defoe's dramatic picture of London and the Thames in 1665 as portrayed in his *Journal of the Plague Year* has little documentary value. He was only five in 1665 and wrote the book fifty-seven years after the event. Then there are the occasional deliberate fakes, such as the remarkably researched *The English Rogue,* a four-volume "Life of Meriton Latroon, And other Extravagants," which describes low life in the reign of Charles II in great detail. Published in an alleged facsimile edition in the nineteenth century, this lively and mildly pornographic work, if authentic, would rival the diary of Samuel Pepys or Ned Ward's *London Spy* (1698) as a portrait of Stuart London. But, alas, it is not—and there's an end on 't.

The suppressed literature of the eighteenth and nineteenth centuries has often been touted as possessing redeeming social value as a source of contemporary information. More often than not, however, it is only the authors' numbingly similar approach to a limited spectrum of sexual gymnastics that has anything to offer, reminding us of something that should be painfully obvious already, to wit: the human animal is an unchanging beast at heart. John Cleland's *Memoirs of a Woman of Pleasure* (1749), better known as *Fanny Hill,* is of disappointingly little value as a piece of social history, being far less interested in furnishings than in fun. On the other hand, the wisely anonymous *My Secret Life,* written in the 1860s, is (in its embarrassing way) a remarkable evocation of the netherworld of gaslight and garters behind the starched façade of Victorian England.

To both the collector and the social historian, the diaries and journals of travelers are generally more helpful than are those of writers who stayed at home. The latter described the unusual but overlooked the commonplace, whereas the foreigner found the other fellow's habitat and daily round interesting and worthy of note. It may be added that, on the whole, diaries, being daily records, were likely to be more detailed and accurate than were journals, which might be written up days or weeks after the described events occurred, time enough for backgrounds to blur and nuances to be forgotten. Although, for the reasons stated, many of the most perceptive descriptions of England were written by German, French, and Dutch diarists, most of the better portraits of the English colonies in America were provided by traveling Britons—from Captain John Smith to Nicholas Creswell. It was a compliment returned, as I noted earlier, by Benjamin Silliman of Yale in his travels through England and Scotland in 1805–1806.

There are, of course, a tremendous number of such sources, and in mentioning any of them I am laying myself open to charges of having deliberately and with malice ignored everybody else's favorites. How can he say that only British visitors wrote about colonial America, and is he suggesting that there were no American diarists who had useful things to say about their own time and place? I am not saying or suggesting either; my point is merely that the inquiring collector need not limit his library visits to the stacks labeled "Collecting." Unfortunately, however, publishers and their indexers are often ill-prepared for our attention; relatively few diary and journal indexes have been prepared with the needs of the student of objects in mind, assuming, instead, that only proper names are worthy of recognition. It is true that to the genealogist the insertion of "buttons" between Butterworth and Buxton may seem jarringly pedantic, but no more annoying than it is for me to find no reference to "tea" in the index to *The London Diary of William Byrd of Virginia*. Indeed, I feel that insult has been added to my injury when I discover that "Andrews, Mrs. (or Miss)" rates no fewer than twenty-five entries—six referring to visits by Byrd to an unspecified address where he found Mrs. (or Miss) Andrews not at home, and thirteen to occasions when she was, and he joined her for *tea!* In short, the collector who expects to make frequent use of such published source material should be prepared for the tiresome chore of making his own indexes.

Hurrying once more to my own rescue, I must insist that I

do not suffer from a hang-up about proper names (though I doubt if it would ever occur to me to look in this index for half of those that are listed); on the contrary the acquisition of an object bearing the name or initials of its maker or owner sends me riffling through the indexes of everything that even remotely relates to the period and the place. For the very reason that they do enable us to take that step, marked antiques are both a better investment and a lot more fun than are those that remain glumly mute. Take, for example, the bell-metal skillet illustrated in Figure 112; it is of a type generally attributed to the eighteenth century, and although little has been written about these once common kitchen utensils, it is sometimes claimed that those made in England were produced either in the southeast or in the southwest. The claim is made baldly and without any supporting evidence, and we can take it or leave it. But the illustrated example has something to say for itself, for cast into the handle is the inscription COX TAUNTON VI, indicating that it is a size six and was made for or by a Mr. Cox of Taunton in Somersetshire—which happens to be on the edge of the English West Country. With that much in hand, the next step is to try to run Mr. Cox to earth in the pages of eighteenth-century county trade directories. I found him in *The Universal*

112.   This bell-metal skillet was made for William Cox, an ironmonger of Taunton, England, in about 1790. Diameter 7¾ inches.

*British Directory of Trade, Commerce, and Manufacture* for 1793, where he was listed as "Cox William, *Ironmonger.*"

In the eighteenth century the business of the ironmonger and brazier were frequently considered as one; thus in 1753 *The General Shop Book* described him as a seller of "stoves, grates, candlesticks, box-irons, jacks, spits, tea-kettles, hinges, kitchen-furniture, and all manner of brass and iron utensils, tho' he seldom makes any of them."[10] There is still no knowing whether William Cox of Taunton cast his own skillets or had them made to his order; but one thing is certain, he was one of very few individuals to have left us examples marked both with their own names and those of their towns. What may be one of the largest collections of these bell-metal skillets (sometimes pedantically called "posnets") is owned by Colonial Williamsburg, yet only two spell out the name of their town, both dating from the late eighteenth or early nineteenth century, and both made, not in England, but in Richmond, Virginia, by or for John Taylor and I. Boulton.

Another example in the Williamsburg collection is marked WARNER PH, and might have been made by Herinemus Warner (c. 1790–1800) of Philadelphia, but other skillets marked WARNER have turned up in England and obviously are not American. After being purchased in England and shipped home by American dealers and collectors, antiques are prone to acquire "colonial" or "early American" credentials simply through losing sight of the fact that they have been imported. Even if the object is demonstrably of English manufacture, the possibility that it may have been in America since it was new makes it vastly more desirable. The fact that most English place names have their American counterparts (or vice versa, depending on your point of view) makes certain identification of marked objects that much more difficult and demands that we make full use of the documentary sources, which, of course, is what this chapter is all about. In the Winterthur Museum in Delaware, a New England kitchen exhibit includes a skillet marked S. C. NEWPORT 1715, the implication being that it was made at Newport, Rhode Island—and perhaps it was. But until someone produces documentary evidence that a brass founder with the initials "S.C." was in business there in 1715, one cannot ignore the possibility that the skillet came from any one of twenty Newports in the British Isles. The same museum also possesses an example elegantly marked AUSTIN & CROCKER Boston, and although there is a Boston in England, this skillet, unquestionably, is American. A Boston, Massachusetts, directory of 1796 lists Robert Crocker as a brass founder, and Richard Austin is known to have been a contemporary Boston pewterer. So here, as with the Cox skillet from England, a city and trade directory provides the proof—as they can for all sorts of antiques from sealed bottles to labeled furniture.

Like all copper-alloy cooking vessels, bell-metal skillets were originally coated on the inside with tin, which gave them a silvery appearance. It was done not for looks, but as a protection against copper poisoning, on which were blamed "palsies, apoplexies, madness, and all the frightful train of nervous disorders which suddenly attack us without our being able to account for the cause."[11] Rarely has the tinning survived; it has either been worn off through the harsh scouring of generations of scullery maids, or has become so dull and patchy that the dealer, knowing that his customers like their brass shiny, has thoughtfully removed what was left. The outsides, on the other hand, are generally heavily blackened from having been thrust countless times into hot ashes and are extremely hard to clean, and just as old iron pots are usually painted black to cover the rust and plugged cracks, so dealers will sometimes smarten up the outside of a bell-metal skillet with a coat of paint. One of Colonial Williamsburg's rare American specimens (the one marked IN. TAYLOR ✷ RICHMOND) was disguised in that way, being painted black both outside and in. It was unmasked by an eagle-eyed curator in a junk shop not ten miles from the city and bought at the modest price that old *iron* pots command.

Objects whose pedigrees were stamped or cast into them when they were manufactured are matched in interest only by those accompanied by genuine written histories. When, as occasionally happens, one comes upon an object possessing both, mountains should be moved and piggy banks broken to acquire it. This happened only once to me, and I really was not at all pleased when it did; not that I disliked the object, it was simply that I did not know what to do with or where to put a massive leather-covered trunk (Fig. 113a). The leather was secured and decorated with patterns of brass studs describing tulips, crowns, and the Hanoverians' "G.R." cipher. Inside, the trunk was lined with marbelized paper, and on the interior of the lid was a large maker's label declaring that it was made by "Smith & Lucas, Coffer & Plate Case Makers to his Majesty and his Royal Highness the Prince of Wales at the Kings Arms & three Trunks Charing Cross London" (Fig. 113b). The label went on to state that Smith and Lucas made and sold "Black Leather Trunks, for Travelling, Carriages, & Exportation." They did not, however, make trunks to be used as fireside log boxes, and that was the fate the dealer told me was in store for this trunk if I decided not to buy it. An American who had recently bought an English house near Winchester was in the process of furnishing it with quaint antiques, and the trunk had taken his fancy. Would I want that to happen to this fine and historically important relic of British royalty? My answer was as predictable as the response of a theaterful of kids to Peter Pan's "Do you believe in fairies?"

Accompanying the trunk was a document listing its owners from 1787, when it was in the possession of "Mr. Philips Morgan, mason" of Bristol, until 1940, when it was willed into the Southampton family from whom the dealer bought it. Checking the late-eighteenth-century Bristol directories proved that a Philips Morgan lived there, and the evidence of the studded decoration and the maker's label left no reason to doubt the document's heading which described the trunk as "A Royal Chest." I at first thought that the cipher was that of George III (1760–1820), but I was to be proved wrong. London's Guildhall Library owns a bill issued by Edward Smith in 1758, at which date he was in business alone, though at the same Charing Cross address printed on the trunk's label. Further evidence was provided by an advertisement in *The Connoisseur* in September, 1958, when a comparable trunk bearing

113a & b.  Made for the household of George II, this important and closely documented leather-covered trunk narrowly escaped ending its days as a log box. The stand is believed to be original. Figure 113b shows part of the lid interior with its marbelized paper lining and maker's label. Before 1751. Length 42½ inches.

a very similar Smith & Lucas label was offered for sale. Unlike the would-be log box trunk, this one's label had incompletely erased the "By Appointment" reference to the Prince of Wales and has substituted "the Princess Dowager of Wales." As her husband, the prince, had died in 1751, and as Smith was no longer in partnership with Lucas in 1758, there was no doubt that *my* trunk could have been made no later than the date of the prince's death, thus putting it in the reign of George II and not George III.

By buying the trunk, having it restored, and bringing it to America I believed I was saving it from a fate worse than death, but after living with it through two Virginia years, I was not so sure that I had done the right thing. In spite of constant attention to prevent mildew developing through the humid summers, and frequent applications of preservatives to discourage the leather from drying and cracking during the centrally heated winters, the patient showed signs of deterioration. Neither air-conditioning the house for the summer nor adding a humidifier to the furnace for the winter seemed to do enough —which is why the trunk is now to be seen in the collection of Colonial Williamsburg. Some museum-quality objects belong in museums and nowhere else, and this was one of them.

Just as the police detective is rarely presented with the same set of clues in any two cases, so the collector must be prepared to pursue each historical hare along different paths and through unfamiliar thickets. Budding Sherlock Holmeses know that fingerprints are good things to look out for and that powder burns around the wound make stabbing the wrong thing to list as cause of death; similarly, the novice collector quickly learns that makers' marks are helpful, and that books and contemporary records are the places to learn more about them. But which book, which records? That they can learn only from experience. In the examples I have discussed, I have tried to demonstrate the diversity of the potential sources: wills, inventories, newspapers, diaries, trade tokens, bills, labels, city directories, encyclopedias, dictionaries, court records, contemporary novels—and these are but a few. My examples have not made use of the British city apprentice lists and burgess rolls which have so much to say about individual tradesmen and craftsmen. I have not mentioned the lists of people who died in the Great Plague of London in 1665, yet they certainly should be checked if one is looking, say, for the death of a tavern keeper in business there in the mid-seventeenth century. If, instead, one is trying to determine the fate of a patient confined to the lunatic asylum in Williamsburg in 1850, the place to begin is in the hospital's annual reports published in the *Journals of the Virginia State Legislature*. It is up to each of us to learn what we need and where to find it, and for that there is no substitute for practical experience.

There is, however, something else that the novice collector-historian can do without first acquiring a large, catalytic collection; he can compile his own reference books, catering precisely to his own interests. For more than twenty years my

114. Stalls in London's Portobello Road—anything and everything from silver to celery.

wife has spent two or three hours a week cutting up magazines, newspapers, and sale catalogues, filing and indexing pictures and articles on antiques, architecture, archaeology, history, rural customs, and suchlike, to create a library of more than a hundred volumes. Particularly valuable are the photographs of thousands of antique objects advertised in such magazines as the American *Antiques,* and the British *Connoisseur, Apollo, Country Life,* and half a dozen others. Mounted on sheets and annotated in volumes under scores of categories (e.g., lighting, silver, architectural hardware, furniture, seventeenth-century paintings, brassware, stoneware, delftware, eighteenth-century glass), the pictures are made easily available for chronological study. Occasionally, we are confronted by an angry book lover who expresses horror at the destruction of magazines and catalogues and threatens to spear us on her hatpin. But in reality there is no other way to put the material to work and to store its information in a reasonably manageable space. Besides, sale catalogues are never indexed, nor are the advertisements which today take up two-thirds of the pages in most antique-oriented magazines.

Although the kind of catholic approach to the paste-and-scissors surgery that I find necessary is equally valid for curators, dealers, and collectors with broad interests, specialists may well be content with less, and if they balk at damaging magazines just to extract pictures of enameled etuis (or whatever it is they collect), photocopying will make fileable substitutes that can be cross-referenced to the still-intact publication. In this way, for example, a silver collector can arrange in chronological order every dated candlestick he can find illustrated, and in doing so assemble a volume of diagnostic examples unequaled in any published book.

While most contributors of articles to the popular antiquarian magazines are content to keep using the same old photographs of well-known specimens in major museums, vastly more examples yearly pass through the hands of dealers and auction houses, surfacing just long enough to be advertised or illustrated in catalogues before disappearing once again into private collections. These are the prizes, and sometimes it is only the hope of landing them that keeps us subscribing to an otherwise dreary magazine. It does not follow that advertisement captions will be accurate; on the contrary, the same item may show up two or three times in a decade as it passes from dealer to dealer and acquiring different attributions each time. Capturing these variations (though not very instructive) can be part of the sport and as satisfying to a cynical cutter-and-paster as being dealt the ace, king, and queen of trumps. Indeed, assembling a pictorial library of antiques becomes such an absorbing occupation that it can rank, in its own right, as a legitimate and highly educational collecting pursuit—one that is a hell of a lot cheaper than buying the antiques themselves!

# TWELVE

# Of Mermaids, Fakes, and Other Grave Matters

BECAUSE ARCHAEOLOGY is a sunshine occupation, most of my visits to London occur in the winter and usually in the rain, not as a rule a hard, authoritative downpour, but a chilling drizzle just persistent enough to cause the mouths of Londoners to droop at the corners and their poodles to smell like wet spaniels. The stall-holders in the street markets huddle under the eaves of dripping canvas roofs, and on Kensington's Church Street the steep sidewalks are slippery and the numerous small antique shops appear less inviting than one had remembered them to be. On such a day an early-nineteenth-century powder horn lay on a Church Street dealer's shelf, wrapped in its memories of equally miserable days in an entirely different clime. Wearing its past like tattoos on a sailor's arm, the horn was inscribed with the emblem of the 33rd Regiment of Light Infantry, with the name J. MITCHELL, and an address: Stony Hill, Jamaica, West Indies (Fig. 115). To most browsers in a shop dealing primarily in ceramics, the horn probably attracted little attention. For me, however, it was to rekindle memories of my first evening in Jamaica—a terrace beside the yacht harbor at Port Royal, colored lanterns swaying overhead in a warm Caribbean breeze, the last pleasure boats

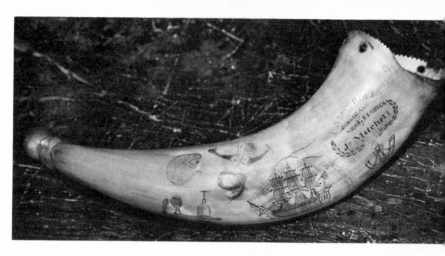

115a, b, & c. J. Mitchell of the
33rd Regiment of Foot left a
powder horn as his only memorial. He presumably served
with the regiment at Stony Hill,
Jamaica, in the 1820s, though
his name has not survived in
British army records. Figures
115b and 115c show the horn's
lively renderings of a mermaid,
a monkey, a centipede, and a
scorpion, details which are less
self-explanatory than they at first
appear. Length of horn 13½
inches.

returning from the cays, cutting their way homeward through the silver water, all beneath a backdrop of blue-black mountains and the firefly lights of Kingston twinkling at their feet. It was a setting as close to a P.R. man's vision of travel-folder paradise as could be imagined. Between sips of my gin and tonic I asked the hotel owner my standard traveler's question: "Are there any snakes, spiders, or biting bugs we should watch out for?"

"None," he assured me. "There's nothing like that to bother you here." The words were still wet on his lips when what felt like a hot needle jabbed my instep, and looking down, I saw an enormous brown centipede backing away. Its brother's portrait is engraved on the side of J. Mitchell's powder horn.

The 33rd Regiment (later the 1st Battalion of the Duke of Wellington's West Riding Regiment) landed at Kingston on February 13, 1822, with an additional detachment arriving on the 17th, in all seventeen officers, twelve sergeants, nine corporals, seven drummers, 362 privates, along with thirty women and thirty-seven children.[1] Somewhere among them was J. Mitchell, but whether he marched ahead or brought up the rear I have been unable to discover. I know only that his absence from the army list precludes him from having been an officer. One wonders what he expected lay ahead, and whether he remained with the regiment for its full tour of duty which would not end until 1832. It took up its station at the barracks on Stony Hill six weeks after landing, and although this encampment was situated at an altitude of about 1,200 feet, seven miles behind the hot and unhealthy Kingston, and was considered a relatively pleasant billet, it was far from being an English country garden (Fig. 116). On April 24, 1802, Maria, Lady Nugent, wife of Jamaica's Lieutenant Governor, noted in her journal that "It is extraordinary to witness the immediate effect that the climate and habit of living in this country have upon the minds and manners of Europeans, particularly of the lower orders. In the upper ranks, they become indolent and inactive, regardless of everything but eating, drinking, and indulging themselves, and are almost entirely under the domination of their mulatto favourites. In the lower orders," Lady

116. Part of Stony Hill Barracks in Jamaica, now used as a reform school. The steps belonged to the men's quarters, the building which may, for a time, have been home to J. Mitchell. An inscribed stone dates the steps to 1808, but the wooden barracks above has probably been rebuilt a number of times.

Nugent went on, "they are the same, with the addition of conceit and tyranny. . . ."[2]

The Mitchell powder horn tells its own story of a side of life in Jamaica that his travel agent forgot to mention. On the underside of the horn and seen only when, like a stone, you turn it over, lurks an unpleasantly lifelike scorpion, along with a snake, an iguana, and the centipede which climbs out from beneath in a remarkably natural rendition of the insect's rippling movement, all recalling Lady Nugent's observation that "The late rains have made the insects and reptiles appear in swarms innumerable."[3] To one side, scratching its ear, sits a monkey resembling the kind that has outlasted the British soldier and is still to be seen scampering through the ruins of his fortress on the island of St. Kitts. There are, however, no monkeys in Jamaica and no real evidence that they ever were indigenous to it, though their bones have twice been found by archaeologists in the middens of Arawak Indians. But just as British troops took occasional monkeys with them to Jamaica in the Second World War so earlier garrisons may have done the same, perhaps having brought them from St. Kitts. Dr. Bernard Lewis, director of the Institute of Jamaica, has noted that even those were not native to the Caribbean but were the offspring of African green monkeys taken to St. Kitts at the end of the seventeenth century. A somewhat unlikely legend has it that a British merchant in Bristol ordered two such monkeys to be shipped to him from Africa as pets, but a practical joker changed the figure to two hundred. When the monkey cargo reached Bristol the merchant hastily transferred the lot to a ship then leaving for St. Kitts.

Below J. Mitchell's monkey is engraved another enigmatic portrait, this of a human hand reaching up to grasp a froth-topped glass; beside it stands a bottle with a corkscrew inserted and waiting only to be pulled, and beneath both are the terse words TAKE HOLD. It is hard to believe that these are nothing more than an invitation to pull the cork or grab the glass, but if there is more to them I have been unable to find out what it may be. I know only that it is not the motto of the 33rd Regiment. The British warship that enjoys pride of place on the horn is seemingly easier to interpret, and I like to think that it was the artist's imagined ship that would one day carry him home to England. The vessel, like most of the creatures and devices, is relatively well executed and easily recognized—which makes it odd that there should be one outstanding exception, the black-armed mermaid. More monster than siren, her tail is barbed with sharklike fins, and her hair streams out to one side from a head more fish than human, yet she holds in her hands the mirror and comb, the traditional attributes of feminine beauty (Fig. 115b). Why did the artist choose to include this one mythical creature in what was otherwise a gallery of realities? It is true that mermaids are common subjects in scrimshaw work by seamen, but from the tail up they are generally provocatively human; yet this one, presumably drawn by a soldier, repels more than it beckons. Her lack of neck, and her flat, slit-nostriled and otherwise noseless face render her less human than is the monkey sitting at her side—and one wonders why.

It is just possible that Mitchell (if it was he who decorated the horn) actually saw such a creature, not the mermaid of mythology but the manatee of the Caribbean. This smaller relative of the so-called sea cow has been credited with giving rise to most of the alleged mermaid sightings. The creature has little or no neck, has prominently slit nostrils, a bald and high-domed head, dark-colored arms or flippers, and a yellow belly, all features of Mitchell's mermaid. Furthermore, the fact that the manatee is still to be seen basking in Jamaican bays and estuaries leaves no doubt that it could have been spotted by the credulous soldiers of the 33rd.

I have dwelt on the horn at some length not because it is one of the world's great treasures but because it can fit into a surprising number of collectable categories. Its ship and mermaid can earn it a place in any collection of maritime antiques, while its regimental emblem and association with firearms makes it desirable to the military or gun collector. Then again, it is of interest to students of West Indian and Jamaican history, to herpetologists, to natural history enthusiasts in general, as well as to those of us who collect contemporary illustrations of bottles. Finally, but certainly not the least important, the horn is a work of what is loosely termed "folk art"; by which one means, I suppose, the relatively successful product of an untrained artist—though just where the patronizing of peasants and the recognition of bad art divide remains open to extended debate. There is no knowing whether J. Mitchell took art classes at school. In any case, working with pencil or brush is very different from scratching on horn. But if we judge him by his monkey or his centipede, Mitchell did a good job, and the same is true if his mermaid is derived from the manatee. If not, and he was trying for a stock, seductive, sex-symbol-of-the-deep-type mermaid, he gets few marks for art and none for anatomy. To me, however, the horn remains an original artistic effort, its interest resting not so much on the competence of the engraving but in its preservation of a soldier's thoughts.

Although original works of art of high quality are likely to be beyond the financial range of the modest collector, much of lesser stature survives in sketchbooks and scrapbooks, scratched on ivory and even window glass, and in my favorite haunt, the flyleaves of old books, particularly old school books. Thus to the connoisseur of doodles Nicholas Wakeham's portraits of his tutor (?) in the back of his 1721 edition of *Aesop's Fables* (Fig. 117) are of greater human interest than a print from the plate of a celebrated engraver. Nicholas Wakeham began his doodles in 1729 and ended them in 1732, and somewhere in between he wrote: "Nicholas Wakeham is my name and England is my Nation and Modbury is my dwelling place and Christ is my Salvation." Suffice it to say that Modbury is a

117.   Something for the doodle collector. Nicholas Wakeham drew these caricatures of his teacher (?) in the back of his 1721 edition of *Aesop's Fables.*

small town in south Devonshire, ten miles east of Plymouth, and that the quest for Nicholas Wakeham is a treat still in store.

The woods are not full of doodle collectors, and consequently treasures of this kind can still be secured at little cost, particularly if the books themselves are of no interest. It is only when other collectors begin to find the same things equally desirable that the supply sinks and the prices soar. Luckily for antique dealers and junk-shop proprietors, there are now collectors of just about everything from cast-iron manhole covers to tobacco tokens and bits of barbed wire. I confess that I have scoffed at all three, just as I have at glass collectors whose interest centers not on the creations of such masters as Verzelini or Amelung but on insulators from late-Victorian telegraph poles. Although I have never encountered a manhole cover aficionado, I have met collectors of insulators, tobacco tokens, and barbed wire, and from listening to them I have learned to appreciate the educational value of them all.

The idea of adults excitedly bidding up to $100 for an eighteen-inch length of "Burrow's Four Point" (1877 patent) barbed wire is initially hard to swallow, but it remains so only until you realize what it is that makes that particular wire so special. The first United States designs for wire to control cattle were patented in 1867, and in the next decade or so literally hundreds of different types were introduced, many of them commercially impractical and so made only in small quantities. These, therefore, have acquired the value of scarcity if not of significance.

Although I have yet to be convinced that barbed wired can be attractively displayed "framed, as a picture, with soft contrasting background and an illuminating light mounted above," as one enthusiast advocates, I readily concede that wire provides an extremely interesting link with the American past and merits the attention both of Americana collectors and of social historians. Numbered among the four inventions that won the West (the others being the revolver, repeating rifle, and windmill), wire was used by homesteaders to keep the ranch herds out of their crops, by ranchers to keep their cattle in, and by everybody to disenfranchise the Indian, the buffalo, and the mustang (Fig. 118). To the archaeologist and local historian, the rusting strands of old wire lying along abandoned fence-lines in the Plains and Western states provide valuable clues to the age of property boundaries, and the discovery of a piece of "Scarlett's Wire-locked Barb" (Patent 190081) shrieks 1877 to anyone who knows his wire. Collectors are not so isolationist as to exalt only over American wire; they have been known to pay up to $40 for eighteen inches of British "Tommy Atkins" wire from the First World War, half as much for a bit of Kaiser Bill's, and less for a nice piece of Nazi. Thus, in wire collecting, as in the more traditional vineyards of antique collecting, the specimen has interest not only for being what it is, but for having been where it has been.

Collecting only the best and rarest may be satisfying to the

118. Barbed wire has not yet been sold at Sotheby's, but it is both collected and historically informative. These pieces, from top to bottom, are examples of Edward M. Crandal's "Zigzag" patented in 1879; Thomas V. Allis's "Buckthorn" variation patented in 1881; and Michael Kelly's "Staple Barb" of 1868, the fifth barbed wire design to be patented in the United States.

egotist or to the person needing aesthetic stimuli to get him through the misery of life in a world of mediocrity, but it does nothing for anyone wanting to know what it was like to live in other centuries. The individual connoisseur is entirely free to collect as he chooses and as his pocket permits, but it is questionable whether today's major public museums should seek and cherish only the superb to the exclusion of the ordinary. There is no denying that the best must be preserved and that museums offer necessary sanctuaries, but at the same time it is important to remember that the character of the museum-visiting public has changed appreciably in the present century. Whereas in the past the majority of visitors were members of the so-called educated classes, and even when they came as school groups there was a sporting chance that Mummy had a Wedgwood vase at home quite as good as the one in the museum or that Daddy's great-grandfather was painted by Reynolds, today's visitors come with no such built-in points of reference. But if they are to learn to appreciate the best, they must be shown it in the context of the average, and if they are to better understand the opportunities and problems of twentieth-century living, they need to know what life was like for people such as themselves in past generations. In an age wherein visual aids have become essential education crutches, today's museums have a chance to contribute as never before. Nevertheless, many of them still see themselves primarily as repositories for great objects, following the instruction of the sixth-century Chinese philosopher Hsieh Ho, who in spelling out the six canons of aesthetics said: Collect masterpieces.

In 1904 the new handbook of English pottery published by the Victoria and Albert Museum in London grandly dismissed the ceramic products of the first half of the nineteenth century in the following sentence:

[From] about the year 1790, the careful and elegant and rich wares which had held their own for nearly half a century were gradually displaced by more gorgeous productions covered with gilding, and possessing even less freedom and spontaneity than the works of Chelsea and Etruria, in fact, vulgar when not merely feeble.[4]

Nine years later, the museum's keeper of ceramics reminded his superiors of Hsieh Ho's advice about collecting master-pieces, adding that this should be "the first principle of any good collection. . . . Only masterpieces," the curator went on, "are the source of inspiration—and by the number of its masterpieces a collection is finally judged."[5]

"By whom?" we may ask.

"Why, by our peers," the curator would reply.

But publicly funded museums are, by definition, for the people, and do not exist for the benefit of connoisseurs or curators—though one might have thought so from reading the Victoria and Albert Museum report of 1913. In it the keeper of ceramics pleaded for increased funds both to buy the best and to keep the curators happy who, he said, were "gifted by nature to feel the difference between a masterpiece and an average work—and entitled after years of training to become heads of departments." The same spokesman argued that it was folly for a great museum to "fall back upon what is cheap—the fatal snare of the second-rate collector" who "soon finds his collection *déclassé*."[6] The italics were the curator's, but they might as well be mine, for the word then, as now, referred to social class and not to the quality of inanimate objects. Thus, therefore, spake the antiquarian snob. An aesthete, a student of aesthetics, is, by definition, one who has or professes to have a high degree of sensitivity toward the beauties of art or nature. But beauty is a matter of taste, and taste is subjective, enabling Professor Church, who so flatly panned English ceramics of the first half of the nineteenth century, to go on to say that "The decadence . . . continued without intermission until the new renaissance of the middle of the nineteenth century. Since then," he went on, "International Exhibitions, loan col-lections, and the multiplication of Schools of Art have greatly changed the character of English ceramic productions."[7] It is true that there were changes—but for the better?

I, for one, would disagree, and I suspect that there are scores of collectors of early-nineteenth-century pottery and porcelain who would join with me. My point, however, is that museums should not make those kinds of judgments for us and certainly should not build their collections on the basis of them. Taste and fashions change with greater rapidity than ever before, and no museum that purports to preserve the art or industry of a nation can afford to leave gaps because they may not be to the taste of a curator, any more than they should deny those of us not "gifted by nature to feel the difference" between masterpieces and the "inferior production of a mere imitator" the opportunity to see the fine alongside the not-so-good, and the mediocre beside the downright shoddy. Only in this way can we improve ourselves and be worthy of the curator and his museum. I am not denying that the goal should always be to secure good, well-preserved examples of whatever it is one collects (whether we do it for ourselves or for a museum), for as a rule, damage detracts from the object and makes it something less than it was. On the other hand, a certain amount of fair wear and tear evident on an object made to expect it enhances rather than detracts from its interest. A butcher's block without the marks of his cleaver, or a tavern table without the stains of mugs and bottles, is sterile and somehow unworthy. But if the block has been split in half and nailed back together, or if the table has had its top replaced by an overzealous restorer, then neither is good of its kind.

The individual who collects as an investment (and who is unlikely to be reading this book) must put quality and condition before all else, but for the rest of us it is better to buy a less than perfect piece which interests us, at a price we can afford, than not to have it at all. If nothing else, it can serve as a stand-in until we can find or afford a better specimen. Both dealers who sell the best and collectors who can afford to buy it will tell the novice that he should shun damaged pieces on the grounds that he will never be able to get his money back when he wants to sell them. Like most generalizations, this one is both true and false. The very fact that a dealer puts a price on a damaged piece and does not simply give it away is evidence enough that there is a market for it. If the collector is fool enough to pay a high price for such an object and then tries to sell soon afterward, he will lose hands down; but if he buys at a bargain price and waits until inflation and increasing

scarcity drive up the so-called bargain prices along with everything else, he will reap a modest harvest—just how modest
depends on the rarity of the object and the extent of the
damage. Repaired furniture (*restored* is the trade word for it)
is the rule these days rather than the exception as past neglect
and present central heating take their toll. Indeed, when I
pointed out that an eighteenth-century oak dresser had had its
back leg broken in half, the dealer replied with pained
hauteur: "Good heavens, you must expect a bit of *age* on an old
piece like that!"

Repaired glass is rarely worth buying except for no-return,
comparative purposes. Relying, as it does, on form and the
transmission or reflection of light, glass loses everything once it
is cracked. There are exceptions; fractures at original construction joints (between foot, stem, and bowl) can be obscured,
and sometimes when the importance of a piece lies, say, in the
diamond-point engraving of its bowl, a broken foot replaced in
silver or ebony can keep the glass alive and clinging to part of
both its interest and its worth. Archaeological museums take a
more liberal view, not only with glass, but with everything that
comes to them from out of the ground. They glue, and patch,
and paint as much as they legitimately can to enable us to
appreciate the objects for what they once were. The same can
be true for the collector who wants to teach or needs to learn.

The student of pottery and porcelain learns by handling,
comparing, and even by the test of his tongue, and therefore
the possession of a number of damaged pieces is vastly more
educational than putting all his money into one unchipped
specimen of what is termed "museum quality." Peering at
specimens through the glass of a gallery case is better than
looking at pictures in a book, but neither is any substitute for
learning through familiarity—and that means through possession. Besides, having for years been a buyer of not-quite-
perfect pieces, I have been pleasantly surprised to find that
"chippy" specimens are today commanding the prices and
respect which ten years ago were reserved for the pristine.

Unlike glass, pottery and porcelain can be skillfully and even
invisibly repaired. Gone are the drilled holes and leaden rivets

that have minimized ceramic tragedies for the best part of two thousand years; in their stead have come epoxy resins and reglazing ovens that obscure the fine line between mending and faking. Alas, the woods are increasingly full of pitfalls, whose bottoms bristle with poisoned stakes waiting to impale the unwary and the unknowing. It would be grossly unfair to label every skillfully concealed repair a fake. The collector whose newly acquired delftware plate is dropped by an inattentive customs official will doubtless want it repaired, and repaired so that the damage does not show. When the plate is sold again it may pass from hand to hand without anyone knowing that it is repaired, but no one is guilty of fakery. But if, on the other hand, the same repair job is done on behalf of someone who plans to sell the object as unbroken, fakery is the proper term. Regardless of who did what and for which motive, the novice (and the experienced collector, for that matter) should question the condition of every ceramic object no matter how unsullied it appears.

A mended and reglazed plate is no better than our hypothetical retopped tavern table, but they are becoming increasingly common. I have even seen a seventeenth-century delftware goblet whose pedestal foot is entirely the invention of a restorer, and were it not for a surface that is slightly less reflective than the bowl, one would never know that the vessel is only half as old as it purports to be. Nervous collectors have grown accustomed to putting their trust in ultraviolet lamps which can expose surface discrepancies in composition invisible to the naked eye, and some buyers even carry small "black light" lamps with them when shopping. Now, however, restorers have begun to use materials indistinguishable under the light from the original, and a few have advertised that their work defies ultraviolet detection. Why, one wonders, does any restoration need to be capable of hoodwinking a lamp?

In the long run, the collector's only real protection lies in the extent of his own knowledge and experience, for it is only a small step from invisibly replacing a foot to replacing the whole thing. That old chestnut about George Washington's ax is less funny than it was—the selfsame, original ax he used to cut down the cherry tree, save for the handle, which was replaced in the nineteenth century, and the more recent substitution of a better blade.

In contrast to extensive restoring, the deliberate faking of pottery and porcelain is generally confined to rare and expensive pieces, and to ornamental rather than utilitarian wares. At the same time, however, because dated anythings always fetch good prices, it is not unusual to find old pieces enhanced by the addition of new dates. Thus, for example, nineteenth-century lead-glazed wares such as inkwells, tobacco jars, and small pitchers are found with enticingly early dates incised on their bottoms, copying the kinds of inscriptions sometimes applied by potters before the wares were fired. But lettering and figures added afterward cut through the skin and surface texture of the baked clay, whereas those scratched beforehand became one with it. Now it is true that owners of domestic wares sometimes added identifying initials and dates after manufacture, but they did so where they could be seen. Letters and dates on the bottom were invariably the marks of the maker and were applied when the clay was in the leather-hard condition and much easier to incise than it would be after firing. Consequently a knowledge of *how* pottery was made and *why* it was inscribed can help to arm the collector against such crude deceptions. More difficult to spot are old pieces that have been doctored and refired or reglazed, such as the genuine, late-eighteenth-century delft ointment pots which turn up blandly sporting seventeenth-century dates or the cipher of Charles II, all in underglaze blue. The forger has usually well mastered the appropriate style for the digits and letters and has accurately captured the tone and texture of the cobalt blue; but he has made one glaring mistake. Unaware that even the simple ointment pot went through an evolutionary progression from the seventeenth to the end of the eighteenth century, he has used shapes unknown in the reign of Charles the Second. Thus the collector who does know the difference is unlikely to be deceived.

Just as desirable as dated pieces of British delftware are the large dishes or chargers decorated with royal portraits or the arms of livery companies, and their value has skyrocketed in the last twenty years. Although a surprisingly large number of good examples keep appearing on the market, some clever forgeries (apparently made in France) were injected into the London shops and salesrooms in the 1920s, and they still surface from time to time, ready to torpedo the unwary. Much more insidious are the copies of once commonplace, eighteenth-century delftware bowls made as recently as 1972 in Spain and sold in New York as antiques. Decorated in polychrome, the example shown to me had a parrotlike bird in a hoop as its principal feature; the quality of the painting was extremely good in that it cleverly captured the confidence of the eighteenth-century brushwork that is usually lacking in modern reproductions. On the other hand, the white tin-glaze, though convincing enough on the wall of the bowl, was less so on the base where it had tended to pool and become suspiciously blue. Somewhere along the line, either at the factory or in the hands of a trader intent on deception, the rim had been chipped and stained, and the foot filed in a less than successful simulation of wear. Nevertheless, the overall effect was so frighteningly good that even knowledgeable dealers have been blighted by these Spaniards.

Just as one cannot learn to identify and date genuine antiques from books alone, so one cannot hope to detect forgeries without a thorough knowledge of the character and feel of the object being copied. Nevertheless, there are some key pieces of information that can best be obtained from books, and these are sizes. The saltglaze figurine illustrated in Fig. 119 belongs to a much-prized class of molded ornaments or "toys" sold by peddlers and at mid-eighteenth-century country fairs. It is visually more or less identical to an example illustrated in the 1908 catalogue of London's Guildhall Museum—except that it is smaller by half an inch. Had it been made from the same mold as the London specimen, both figures would have been virtually identical in size; instead, the loss of the half inch indicates that the smaller example is a copy once removed from the original mold. It was actually shaped in a matrix taken from a plaster

119.   Diminished size and sharpness can be clues that unmask a ceramic impostor. *Left*, a modern copy of an English white salt-glazed stoneware figurine, its height 4 inches. *Right*, the original dating from about 1745 and 4½ inches tall.

cast of the original and was made at the Williamsburg Pottery, one of the few factories still producing white salt-glazed stoneware. The reproduction was made with no intent to deceive ( and no expert handling it would be fooled ); the point is simply that Staffordshire figures made in England in the same way do deceive collectors who do not know the measurements of the originals. I should add, however, that overall size variations are not infallible guides, as the two statuettes of Lord Rodney ( Fig. 120) demonstrate. They are painted in different colors, one has a hat and the other does not, and their bases are not in the least alike. Nevertheless, both are genuine, the figures themselves being cast from molds taken from the same master matrix—though admittedly the hatless example is a pretty

120. Differences in overall size can themselves be deceiving. These pearlware figures of Lord Rodney are both genuine and cast from the same original pattern, but they have been attached to different bases, were painted in different colors, and one, of course, has his hat on. About 1782. Height of example at right 7 inches.

miserable product. In such cases it is only by careful comparison that one can be sure that the figures are genuine, which makes it tough on the novice collector who has never before seen one example, let alone having access to two or three.

In America, as interest in the Colonial and Federal periods has increased, a number of museums and historic places have sponsored the reproduction of items in their collections in the thoroughly praiseworthy belief that the past can contribute as much to twentieth-century taste in private homes as it can from the confines of public museums. Tremendous care is taken to insure that the reproductions (be they of furniture, silver, brassware, engravings, ceramics, or glass) are as exact duplications of the original antiques as modern materials and skills will allow. All are clearly marked when they leave the museums, but clarity and permanence are not necessarily synonymous. On the contrary, countless thousands of pieces of reproduction glassware ranging from eighteenth-century-type drinking glasses to commemorative American spirit bottles have been distributed with no more lasting identification than a gummed label intended to be removed as soon as the buyer got home. Proposed legislative action calling for the permanent marking of all reproductions of antique glassware that had long languished in Congressional committee was expected to pass in 1973, but the closing of the stable door would do nothing to recapture the hundreds and thousands of unmarked copies already away and running. To add further hazards to the course, there are some deliberate and extremely skillful fakes of early-eighteenth-century glasses on the market, most of them doctored to exhibit the right appearance of age and usage.

The presence or absence of wear under the foot of a glass is not an infallible test, for old specimens that received little use can have come through with virtually no abrasions. It is worth remembering, however, that when the wear is genuine the scratches go in all directions, having been acquired one at a time, but fake wear has usually been applied in one operation (either by the deft use of sandpaper or by rotating the foot on a rough surface) creating a degree of uniformity in the direction of the scratches. Just to make sure that nothing is simple, I must add that the presence of bogus wear does not necessarily mean that the glass is also spurious. A distinguished ceramics collector visiting one of the London antiques markets came upon a customerless merchant filling in time studiously abrading the base of a wine glass with emery paper.

"What are you doing that for?" the amazed collector inquired. "That's a perfectly good eighteenth-century glass."

"I know," replied the dealer, "but Americans won't believe it unless they can spot a bit of wear on the bottom."

Glasses with solid rather than folded feet were frequently chipped in the course of normal use, and chips mean cheap in the antique market; so it is not uncommon to find that feet have been carefully ground down and repolished. The result is a foot of slightly, yet noticeably smaller diameter and an edge that is sharper than it should be. Sometimes there is nothing wrong with the foot or with the rest of the glass for that matter—except that they did not start life together. A valuable glass that has been made almost worthless by the loss of its foot has sometimes been the beneficiary of a foot transplant, a fraud that should be detectable under the right ultraviolet light.

Museum distributors of ceramic reproductions are generally very conscious of their responsibility not to mislead, and they make sure that their wares are firmly marked, yet even the best of them may not be safe from the attentions of black-hearted villains willing to buff, grind, and chisel. Even though the recorded examples are relatively few in number, they are enough to warrant collectors to examine carefully those places where marks are usually applied. Irregular concavities on a ceramic base, unusual thinness, smoothness where wear might be expected, or an unusual absence of glaze are all causes for alarm. I might add, too, that the grinding wheel of a deftly handled file can also do wonders for a genuine but damaged antique by trimming down and reshaping a broken spout or whittling away the chipped rim of a tea bowl—sometimes creating some unusual (and expensive) shapes in the process.

Reproductions of German stonewares have received more than their fair share of name grinding. Skillfully manufactured in the Rhineland in the nineteenth century to take advantage of the Gothic revival, vases, jugs, and *steinzeugs* of great elaboration closely resembled their sixteenth- and seventeenth-century predecessors—all the way to the inclusion of contemporary dates and the initials of well-known master potters. These reproductions were nearly always cast rather than thrown on the wheel, and careful examination reveals traces of vertical moldmarks as well as molded and not folded terminals to handles. But in spite of these telltale details which cannot be hidden, Victorian makers' marks have been ground off the bottoms to add three centuries to the pots' age. There is, of course, a much greater temptation to play games with reproductions which also bear the date of the original, for by removing the modern dating evidence and leaving only the lying digits, the objects can be left to make their own sales pitch without any help from the dealer.

The importing of antiques into America from Europe is a trade of such proportions that it is hard to believe that any water remains in the well. As the supply drops and prices rise, small traders are forced to supplement their stocks with what they hope customers will consider tasteful household accessories—reproduction delftware, glass, and brassware from Holland, gaudy faïence from France, bone china from England often bad enough to make Professor Church spin in his grave, tinware from Italy, porcelain from Japan, and cute clocks from Germany. When mingled with genuine antiques, the line between old and new can become unintentionally unclear. This was brought home to me while visiting a large American import warehouse in an East Coast seaport, a warehouse doing business solely with the antique and decorating trades. The building was stacked high with furniture of every age from sixteenth-century Spanish to late-Victorian English, much of it in need of repair but all marketable after appropriate face-lifting. Tall case clocks of eighteenth- and nineteenth-century dates stood in dusty rows against the walls like old soldiers on their last parade; paintings of disapproving ancestors were stacked six deep awaiting their passage from purgatory, and piled in cupboards and standing about on chests and any available flat spaces were smaller antiques: ceramics, pewter, miscellaneous bric-a-brac—including an interesting box iron of brass with what appeared to be a Delftware handle. The metal was dull and spotted with corrosion, but it could easily be cleaned. However, when I picked the iron up I knew that the brass was too thin to have withstood real usage, and the handle, once deprived of its dust, was too bright to be old. Nevertheless, the iron was an attractive, if none too convincing "bygone," and I wondered whether the importer had been deceived by it. The answer was not long delayed, for while he was showing me his stock of porcelain my eyes wandered to a shelf whereon, sealed in individual plastic bags, stood twenty or thirty bright new box irons, all fresh from the factory.

I know from bitter experience that antique buying outside one's area of specialization can be a costly business. Most authorities advise the neophyte to admit his ignorance to a reputable dealer and place himself in the expert's hands. Although I am sure that broadly speaking this is sound counsel, the only time I tried it I was taken to the cleaners by one of London's best-known and oldest established dealers in antique weapons. When I complained that the alleged Brown Bess musket (c. 1780) had a barrel stamped with proof marks not used before 1813 and that the lock bore an ordnance mark not used before 1841, my gentle mentor had the gall to remind me that in the antique business the watchword was *caveat emptor*. I say "was" and not "is" because today collectors buying in Britain are better protected, thanks to the Misrepresentation Act of 1967, which gives an unhappy customer civil recourse, and the 1968 Trades Descriptions Act that lays violating traders open to criminal prosecution.

The novice collector who decides that he can buy more advantageously in reputable salesrooms than in shops is probably quite right. After all, he is going only one step further on a limb than the last bidder to think the object worth having at approximately that price. Nevertheless, it is unwise to put total trust in the catalogue descriptions. Although major auction firms in America and Britain have specialists on their staffs to write the texts, a Meissen porcelain expert who happens to be the company's current "ceramics man" might well find himself cataloguing Staffordshire earthenwares. He then does the best he can, based on the owner's descriptions, checked against available reference books and his own good judgment. If, as sometimes happens, the books are wrong, then an uncommon object may be given less or more than its due. Thus, for example, I have seen some very ordinary seventeenth-century kitchen earthenwares offered as medieval rarities, and being knocked down at very uppity prices. Careful reading of the fine print generally shows that the auctioneers take no responsibility for such honest errors, though they will usually take back any item that can be proved to be a forgery, but only within a specified time after the sale.

From my own, admittedly limited experience, I have found that buying at long range from a catalogue description alone can be an exhilarating but dangerous sport. In theory, one should only land a single "going, going!" deeper in the hole than bidders who have had the advantage of examining the object. In practice, however, it may not work out that way. Instead, one can wind up bidding against a rich idiot, or worse still, another blind postal bidder willing to go within one piaster of your limit. In this way it is possible to be landed with a damaged item at much too high a price. Therefore, if condition and quality are important to the long-distance bidder, it is much wiser to invest a little more and let a competent dealer act on his behalf. This is equally true if one is bent on acquisition regardless of cost, for it is as easy to submit too low a postal bid as it is to go too high. Auction houses will generally be willing to provide an estimate of the price they expect an object to command, but experience has often shown such estimates to be far too conservative, sometimes by as much as 40 percent. Thus the absentee bidder who allows himself to be closely guided by them can expect frequent disappointments.

Even if one collects as I do, more for pleasure and education than for investment, it is imbecilic not to protect one's assets. In spite of the fact that fashion and attendant band-wagons make prices move in cycles, the value of antiques, prudently acquired, steadily increases and can offer a better hedge against inflation than can many another investment. It is important, therefore, that antiques of any consequence should be individually insured under a fine arts policy, and unless accidental breakage coverage is included, protection against fire, theft, and weather damage is relatively inexpensive and is well worth its premiums in peace of mind. Although a one-line description and an appraised (or documented purchase price) value is generally all that is necessary for an insurance company to issue a policy, it may become more picky when the hat is in the other hand. Thus, to avoid any danger of the company, which has so smilingly accepted one's premiums these many years, from turning tiresome, each insured object should be catalogued and photographed—with a copy of the card being housed somewhere other than the home that may be burned or burglarized.

Figure 121 illustrates the card format that I have adopted for my own collection and which seems to fulfill most needs. The picture (in this case a contemporary portrait of Charles II) goes on the right and the description on the left; the latter includes measurements, date, salient features, and so forth. Additional boxes are provided for the date of acquisition, the purchase price, currently insured value, and the photo negative number, along with the name of the dealer from whom the object was bought. The back of the card provides ample space for extra descriptive information, published parallels, experts' comments, notes on any repairs that may have been made, and references to exhibitions or publications in which the object has figured. The space for the photograph provides room enough for a standard 4¼″ x 3⅜″ Polaroid print.

All this museumy regimentation may at first appear to take

| Portrait: CHARLES II (1630-85) | NO: 99 | NOEL HUME COLLECTION |
|---|---|---|

DESCRIPTION: Oils on canvas (rebacked), chest-length portrait of the king to right, wearing a cuirass, full black wig, sleeve worked in gold, a blue sash below the lace cravat, all within a painted oval frame. A contemporary copy of the original by Mary Beale (1632-97) in the Nat.Port. Gallery (London); copies in colls. of Lord Montague of Beaulieu, at Pencurrow House, Cornwall; and Haddon House, Scotland.All have Order of Garter in place of sash.    DATE: c.1660-70.

(Other details see Back)

MEASUREMENTS:
30 1/2 by 25 1/2 inches.

| PURCHASED: | PRICE: | INSURED: | PHOTO: |
|---|---|---|---|
| 1962 | LEA | SBFAA | Bk.V.43 |

SOURCE:
Salisbury, England.
(No pre-dealer provenance recorded.)

121. A specimen catalogue card.

the fun out of collecting and reduce the very objects we are trying to bring to life to the level of impaled butterflies in a glass case. In reality, however, the process of cataloguing forces us to examine an object in far greater detail than ever we would if it was simply brought home and set on a shelf to be admired but never touched. Not only do we consider its size, color, age, provenance, and the materials from which it was made, we examine and record the chips, cracks, and scratches that make this antique like no other. This last information can sometimes provide clues to the way and extent that an object was used—though that is not the primary reason for noting it on the card. Insurance companies like it that way, for it enables them to make positive identification if a thief is caught with your loot in his knapsack.

Beside keeping one's collection in order and one's insurance agent happy, there is another excellent reason for keeping a detailed catalogue. If, like my godfather (who inadvertently dropped dead in the foyer of the London Coliseum while escorting a lady of the chorus), you leave a valuable but undocumented collection behind you, the chances are that it will be sold up by executors who do not recognize its worth or know how to dispose of it advantageously. My godfather, incidentally, collected both chorus girls and European armor, and while the girls were able to fend for themselves, the merits of the armor were less obvious. The whole lot was put up for sale at a local and very rural auction where it was knocked down for virtually nothing. Although this happened during the Depression, when antique prices were low, equally philistine executors may today see as little in one's prized collection of barbed wire or bottle caps. Consequently it behooves us to be sure that our postfuneral voices are capable of being heard from the depths of our safe-deposit boxes.

All this may sound very crass, and I suppose it is. But the sad truth remains that serious collecting blossoms with middle age and bears its richest fruit toward the end of a collector's life. Consequently the inheriting generation is more likely to sell the plums than cherish them. If the treasures were originally assembled only to feed their owner's ego or to be decorative around the home, then their dispersal at his death is no cause for dismay; on the contrary, their return to the salesroom (and the opportunity for them to be acquired by public museums) is all to the good. If, on the other hand, the collection is the product of extensive research and refinement and, as a unit, represents a contribution to the history of art, technology, commerce, or society, then its dismemberment is to be deplored. Similarly, the parting of an antique from the information about it that the collector may have garnered represents a sorry waste of knowledge. But how is it to be prevented?

The obvious answer is to give both the collection and the associated research notes to a museum—with or without claiming a tax deduction—while one is still around to do it. Simple as that solution may sound, it oftens turns out to be much harder to accomplish. Many museums do not like collections; they like *objects!* Collections demand blocks of storage space and cataloguing in a way that may be at odds with established practice. I found this to be the stumbling block when I tried to give my Thames collection to two London museums before moving to America. As the artifacts had been found in certain recorded localities and so were to some degree associated in place if not in time, I wanted them accessioned and stored as a unit. Neither museum would accept that restriction, and so, with the exception of a piece of a Roman helmet which went to the British Museum, the best of the collection came with me to America.

This kind of problem is particularly common among archaeological collections where the relationship between otherwise disparate items lies only in the fact that they were found at a certain spot. If that happened to be the home of a Founding Father or a popular pirate, then a museum might be glad to accept the inconvenience along with the collection. If, on the other hand, the location is of no general interest, then it becomes a liability that curators may be loath to accept. They are liable to be equally unenthusiastic about accepting anything encumbered with restrictions limiting the museum's freedom to store or exhibit as it chooses. It is a reluctance that can burgeon into a flat refusal if the collection includes mediocre specimens along with the good. Of course all these objections can be routed like vampires at the sunrise if the donor is prepared to endow a building, a wing, or equip and staff a gallery. Alas, the kinds of collections and collectors I am thinking about are not in that league.

Even if we give our collections to museums without any strings attached, just to prevent the pieces disappearing again, there may be no guarantee that they will be safe as long as the museums endure. A museum must change its policies and points of view to keep pace with popular interest, to combat economic strictures, and to reflect the taste and scholarship of its curators. A director whose specialty is Korean bronzes may have scant regard for his museum's collection of Roman glass, just as a connoisseur of *art nouveau* may use the current fashion for Edwardiana as an excuse to dispose of the medieval ivories acquired under a predecessor's regime, using the proceeds to invest in Limoges enamels and Tiffany glass. Furthermore, the masterpiece philosophy of giving the Hsieh Ho to second-rate treasures can mean that anything is vulnerable when a better example is offered.

The trading and selling of museum specimens is more common in the United States than in England, but even in Britain it is an idea that finds increasing favor as spatial problems mount along with costs of maintenance and acquisition. In 1972 the director of Britain's Colchester Excavation Committee proposed the raising of funds for further digging on the site of the Roman city by selling "priceless mosaics in Colchester Museum" to America. Later in the same newspaper interview he allegedly managed to put a price on the priceless, and suggested that one mosaic might fetch as much as $125,000, which sum could finance a major excavation in the downtown area and might lead to the finding of "maybe four or five more floors."[8] The need for the money and for the digging to be done cannot be questioned, but this proposal would not merely ask the museum to exchange one unique object for another it desired more, but to gamble away a national treasure on a chance that it *might* secure four others—others that no one could guarantee even existed.

We might be tempted to seek comfort in the knowledge that most collections of yesterday's best rubbish are not blessed with Van Gogh and Modigliani canvases or with priceless Roman mosaics, and therefore once in a museum, curators will not be tempted to use our lesser treasures to solve their financial problems. Instead, the danger lies in the staff thinking so little of the objects that it gives them away, stores them with too little regard for their safety, or throws them out (or burns them like the Ashmolean's dodo), to make room for new, nine-day wonders. The disposal of museum objects, in whatever manner or for whatever reason, has a reassuringly scholarly name; it is called "de-accessioning." When the objects to be de-accessioned were acquired by purchase, their rejection is really only a repudiation of a previous curator's judgment; but when gifts or bequests are involved, or when the objects are the product of neighborhood excavations and thus are pages from local history, other more cogent issues are at hazard. It would be grossly unfair, however, if I were to leave the impression that museum staffs and trustees glibly accept responsibilities they have no intention of honoring. Although I admit to having been mildly piqued to find that an item given to a museum in 1956 could not be found there in 1972, I am sure that this was an extreme and unfortunate instance, offset a thousandfold by its galleries and storerooms filled with not-so-marvelous objects accessioned before 1872. In short, few museums are out to break the Metropolitan's reported record of dispensing with fifteen thousand objects in twenty years.

In the final analysis, the mere bringing together of objects into a collection does not make that assemblage of importance to anyone but the collector. Therefore, unless the material, collectively, has something new to say, it is better broken up and a safe museum home found for individual items that are of premier importance. It is obviously a great deal easier to get a museum to accept two or three choice pieces than a collection of three hundred of which those three are the only items really worth having. As for the remaining 297, their return to the marketplace provides another generation with the opportunity to acquire and enjoy them. To the specialist who has used his collection as the basis for research, I would urge worrying more about publication than preservation. All too often a collector has devoted the best years of a lifetime to assembling and studying a definitive collection of something, only to die without ever making the results of the work lastingly available to others. Fear of "rushing into print" (the favorite charge of critics who planned to write on the same subject but didn't) after only forty years of research, lest some new specimen or fact should turn up tomorrow, has resulted in losses far more deplorable than the dispersal of fine collections. In sum, therefore, and before the last trump sounds, if your collection has something to say, let it say it—if not, sell it.

## ᴥ THIRTEEN

# *And Then What?*

W E TAKE A DEEP BREATH, try to control the choke in
our voices, and consign our treasures to the salesroom. If we
have done our homework properly and the pieces are thoroughly documented (and always supposing that we have
struck when the market is hot), the parting may be turned to
a sorrow sweetened by lots of lovely money. Is that then to
be the end of it?

As Eliza Dolittle might piquantly have put it: Not bloody
likely!

Collecting is an incurable habit, and both the empty cabinets at home and the siren songs of grieving dealers will ensure
that even after taking the cure we remain forever hooked. Only
our new direction remains in doubt—if, indeed, we do elect to
begin again at some other beginning. Many specialist collectors
have no intention of breaking new ground. Having extracted
all the information that their best pieces have to offer, and
having drawn and photographed them from every angle, they
send them back to the marketplace to obtain funds to buy
other, better examples. These dogs are too old to learn new
tricks, and they prefer to continue to the end learning more
and more about less and less. For the average collector, however, who does not aspire to being an acknowledged pundit or
the breaker of new ground, starting again at the gate to a field

that is new only to *him* may offer all the stimulation he can stand.

It would be presumptuous to advise a recently abdicated English porcelain collector to try glass paperweights or player pianos. It is also unsporting to suggest that he should have nurtured the saplings of potential new interests before putting his ax to the old, yet I know from my own experience that the diversity of my collecting has developed out of itself. So, being in no position to pontificate, I can only try to answer the "Where do we go from here?" question by reviewing my most recent digressions, even though (like Mr. Toad's springtime enthusiasms) there is no guarantee that they will be my last.

As I noted earlier, my need to learn to date the tapestry of soils beneath London's bombed buildings generated an interest in the evolution of glass wine bottles. From there it was an easy step to learning about the stoneware wine bottles that preceded the use of glass and were ousted by it. These were the so-called bellarmine bottles from the Rhineland, which, when I began, could be picked up in English antique shops for four or five dollars. Collecting Rhenish bottles in turn led to an interest in the British brown stonewares that became an important part of her ceramic industry after John Dwight of Fulham had discovered in 1671 "the misterie of the stone ware vulgarly called Cologne ware."[1] My pursuit of English stonewares through the eighteenth century inevitably ran on into the nineteenth century, but there enthusiasm drained away. The shapes, decorative techniques, and designs settled into a dreary sameness—except in one area, a new class of ornamental gin flask molded to catch the mercurial enthusiasms, causes, and hatreds of public-house tipplers.

The flask illustrated in Figure 122 is typical, but it is up to its ring neck in history. The design is one that was fairly common (and so relatively inexpensive), though the figure is usually incorrectly described as "The Drunken Sailor." It is, instead, a portrait of the American vaudeville performer Thomas Dartmouth Rice who, in 1828, while playing at a theater in Louisville, Kentucky, appeared during an intermission between the acts of a play performing a song and shuffling

122. An English brown stoneware gin flask commemorating the 1836 London debut of Thomas "Jim Crow" Rice, the first American black-face minstrel. Height 6¾ inches.

dance that aped an old Negro named Jim Crow. Rice's routine was an instant success and his song "Jump Jim Crow" with its nonsense lines "Turn about an' wheel about an' do jis so / An ebery time I turn about I jump Jim Crow" became a popular hit. Rice sang it at the Royal Surrey Theatre in London on his first visit to England in 1836, and, as ceramic historian Anthony Oliver has discovered, it was the poster for that engagement (Fig. 123) that provided the stance and costume for the dancer on the flask. Rice was the first black-face minstrel, and it was he who was responsible for introducing Jim Crow (the white man's black man) into the American language. Thus this

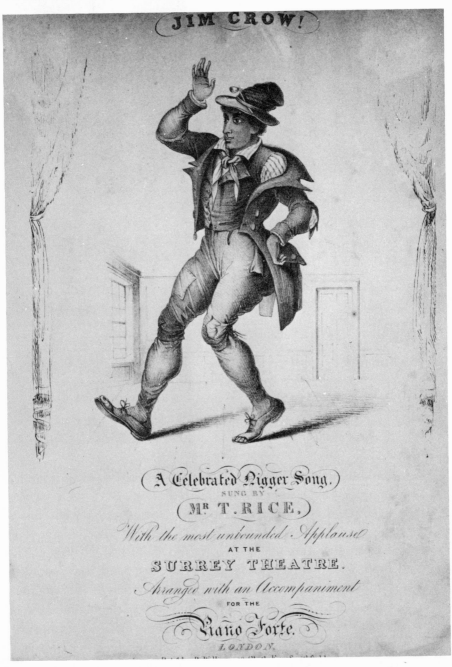

123. The sheet music and poster design used when Thomas Dartmouth Rice appeared at London's Royal Surrey Theatre in 1836, and from which the gin flask was modeled.

124. Another brown stoneware flask, this one said to represent Jenny Lind but more probably the figure of Peace holding a dove. Stamped on the back BOURNES' POTTERIES, DENBY & CUDNOR PARK. DERBYSHIRE, the bottle probably dates from about 1840 and some years before the "Swedish Nightingale" made her British debut. Height 8 inches.

flask merits a place in any collection devoted to black America or to theatrical history.

Inspired by acquiring the Jim Crow flask, I went on to obtain (at a much steeper price) the example illustrated in Figure 124, this one allegedly also theatrical in origin. The figure was claimed to be that of Jenny Lind, the "Swedish Nightingale," who became the toast of London in 1847 and, ten years later, by arrangement with P. T. Barnum, the rage of America. The flask bears no identifying inscription, and the Jenny Lind association stemmed from the fact that the lady holds a bird which, to a myopic non-ornithologist, might pass for a nightingale. It turns out, however, that the back of the figure is almost identical to that of another figure made by the same factory and marked "Queen Alexandrina Victoria." To make matters worse, the hair style and the support for one arm of the "Jenny Lind" flask match details of the front of the Victoria, which shows the young queen holding a scroll bearing the words "May peace and prosperity prevail."[2] On the eve of her coronation she had said to Lord Melbourne, "I pray God my reign will be one of peace," and it seems likely therefore that the "Jenny Lind" is actually a companion flask to the Alexandrina Victoria and is intended to portray Peace holding a dove. Anthony Oliver has since advised me that he has seen Jenny Lind in sixteen Staffordshire figure versions, only one of them with its hair in ringlets, and none carrying a bird. So there went Jenny Lind.

There is no denying that my new beginning as a collector of gin flasks got off to a poor start, for even the example showing Victoria beside her coronation regalia was bought as something else (Fig. 70). The figure was claimed to be that of the luckless Caroline until the pose was found to have been taken from Sir George Hayter's 1833 portrait of the Princess Victoria. I knew my stoneware but I did not have a sufficient knowledge of nineteenth-century art history—and that's the point of the story.

In spite of the foregoing evidence to the contrary, there are obvious advantages to exploring new collecting byways while still heading in more or less the same direction as before. Brave spirits may counter that this is a cowardly solution that narrows one's perspective instead of providing new and exhilarating vistas. But even a totally new direction must have a point of departure, and to string out the metaphor till it chokes, travel is the ideal provider. For me it was a journey down the Nile, although it was not so much a *new* direction as an old one repointed. It took me back to my childhood and the day when a wealthy uncle (who happened to be paying my school fees) demanded to know what I intended to do with myself when I grew up. I had just spent the last of my pocket money on a secondhand copy of Gaston Maspero's *Dawn of Civilization*, and for want of a more intelligent answer, I replied that I intended to become an Egyptologist.

My uncle's neck reddened. "I'm not asking you to choose a hobby. I want to know how you plan to make a living!"

I never did study Egyptology beyond reading a book or two, and instead my archaeological career drifted onward through the centuries until it came to rest at the gates of the Industrial Revolution. Along the way I slowly became aware that although technology has carried us onward and upward, man himself has changed little. On the contrary, his aspirations, ethics, and passions have remained almost defiantly earthbound, enabling him to boast that he is what he is, untainted by the experience of history. Thus it was in search of perspective and, above all, a sense of scale, that I went to Egypt. I returned convinced that we have been as we are for thousands of years.

The unlearned lessons of ancient Egypt are legion, paralleling to a remarkable degree, for example, the failures of modern Middle Eastern alliances. That a single nation could have endured, waxing and waning in so relatively orderly a fashion, through three millennia, is amazing enough in itself, but that this people could design, build, and decorate structures of such prodigious size with little more than levers and copper tools to aid them, is almost beyond belief. To learn that those achievements were less the work of slaves than of willing hands dedicated to the greater glory of the gods came as no small shock—as did the discovery that the building blocks of those religious beliefs were borrowed to construct the Christian Trinity. The experience left me awed, uneasy, and yet exhilarated—as one should be in the presence of the gods, the sensations magnified by the knowledge that they had been shared by great literary names of the past from Herodotus to Flaubert. Unfortunately, one was constantly mindful of innumerable less-illustrious names carved, scratched, and painted on every wall and pillar within reach (including R. K. HUME 1836 on the roof at Dendera), the vandalism of Greeks, Romans, Coptic Christians, British, French, and Americans, proving that no matter how civilized we may appear, we are still barbarians at heart (Fig. 125). Although nothing could have induced me to follow in my predecessors' monstrous foot-

125.  The scourge of the tourist. A wall painting in the tomb chapel of
the ancient Egyptian provincial governor Pahari at El Kab, embellished
with a graffito proclaiming that D. BUSHNELLS OF OHIO was there on November 14, 1839. He was not the first, for there are many other names
on these walls, the earliest dated 1804. His is simply the largest. The
painting dates from the Eighteenth Dynasty and is of great cultural importance.

steps, I found myself sharing their compulsion to leave a mark
at the fountainhead of history and, picking up a piece of flint, I
scratched my initials on a modern Arab potsherd and left it in
the desert somewhere south of Tell el-Amarna. Why? I asked
myself. Perhaps because no matter how firm or shattered are
our religious beliefs, we all seek some measure of immortality,
even if it is no more than a personalized potsherd to remind
posterity that we once were here.

I doubt whether my efforts to learn to read hieroglyphs will
go beyond interpreting a few royal cartouches and a handful of
useless words (vastly more is needed to become proficient in
identifying Egyptian antiquities), but I can already look with

new perception at the shawabti figures and other odds and ends—even the mummified hands—that I acquired in youthful bouts of Egyptomania. Now, however, enthusiasm is tempered with caution, as I remember, for example, the warning of Lady Lucie Duff-Gordon who, while in Luxor in 1864, met a Coptic priest who "fabricates false antiquities very cleverly."[3] Ten years later, her literary successor Amelia B. Edwards would make the point even more sharply, declaring that "every man, woman, and child about the place is bent on selling a bargain; and the bargain, in ninety-nine cases out of a hundred, is valuable in so far as it represents the industry of Luxor—but

126. An alleged funerary figure of the Ptolemaic period. Made of painted wood and covered with the remains of fabric which a textile specialist has stated to be "at least several hundred years old," the figure is nevertheless a fake. The paint colors are too glossy, and the textile seems to have been attached in small pieces with a mixture of glue and animal dung, effacingly and convincingly obscuring the bogus hieroglyphs that begin to be revealed for what they are as the dirt is removed. Height 12¼ inches. When Egyptian fakes are good, they are very, very good . . .

no farther" (Fig. 126).[4] It should surprise no one that a peasant culture which has changed so little in five millennia should continue to operate today as it did a mere century ago. The descendants of Egypt's Billies and Charlies are still at work, disarmingly tempting tourists with the same travesties and the same lies that they were dispensing when Victoria was queen (Fig. 127).

Expert collectors who find that they have made embarrassing and costly mistakes naturally condemn the forgers and would like to see them hung up by their ears. Egyptologists, on

127. . . . but when they are bad, they are horrid. An ancient fellah tries to sell scarabs and alabaster figures of Horus to apathetic tourists at Thebes. His talent for mewing like a cat when offering statuettes of the cat-headed deity Bastet was much more impressive than his treasures.

the other hand, regard them as a useful evil, discouraging the elicit digging for genuine antiquities in favor of selling equally profitable fakes. As for the naïve, novice collector, as long as he can happily believe that his plaster head of Nefertiti was created in the ancient workshops of Akhetaten, his cerebral excursions into history remain real and exciting. For my part, I find the bogus antiquities manufactured in the days of Lady Duff-Gordon and Amelia Edwards of interest in their own right, as relics of that Victorian world which (as I have tried to show in these chapters) remains as intriguing and different from our own time as were the centuries of the pharaohs.

It is partly for this reason that my renewed interest in Egypt is fueled, not by a desire to possess, but by the pleasures of vicarious travel and adventure to be derived from the often marvelously literate journals of nineteenth-century antiquaries and tourists. I intend to journey with Belzoni, the one-time circus strong-man, as he digs into the tombs and temples of

128.  An Egyptian woman searching for portable valuables in what, in 1841, was described as a "mummy pit." From Sir J. Gardner Wilkinson's *Manners and Customs of the Ancient Egyptians*, 2nd Series, vol. II, p. xxxi.

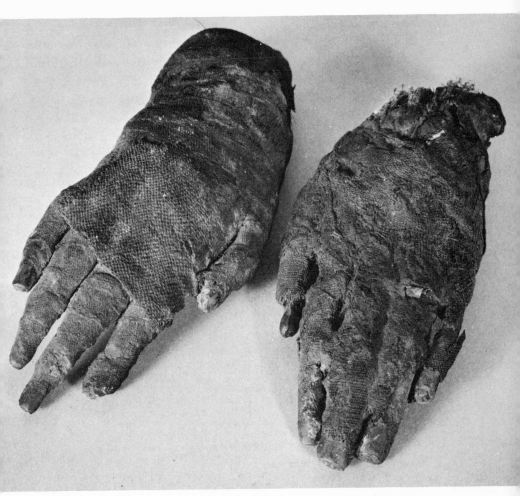

129.   The dry black hands of Egyptian mummies were popular tourist trophies in the nineteenth century, particularly among those who lacked the fortitude or the room in their bags to carry off the whole thing. In the preceding centuries, however, there had been a brisk trade in mummy parts for the use of European apothecaries who ground them up as components for medications to cure almost anything from bruises to epilepsy. It was a business that did the future of the Egyptian past no good at all. The hand on the right still wears part of a blue faience ring, and the nails of both are henna stained, an embalmer's technique for enlivening the "loved one."

Thebes for treasures that would enrich the British Museum; I shall stop my ears as that dubitable Briton Colonel Howard Vyse blasts his way through the pyramids and drills holes in the Sphinx; and I shall share the fears and excitement of the Frenchmen Mariette and Maspero as they creep through rock-hewn tunnels, their flickering lamps revealing the awesome painted figures of Re, and Seth, and Sobek, and of servants and handmaidens, all enjoining us to trespass no farther.

In short, a new world and a lifetime of adventure have opened for me, and although I have no intention of becoming an avid collector of canopic jars or mummy cases, I am willing to bet beans to a belly dancer's button that space will have to be found for the occasional Egyptian *bargain*.

# Notes

ONE: *"What's Past Is Prologue . . ."*

1. Maurice Rheims, *The Strange Life of Objects* (New York, 1961), p. 211. Originally published in France in 1959, and subsequently in England as *Art on the Market.*
2. *Webster's Seventh New Collegiate Dictionary* (Springfield, Mass., 1963), n.p.

TWO: *To Have and to Hold*

1. John Nichols, *Literary Anecdotes of the Eighteenth Century* (London, 1812–1815), vol. VIII, p. 68.
2. Quoted by Mea Allen, *The Tradescants, Their Plants, Gardens and Museum, 1570–1662* (London, 1964), pp. 114–15.
3. *Ibid.*, p. 175.
4. *Elias Ashmole 1672–1692,* C. J. Josten, ed. (Oxford, 1966), vol. IV, p. 1607.
5. Allen, *op. cit.*, p. 215.
6. *The Diary of John Evelyn,* William Bray, ed. (London, 1952), vol. II, p. 124, entry for July 23, 1678.
7. Anon., *Old England: A Pictorial Museum* (London, 1845), vol. II, p. 287.

THREE: *Cabinets, Closets, and Dubitable Curiosities*

1. Richard Steele, *The Tatler* (London, 1709), No. 34.
2. Quoted by William Kent, *An Encyclopaedia of London* (London, 1937), p. 484.
3. Benjamin Silliman, *A Journal of Travels in England, Holland and Scotland, and of Two Passages over the Atlantic, in 1805 and 1806,* 3 vols. (New Haven, Conn., 1820), vol. II, p. 73.

4. *Ibid.*, p. 71.
5. *Ibid.*, vol. I, p. 257.
6. William Hone, *The Every-Day Book* (London, 1825), vol. II, p. 495.
7. Ephraim Chambers, *Cyclopaedia* (London, 1738), vol. I, n.p.
8. As Figure 125 (p. 297) demonstrates, those Americans who did travel made sure they were remembered.
9. Frederick Marryat, *A Diary in America, With Remarks on Its Institutions*, S. W. Jackman, ed. (New York, 1964), p. 148.
10. Edward Hingston, *The Genial Showman, Being Reminiscences of the Life of Artemus Ward* (London, 1870), vol. I, pp. 11–12.


FOUR: *In Search of Bald Sextons*

1. *King John*, III, 2.
2. Quoted by Ernest Morris, *Tintinnabula* (London, 1959), p. 126.
3. Benjamin Silliman, *A Journal of Travels in England, Holland and Scotland, and of Two Passages over the Atlantic, in 1805 and 1806* (New Haven, Conn., 1820), vol. II, p. 92.
4. *North Devon: The Buildings of England* series (Harmondsworth, Middlesex, 1952), p. 85.


FIVE: *Something for Nothing*

1. Ivor Noël Hume, "Present from America—A New Addition to a Fine Bottle Collection," *The Wine and Spirit Trade Record* (London), September 18, 1962, p. 1246; also *The Philadelphia Inquirer*, August 29, 1948.
2. Carl J. Clausen, "The Box—A Mystery on Its Way to Being Solved," *Archives & History News* (Tallahassee, Fla.), vol. 2, no. 2, September–October, 1971, p. 3.
3. *The Merchant of Venice*, III, 1.
4. Homer L. Ferguson, *Salvaging Revolutionary Relics from the York River* (Newport News, Va., 1939), Mariners' Museum Publication, no. 7, fig. 3.
5. John E. Price, *Roman Antiquities Illustrated by Remains Recently Discovered on the Site of the National Safe Deposit Company's Premises, Mansion House, London* (London, 1873), pp. 78–79.


SIX: *Billie and Charlie and Margaret North*

1. Ronald Jessup, *The Story of Archaeology in Britain* (London, 1965), p. 147.
2. *The Journal of John Gabriel Stedman 1744–1797*, Stanbury Thompson, ed. (London, 1962), p. 364.
3. E. T. Hall, research laboratory head, Ashmolean Museum, to C. H. V. Sutherland, February 12, 1957.
4. Eric P. Newman, "First Documentary Evidence on the American Colonial Pewter 1/24th Real," *The Numismatist*, July 1955, p. 3, quoting the Out-Letter Book of the Treasury, Tome 27/11, p. 424.
5. Frank Cundall, *Historic Jamaica* (London, 1915), pp. 78–79.

SEVEN: *Of Mud, and Pots, and Puppy Dogs,*
*and Mistakes that Come Back in the Night*

1. George Payne, *Collectania Cantiana* (London, 1893), p. 74.
2. *Ibid.*
3. Thomas Wright, *The Celt, the Roman, and the Saxon* (London, 1875), pp. 259–260.
4. Payne, *op. cit.*, p. 79.
5. J. M. C. Toynbee and I. Noël Hume, "An Unusual Roman Sherd from the Upchurch Marshes," *Archaeologia Cantiana*, Vol. LXIX (Ashford, Kent, 1955), p. 74.


EIGHT: *Adam and Eve to Caroline, with Intermediate Stops*

1. Samuel Smiles, *Josiah Wedgwood F.R.S., His Personal History* (New York, 1895), p. 62.
2. Katharine Morrison McClinton, "Brass Tobacco Boxes," *Antiques*, vol. L, no. 3 (September, 1946), p. 176.
3. *Daily Mail* (London), June 23, 1897, p. 4.
4. Henry Mayhew, *Mayhew's London, Being Selections from 'London Labour and the London Poor,'* Peter Quennell, ed. (London, 1969), p. 182. Mayhew's original work was first published in 1851.
5. *Pennsylvania Gazette* (Philadelphia), July 19, 1733.
6. *Gentleman's Magazine* (London), August, 1785, p. 603.
7. *Ibid.*, p. 760.
8. John Brand, *Observations on the Popular Antiquities of Great Britain: Chiefly Illustrating the Origin of Our Vulgar and Provincial Customs, Ceremonies, and Superstitions* (London, 1849), Vol. II, p. 235. Brand's manuscript was completed in 1795, and considerably revised when it was published under the editorship of Sir Henry Ellis in 1813.
9. Ray Fremmer, "Dishes in 18th Cent. Tombs," *The Weekend Star* (Jamaica), May 12, 1972, p. 6.


NINE: *History in a Green Bottle*

1. *The Diary of Samuel Pepys Esquire F.R.S.*, Lord Braybrooke, ed. (London, 1902), p. 675.
2. *Ibid.*, p. 735, entry for May 18, 1668.
3. *The Scowrer*, 1691.
4. *The Recruiting Officer*, V. 6.
5. E. G. Swem, ed., *Brothers of the Spade* (Barre, Mass., 1957), p. 47. From page 79 of the Custis Letter-book in the Library of Congress; Custis to Collinson, probably August 28, 1737.
6. Custis Letter-book p. 192; letter undated. Text from typescript in the collection of the Virginia Historical Society.
7. *William and Mary Quarterly*, 1st series, Vol. 7 (1898–99, reprinted New York, 1966), p. 152.
8. Quoted by Geoffrey Wills in *English and Irish Glass* (London, 1968), signature 10, p. 13.
9. From a promotional broadsheet published c. 1755–57.
10. Lord Tennyson, "Song of the Lotos-Eaters," 1832.

TEN: *"All the Best Rubbish Is Gone"*

1. John Dryden, *Absalom and Achitophel* (London, 1681), Part I, lines 801–804.
2. Alexander Laing, ed., *The Life and Adventures of John Nicol, Mariner* (London, 1937), pp. 128–144. The original manuscript was edited by John Howell and published in Edinburgh.
3. Arthur Griffiths, *The Chronicles of Newgate* (London, 1884), p. 279.
4. Since this book was written, the Corporation of London has agreed to accept the return of the salvaged documents and to see that they are restored and preserved.
5. Jonathan Swift, *Journal to Stella*, 1710.
6. Richard Steele, *The Spectator*, Henry Morley, ed. (London, 1888), p. 51; No. 30, Wednesday, April 4, 1711.
7. James Howard, *The English Mounsieur* (London, 1674), p. 45.


ELEVEN: *A Word in Your Eye*

1. James Mountague, ed., *The Old Bailey Chronicle* (London, 1788), Vol. I, p. 328; trial of Joseph Blake, alias Blueskin, for burglary, October, 1724.
2. *Ibid.*, p. 172; trial of Arthur Gray, for burglary, December, 1721.
3. Henry Mayhew, *Mayhew's London, Being Selections from 'London Labour and the London Poor,'* Peter Quennell, ed. (London, 1969), pp. 199–200. Mayhew's original work was first published in 1851.
4. Flora Thompson, *Lark Rise to Candleford* (London, 1971), pp. 135–136; first published as three books, 1939–1943.
5. *Ibid.*, p. 134.
6. *As You Like It*, II, 3.
7. John Ireland, *Hogarth Illustrated* (London 1791), Vol. I, p. 39.
8. *The General Shop Book: Or The Tradesman's Universal Director* (London, 1753), n.p., article under "NEGRO'S, a kind of black slaves, which makes a considerable article in the modern commerce."
9. *Daily Sketch* (London), March 4, 1961.
10. *The General Shop Book*, n.p. (see footnote 8).
11. J. Seymour Lindsay, *Iron and Brass Implements of the English and American Home* (London, 1964), p. 27, quoting from a 1755 pamphlet headed "Serious reflections attending the use of copper vessels."


TWELVE: *Of Mermaids, Fakes, and Other Grave Matters*

1. Information provided by T. A. L. Concannon from manuscript notes, "Report on British Troops in Jamaica 1818–1823," compiled by Lt. Col. M. E. S. Laws, Royal Artillery (Retd.), March 19, 1970.
2. Philip Wright, ed., *Lady Nugent's Journal of her residence in Jamaica from 1801 to 1805* (Kingston, Jamaica, 1966), p. 98.
3. *Ibid.*, p. 208.
4. A. H. Church, *English Earthenware* (London, 1905), p. xi.
5. Frank Hermann, *The English as Collectors: A Documentary Chrestomathy* (London, 1972), p. 47; quoting the Victoria and Albert Mu-

seum's Advisory Council, "Reports of the Sub-Committees upon the Principal Deficiencies in the Collections," 1913.

6. *Ibid.*
7. Church, *op. cit.*, pp. xi–xii.
8. *Essex County Standard*, August 25, 1972.

THIRTEEN: *And Then What?*

1. Patent granted by Charles II to John Dwight (No. 164) for the manufacture of china and other ware, 1671–84.
2. André L. Simon, *Wine Trade Loan Exhibition of Drinking Vessels . . . &c.*, Vintners' Hall (London, 1933), p. 29, no. 62B1.
3. Lady Lucie Duff-Gordon, *Letters from Egypt 1862–1869*, Gordon Waterfield, ed. (London, 1969), p. 157; letter of April 14, 1864.
4. Amelia B. Edwards, *A Thousand Miles Up the Nile* (London, 1889), pp. 410–11.

# Bibliography

The following short list of books is intended to provide the reader with points of departure or an opportunity to explore in greater depth some of the sources over which I have enthused. To provide a full bibliography for all the subjects touched on would require a volume on its own, and most of its entries would cite magazine articles, papers in hard-to-find scholarly journals, and long-out-of-print books wherein only a few pages are relevant. It is true that some of those listed below are no longer in print, but they are included because there are as yet no substitutes for them and because they are wholly pertinent.

CHAPTER ONE
> Maurice Rheims, *The Strange Life of Objects*, Atheneum, New York, 1961.

CHAPTER TWO
> Mea Allen, *The Tradescants, Their Plants, Gardens and Museum 1570–1662*, Michael Joseph, London, 1964.

CHAPTER THREE
> Whitfield J. Bell, ed., *A Cabinet of Curiosities*, University Press of Virginia, Charlottesville, 1967.

CHAPTER FOUR
> Benjamin Silliman, *A Journal of Travels in England, Holland and Scotland, and of Two Passages over the Atlantic, in 1805 and 1806*, 3 vols., New Haven, Conn., 1820.

CHAPTER FIVE
> Ivor Noël Hume, *Treasure in the Thames*, Muller, London, 1956.

CHAPTER SIX
> Ralph Merrifield, *The Roman City of London*, Benn, London, 1965.

CHAPTER SEVEN

Robert Charleston, *Roman Pottery*, Faber, London, 1955.

CHAPTER EIGHT

Geoffrey A. Godden, *An Illustrated Encyclopedia of British Pottery and Porcelain*, Crown, New York, 1966.

John and Jennifer May, *Commemorative Pottery 1780–1900*, Heinemann, London, 1972.

P.D. Gordon Pugh, *Naval Ceramics*, Ceramic Book Co., Newport, England, 1971.

CHAPTER NINE

Ivor Noël Hume, *A Guide to Artifacts of Colonial America*, Knopf, New York, 1970.

Cecil Munsey, *The Illustrated Guide to Collecting Bottles*, Hawthorn Books, New York, 1970.

Shelagh Ruggles-Brise, *Sealed Bottles*, Country Life, London, 1949.

Earl G. Swem, ed., *Brothers of the Spade*, Barre Gazette, Barre, Mass., 1957.

CHAPTER TEN

Alexander Laing, ed., *The Life and Adventures of John Nicol, Mariner*, Cassell, London, 1937.

CHAPTER ELEVEN

Peter Quennell, ed., *Mayhew's London*, Spring Books, New York, 1969.

Flora Thompson, *Lark Rise to Candleford*, Oxford University Press, London, 1971.

CHAPTER TWELVE

Robert T. Clifton, *Barbs, Prongs, Points, Prickers, & Stickers: A Complete and Illustrated Catalogue of Antique Barbed Wire*, University of Oklahoma Press, Norman, Oklahoma, 1970.

Frank Herman, *The English as Collectors: A Documentary Chrestomathy*, Chatto and Windus, London, 1972.

CHAPTER THIRTEEN

J. F. Blacker, *The A.B.C. of English Salt-Glaze Stoneware from Dwight to Doulton*, Stanley Paul, London, 1922.

Amelia B. Edwards, *A Thousand Miles Up the Nile*, 2nd ed., Routledge, London, 1889.

Anthony Oliver, *The Victorian Staffordshire Figure: A Guide for Collectors*, Heinemann, London, 1971.

Francis Steegmuller, ed., *Flaubert in Egypt: A Sensibility on Tour*, Atlantic-Little, Brown, Boston, 1973.

Gordon Waterfield, ed., *Lady Lucie Duff-Gordon's Letters from Egypt 1862–1869*, Routledge & Kegan Paul, London, 1969.

# Index

Leicester, churchyard discoveries at, 170
Leicester House (London), 39
Lever, Sir Ashton, 38–40
Lewis, C. Bernard, 265
Lind, Jenny, **294**, 295
Lock, brass rim, 233, **234**, 235
    spring, 233–34
    stock, 234
London Bridge, 85–86, 123
London, Corporation of, 54
*London Journal, The:* quoted, 247–48
*London Labour and the London Poor,* Henry Mayhew's: quoted, 159, 236–37
London, Roman, 54–55, 85, 90–96, **92, 95,** 141, 173
"London" ware, 127, **128**
Lords, House of, 159–60
Long, William and Mary, 177–78
Lottery, museum, 37, 40
Louisbourg, Nova Scotia, 148, 154
Louisville, Kentucky, 291
Love spoons, Welsh, 64
Loyd and Cooper, London mercantile agents, 187
Lunatic asylums: *see* Bedlam

Machapunga River (now Pungo), North Carolina, 121
Madagascar, 33
Maine, artifacts from, 111–12, 183
Manatee, 266
Manhole covers, 268
Marathon, Florida, 75–76
Marryat, Frederick: quoted, 46
Martinique, capture of (1762), **149**
Mary Queen of Scots: cannonball shot at, 46
Marx, Robert F., 114
Mason jars, 201, **202**
Maspiro, Sir Gaston, 295
Masterpiece, cult of, 271
Mauritius, dodo from, 27, 33, **34**
Mayhew, Henry: quoted, 159, 236–37
McClinton, Katharine, 149
McKinley Tariff Act (1891), 144
Medicines, patent, 199, **200**
Medway Marshes: *see* Upchurch Marshes
Mermaid, **262,** 265–66
Merrifield, Ralph, 122
Microfilm, 217
Milan Commission (1818), 160
Milk bottle collectors' club, 14–15
Mill Hill, London, 187
Minories, The (London), 141

Mint, Royal, 108, 113
Miseno, Italy: discoveries at, **4**
Mitchell, J., 261–66, **262**
Mithraeum, in London, 91, **92**
Modbury, Devonshire, 267
Molding, ceramic, **11, 12, 13,** 151–53
Monk, William, 103
Monkey, African green, **262,** 264–65
Montgomery Ward, Inc., 228
Moody, Anne, 189–90
Moorfields, London, 223–24
Morgan, John Pierpont, 42
Morgan, Philips: mason, 255
Mosaic, Romano-British: proposed sale of, 287
Mudlark, **88,** 98, 236
Mug, meditation on a quart, 163, 165
    pewter, **116,** 118–20
    stoneware, **164**
*Mulberry Garden, The,* Sir Charles Sedley's, 178
Mummy, hands from, **301**
    head from, **36**
Murray, Grizel, 233, 235
*Musaeum Tradescantianum,* 26, 35
Museums, American:
    Charles Willson Peale's, 46, **47**
    Henry Francis Du Pont Winterthur (Delaware), 229, 253–54
    Mariners', Newport News, Virginia, 81
    Metropolitan Museum of Art, New York, 2, 42, 288
    Smithsonian Institution, Washington, D.C., 35, 48, 96
    Wadsworth Atheneum, Hartford, Connecticut, 42
    Western Museum of Cincinnati, 46–47
Museums, attitudes toward private collections, 286–88
Museums, British:
    Ashmolean, Oxford, 23, 25–26, 28, 30, 32–33, 107, 173
    Brentford Public Library, 85
    British Museum, 23, 37, 41, 85, 210, 229, 231, 286, 302
    Guildhall, 84, 93, 95, 141, 276
    Leverian (London), 38–41, **39**
    London, 85, 181–82
    Maidstone Museums and Art Gallery, Kent, 128
    Northampton Central, 182
    Rochester's Eastgate House (Kent), 19–20, 128
    Victoria and Albert (London), 229, 270–71

Shield, Iron Age, 84
Ship Tavern (London), mug from, **116**, 119–20
Shipwrecks, artifacts from, 71–82, **72, 76, 77**, 81
*Shop Book, The General* (1753): quoted, 246, 253
Shrines, Roman, 4, 91, **92**
Shrouds, woolen, 169
Silliman, Benjamin, 37, 63, 251
Skillets, bell metal, **252**, 253–54
Slang, underworld, 232
Slaves, runaway: described, 235
Sloane, Sir Hans, 37
Smith, Edward: trunkmaker, 255, **256**, 257
Smith, John, 251
Smith, William: *see* Billie and Charlie
Smithson, James, 48
Smithsonian Institution: *see* Museums, American
Snobbery, antiquarian, 49–50, 271
Snuffbox, silver gilt, 233
Societies: *see* individual names
Sotheby & Co. (London), 104, 166, 175
Southwark Bridge (London), **88**, 90, 107
Space, collectors' need for, 51–52
*Spectator, The:* quoted, 222
*Spy, The London:* Ned Ward's, 250
Stathams, Sir John, 221
Stedman, John: quoted, 105–6
Steele, Sir Richard: quoted, 35–36
Stoneware, British: origins of, 146
   brown, 123, **157, 158**, 291, **292, 294**, 295
   white salt-glazed, 148, **152**, 171, **277**
Stoneware, Rhenish, 108, **109**, 110, 149, **164, 244, 245**, 280, 291
   found in Virginia, 108, **109**
   reproductions of, 280
Stony Hill Barracks, Jamaica, 261–63, **264**
Stoughton's Elixir, 200
Swansea, ceramics, **162**, 163
Swem, Earl G., 187
Swift, Jonathan: quoted, 222

Tablets, Roman writing, 91, 134
Target, Ann: porcelain made for, **167**, 168
Target, Thomas, 168
*Tatler, The:* quoted, 35
Taunton, Somersetshire, 252

Taverns: *see* individual names
Taverns, museums in, 35–36
Taylor, John: Virginia brazier, 253–54
Tea bowls, Bow porcelain, 166, **167**, 168
Tea drinking, 251
Teapot, Wedgwood black basaltes, 140
Tell el-Amarna, 297
Teniers, David, Elder and Younger, 241
Tennyson, Alfred: quoted, 203
Thames river, antiquities from, 84–90, **86, 88, 90**, 98, **99, 105**, 106, 110, **111, 112, 113**, 236, 286
Theatre Royal (London), 223:*see also* King's House theater
Thefts of antiques, 20–21
Thirty-Third Regiment of Foot (British), 261, **262**, 263
Thompson, Flora: discussed and quoted, 238–40
Thurlow, Edward: quoted, 147
Titus: statue of, **4**
Tobacco boxes, 148, **149**, 159, 233
Tokens, plantation, **113**, 114
   tobacco, 268
   tradesmen's, 117–18, 177, **178**, 236
Tomb robbing, Egyptian, 300
Towneley, Charles: 18th-century collector, 2, **3**
Tourists, barbarism of, 296, **297**
Toynbee, Professor Jocelyn: quoted, 138
Tradescant Collection, 23–33, **28, 34**
Tradescant, Hester, 24–31
Tradescant, John I and II, 23–31, **25**
Tradescant's Ark, 24–29, 33–34
Tradescant, tomb of, 30, **31**
Trafalgar, Battle of (1805): commemorated, 154, **155**, 156
Travelers, 204, 243, 250–51, 296, **297**
"Treasure Chest," 75, **76**
Trunk, 79, 255, **256**, 257
Turpin, Richard "Dick," 248–49
Tutankhamen, tomb furniture, 18–19
Tutter's Neck (Virginia), delftware found at, 87, **88**

Ubilla, Juan Estéban de, 72
Uffenbach, Jacharius Conrad von: quoted, 36
Ultraviolet light, 274, 280
Unicorn, 27

## About the Author

IVOR NOËL HUME has been the Director of the Department of Archaeology for Colonial Williamsburg since 1957. He was formerly the archaeologist responsible for the recovery of antiquities in postwar London at London's Guildhall Museum, from 1949 to 1957. He has also been an honorary Research Associate of the Smithsonian Institution since 1959.

Mr. Noël Hume's previous books include: *Archaeology in Britain; Treasure in the Thames; Great Moments in Archaeology; Handbook of Tortoises; Terrapins and Turtles; Here Lies Virginia; 1775: Another Part of the Field; Historical Archaeology; A Guide to Artifacts of Colonial America*. He is the author of many articles on glass, ceramics, and other subjects, and lectures frequently on archaeology and antiques.

73 74 75 76 77 10 9 8 7 6 5 4 3 2 1